THE BEST-EVER BOOK OF
CAKES

THE BEST-EVER BOOK OF
CAKES

165 utterly irresistible and foolproof cakes to bake
for everyday eating and special celebrations,
shown in 800 delectable photographs

  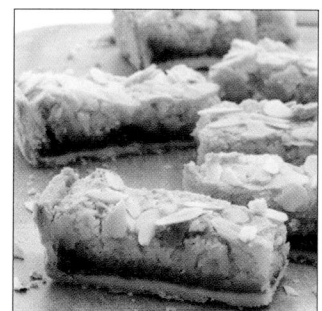

ANN NICOL

LORENZ BOOKS

Contents

Cake-making basics

This chapter will help you master all the basic preparation that leads to successful baking. Good-quality ingredients are the foundation of well-made cakes, so information is provided on the basics such as sugar, eggs, flour, fats and spices. Using good quality baking equipment is vital for cake-making, but only a few items of bakeware are needed, and the essentials are all described here. Learning how to bake is a key skill and often we find it easiest to make the foods we most love to eat. The many methods of making cakes, such as creaming, all-in-one, rubbing-in, melting and whisking, are illustrated with photographs and described step by step. To finish a cake you may like to add fillings and toppings – recipes for buttercream, chocolate icings, almond paste, royal icing and sugarpaste are all provided. The final section explains what can go wrong and the reasons why.

Left: Eggs, sugar, butter and flour are basic ingredients for cake making. Chocolate is a luxury ingredient.

Essential ingredients

Fat, sugar, flour and eggs are the four ingredients that form the basis of many recipes. To these, a whole array of flavouring ingredients can be added, such as chocolate, coffee, lemon juice and zest, nuts, and dried fruits, to name just a few. Each addition alters the basic cake flavour.

Sugar

Not only added for sweetness, sugars produce the structure and texture that make a cake tasty, so it's important to use the correct type:

Caster (superfine) sugar is available in white and unrefined golden varieties. It blends easily with fats when beaten or 'creamed' into light sponge mixtures.

Granulated sugar may be coarse white or golden and unrefined, and is used for toppings.

Demerara (raw) sugar is golden in colour and has a grainy texture.

Below clockwise from bottom left Caster sugar, runny honey, granulated sugar, demerara sugar, soft light and dark brown sugar, black treacle, golden syrup, icing sugar, and muscovado sugar are all sweeteners with their own clearly defined flavours.

It is often used for recipes where sugar is melted over heat, or as a decorative topping.

Soft light and dark brown sugars cream well and usually form the base of a fruit cake, or are used in recipes where a rich flavour is required. Store them in an airtight container.

Muscovado (molasses) sugar is natural and unrefined, with an excellent dark colour and richer flavour. It makes fruit cakes and gingerbreads extra special.

Icing (confectioners') sugar is sold as a fine white powder or in an unrefined golden form. It is used for icings, frostings and decorations. Store the sugar in a dry place, as it tends to absorb moisture. Sift the sugar at least once, or preferably twice, before you use it, as it may form hard lumps during storage.

Above Eggs and buttermilk.

Golden (light corn) syrup, honey, treacle and molasses are thick liquid sugars. They can be used in cakes made by the melting method.

Eggs

Although eggs are often stored in the refrigerator, better baked results will be achieved if they are at room temperature when they are used. The eggs will then whisk better than those kept refrigerated, and will achieve more aeration. Aeration gives more volume but also allows the eggs to blend into mixtures more easily. Cold eggs will tend to curdle a mixture more quickly.

Medium-size eggs are used in the recipes in this book, unless otherwise stated in the recipe.

Dried egg-white powder gives excellent results and can be substituted in royal icing recipes, or in recipes where you are unsure about the suitability of using raw egg whites. **Raw eggs are unsuitable for the elderly, pregnant women, babies and young children.**

Flours

Plain (all-purpose) flour provides the structure of a cake but contains nothing to make it rise. Richer cakes that do not need raising agents are made with plain flour.

Self-raising (self-rising) flour has raising agents mixed into it. These create air in the batter to make a cake rise, so self-raising flour is used for sponges and light mixtures that contain little or no fruit. If you have only plain flour, add 12.5ml/2½ tsp baking powder to every 225g/8oz plain flour to make it into a self-raising flour.

Wholemeal (whole-wheat) and brown flours contain bran from the wheat, which provides a good

Above, clockwise from left Baking powder, bicarbonate of soda, and cream of tartar.

texture with extra fibre. This tends to keep cakes and breads moist and gives a mellow flavour. If you are substituting brown flour for white in a recipe, you will need to add extra liquid, as the bran in brown flour will absorb more fluid.

Gram flour is made from ground chickpeas and retains moisture.

White flours can be kept in a cool dry place for up to six months, but wholemeal flours will not keep for as long because they have a higher fat content. Check the use-by date on packs of all types of flour. Flour is best stored in an airtight container, which should be thoroughly washed and dried before refilling. Don't add new flour to old, as eventually small micro-organisms that look like tiny black specks may form, and will spread into new flour. Make sure all flour is kept dry, as damp flour weighs more and therefore alters the measurements in a recipe, which could lead to failure.

Raising agents

There are a number of raising agents that, when added to flour, make cakes rise. They produce an airy and light texture. As they are added in small quantities, it is important to be

Above, clockwise from bottom left Plain, strong, wholemeal, brown, and self-raising flours.

accurate when measuring them out.

Baking powder is a ready-made mixture of bicarbonate of soda (baking soda) and cream of tartar. When liquid is added, the powder bubbles and produces carbon dioxide, which expands with heat during baking and creates an airy texture in the cake.

Bicarbonate of soda (baking soda) is a gentler raising agent than baking powder and is often used to give heavy melted or spicy mixtures a lift. It can create a bitter flavour if too much is added.

Cream of tartar is a fast-acting raising agent that works immediately it touches liquid, so bake the mixture as soon as possible after adding it.

Buttermilk

When added to recipes that use bicarbonate of soda (baking soda), buttermilk acts as a raising agent. The acidity in the buttermilk combined with the bicarbonate of soda produces carbon dioxide, which raises the mixture as it cooks. If buttermilk is not available, make your own souring agent by mixing 290ml/10fl oz low-fat yogurt or milk with 5ml/1 tbsp lemon juice.

Above, clockwise from left Vegetable shortening, soft margarine, hard block margarine, butter and oil.

Fats

As well as giving flavour and texture to cakes, fats improve their keeping qualities. For cake-making (apart from mixtures that use the rubbed-in method), always use fats at room temperature to make mixing them into the other ingredients easier.

Butter and hard block margarine can be interchanged in a recipe, but butter will always give the best flavour to cakes, so it is well worth spending that little extra.

Soft tub margarine is suitable only for all-in-one sponge recipes where all the ingredients are quickly mixed together in one bowl. These cakes usually require an extra raising agent. Don't overbeat recipes using soft tub margarine, as the mixture will become wet and the cake will sink. Do not substitute this fat for butter or block margarine as it is a totally different kind of fat, and it will not produce the same results.

Vegetable shortenings are flavourless but can be used to produce very pale, light cakes.

Right, clockwise from left Whole hazelnuts, whole walnuts, blanched almonds and ground almonds.

Above, clockwise from left Raisins, currants, glacé and crystallized fruit and sultanas.

Cooking oils can be used successfully in moist cakes such as carrot cake. As they do not hold air, the mixture cannot be creamed and these cakes have a dense texture.

Dried fruits

Sultanas (golden raisins), raisins and currants are usually sold pre-washed and cleaned, but it is still worth picking them over for pieces of stalk and grit. Dried fruit benefits from soaking in dark sherry, brandy or rum, which will make the fruits extra plump and succulent.

Glacé (candied) and crystallized fruits, such as cherries, ginger or angelica, need to be rinsed and dried

Above, from left to right Whole nutmegs, cinnamon sticks, ground ginger and cloves.

before use to wash away their sugary coating. If you do not do this, the sticky coating may cause the fruits to sink during baking.

Spices

Frequently used spices for baking include nutmeg, ground ginger, cinnamon, cloves and mixed (apple pie) spice, which all add warm and fragrant tones to cakes. Dried spices have a long shelf-life but will not keep indefinitely and will gradually lose aroma and flavour. Buy them in small quantities when you need them. Light and heat will affect the flavour of spices, so keep them out of the light. For a longer life, store them in a cool dry place.

If you add spices to hot mixtures, don't measure them into the mixture straight from the jar, as steam may get into the jar causing the spice to become damp and deteriorate.

Nuts

Because nuts are expensive and will deteriorate quickly, buy them in small quantities. If you buy a large pack of nuts that you are not going to use immediately, you can freeze them for up to six months.

Almonds are bought blanched, slivered, flaked (sliced), ground or whole. To remove the skins from shelled almonds, place the nuts in boiling water for 2–3 minutes. Drain and rub off the skins. Ground nuts have a fine, powdery texture.
Hazelnuts are bought whole, skinned, unskinned or ground.
Walnuts contain more oil than most other nuts and will quickly become rancid, so don't buy them in bulk. Walnut halves are more expensive, so if you need chopped walnuts, buy walnut pieces.

Chocolate

For a professional finish and fine flavour buy the best quality chocolate. Good chocolate is sleek and shiny and will snap easily. It also contains a higher percentage of real cocoa fat, which gives a superior flavour and texture. The amount of cocoa fat or solids will be noted on the wrapper of any chocolate. Those marked as 70 per cent or more cocoa solids will give the best results.

Above, clockwise from top left
Unsweetened cocoa powder, milk, white
and plain chocolate.

Cocoa powder needs to be cooked so that its full flavour will be released. Blend it with boiling water to make it into a paste, then cool it before adding to a recipe.

Drinking chocolate contains milk powder and sugar. Don't substitute it for cocoa powder, as it will spoil the flavour of a cake.

White chocolate may be difficult to work with. Grate it finely, or, if melting it, keep the temperature low.

MELTING CHOCOLATE

Melting chocolate needs care and attention. To melt chocolate, break the bar into small pieces and put it in a heatproof bowl standing over a pan of warm water. Make sure the bowl containing the chocolate is dry and that steam cannot get into the bowl. Heat the water to a gentle simmer only and leave the bowl to stand for about five minutes. Do not let the water get too hot or the chocolate will reach too high a temperature and will lose its sheen.

TOASTING NUTS

The flavour of nuts is improved by toasting them for a few minutes before use. To do this, place them in a single layer on a baking tray lined with foil and grill (broil) them lightly.

GRINDING NUTS

If you don't have ground nuts available, place whole or flaked (sliced) nuts in a food processor and grind until they form a coarse powder. Do not over-grind or the powder will be oily rather than dry.

SKINNING HAZELNUTS

For the best flavour in cakes, choose whole nuts, then toast them quickly under a grill until the skins loosen. Rub the nuts in a dish towel to remove the skins. Chop or grind. Use immediately.

Basic equipment

For successful cake making you need an oven that will retain an accurate and even temperature. If you're new to baking, start off with some mixing bowls and utensils and a few pans. A 900g/2lb loaf tin, a muffin tin and a 20cm/8in cake pan are useful sizes to have.

Baking papers, paper cases and foil

For lining tins (pans) and baking sheets use baking parchment, which is non-stick, or greaseproof (waxed) paper. Paper cases can be purchased in many different and convenient sizes to fit round or square cake tins or cupcake and muffin tins. Waxed paper is a useful surface to pipe royal iced decorations on to, as they will peel away easily once dry. Kitchen foil is handy for wrapping rich fruit cakes or for protecting wrapped cakes in the freezer.

Baking sheets

Choose large, heavy-duty baking sheets that will not buckle at high temperatures. Non-stick sheets are useful, but avoid thin, cheaper bakeware, which might bend during baking and cause sloping cakes or burnt edges.

Below Paper cases can be purchased to fit an exact tin size, but you can make your own lining from sheets of baking parchment or greaseproof paper.

Above Mixing bowls, wooden spoons, palette knives, flexible scrapers and a skewer or cake tester are basic items of baking equipment.

Bowls

You'll need a set of different sizes of bowls for mixing and beating small and large amounts of cake batters, eggs, cream and other liquids.

Electric whisk

A hand-held electric whisk makes quick work of whisking cake batters and egg whites, and is an invaluable aid for cake-making.

Flexible scraper

A flexible scraper is perfect for getting the maximum amount of cake batter out of a bowl. Scrapers become softer with use.

Grater

A grater with a fine and a coarse side is useful for grating citrus rinds, chocolate and marzipan. You can also use a zester for citrus rinds.

Kitchen scales

Accurate kitchen scales are a vital piece of equipment for a baker. Old-fashioned scales with a pan and a set of weights are equally as good as a modern set with a digital display screen as long as they are accurate.

Measuring spoons and cups

Use a set of standard measuring spoons for accuracy of small quantities of ingredients. Sets of plastic or metal measures are sold specifically for this purpose. Remember that all spoon measures

Above Essential kitchen equipment includes sieves, graters, scissors, pastry brush and a large palette knife.

should be level. Standard kitchen tablespoons or teaspoons may be inaccurate measures.

Metric and imperial are given in the recipes. Follow one set of measurements, as they are not exactly equivalent.

Graded measuring cups are used in many countries in place of kitchen scales and are handy for quick measuring. A measuring jug (cup) is vital for liquids and it needs to be graduated in small measures.

Below An electric mixer and whisk are helpful and time-saving kitchen tools, making light work of beating cake batters.

Oven

Each recipe usually begins with the oven setting (unless some form of preparation needs to be done in advance). It is important to preheat the oven to the correct temperature before putting a cake in to bake. Before you switch on the oven, it is also essential to arrange the shelves so that the tins (pans) will fit.

Fan-assisted ovens circulate hot air around the oven and will heat up very quickly. If you are using a fan oven, you will need to reduce the temperature stated in the recipe by 10 per cent; for example, if the baking temperature is 180°C/350°F/Gas 4, reduce it to 160°C/325°F/Gas 3. If the oven is too hot, the outside of a cake will burn before the inside has had time to cook. If it is too cool, cakes may sink or not rise evenly. Try not to open the oven door until at least halfway through the baking time when the cake has had time to rise and set, as a sudden drop in temperature will stop the cake rising and it will therefore sink.

Palette knife or spatula

These are ideal for many jobs including loosening cakes from their tins (pans), lifting cakes and smoothing on icing and frostings.

Pastry brush

A pastry brush is necessary to brush glazes over cakes and to brush melted butter into tins. Brushes wear out and start to shed bristles if used regularly, so keep a spare one handy.

Scissors

These are essential for cutting lining papers to size and snipping dried fruits or nuts into chunks.

Below Measuring jug, kitchen scales, measuring spoons and cups are essential for accurate baking.

Muffin tins are available in sets of six or 12 indentations and have deep-set muffin holes for larger individual cakes.

Fairy cake, bun or patty tins are similar to muffin tins but have shallower indentations for making smaller cakes. Line each indentation with a paper case.

Ring moulds and Kugelhopf tins are round metal moulds with a hole or funnel in the centre, and are specially designed for baking angel cakes and ring-shaped cakes. Grease these moulds well with melted butter, and put small strips of baking parchment in the base of plain ring moulds to aid the release of the cake.

Sieves (Strainers)

A large wire sieve is useful for sifting flour and dry ingredients, and a smaller nylon sieve can be kept just for icing (confectioners') sugar.

Skewer or cake tester

A thin metal skewer can be used to test if a cake is ready.

Spoons

Keep a large wooden spoon just for baking, for beating mixtures, butters and creaming. Don't use one that has been used for frying savoury things such as onions, as the flavours may taint the cake batter. Use a metal spoon for folding flour and beaten egg white into batter.

Tins (Pans)

Always use the size of tin stated in the recipe. If you use too large a tin, your cake may be too shallow when it is baked. Too small a tin may cause a peak in the mixture to form, which will then crack or sink in the middle.

Above A selection of tins (pans) in different sizes and shapes increases the range of baked goods you can make.

Choose good-quality rigid bakeware. When buying new tins, remember that top-quality tins will last longer and give better results. Non-stick coatings on some of the new ranges of bakeware need almost no greasing and cakes turn out beautifully, as do cakes cooked in the new heatproof flexible muffin and loaf moulds.

Sandwich tins and shallow round tins are designed to bake light sponges quickly.

Loaf tins in small and large sizes are ideal for teabreads and loaf cakes.

Deep round and square heavy-duty cake tins are ideal for baking rich fruit cakes.

Springform tins are round baking tins with a clipped side that can be loosened and removed easily from delicate bakes such as light sponges or cheesecakes. A loose-based tin makes a good substitute.

Wire racks

These cooling racks allow air to circulate around the hot baked cakes so that they will cool without becoming moist underneath.

ROUND OR SQUARE TINS AND COMPARABLE SIZING

If you use a tin (pan) that is a different size from the one stated in the recipe, the baking time, height, texture and appearance of the cake may be affected, as the quantity of mixture you have prepared will not be correct for that size of tin. Although you can use a square tin instead of a round tin, the sizes are not exactly equivalent, as there is a 2.5cm/1in size difference. A square tin will have a larger area than a round one; for example, a 20cm/8in round cake tin will take the same quantity of mixture as an 18cm/7in square tin.

Successful cake-making

Paying attention to the detail of a recipe will help to ensure a perfect cake. First, get all your equipment ready and prepare your cake tin. Take care with accurate measuring, and know how to test that the cake is cooked so that your hard work is rewarded with a delicious treat.

Assembling the ingredients

Ensure that you have all the necessary ingredients before baking.

Sifting flour makes a fine-textured product that is light and airy.

Accurate weighing and measuring

Recipes usually specify imperial, metric or cup weight. You must follow one set only and never use a combination, as they are not exact equivalents. If the measurements are muddled, it will affect the quality of the baked goods.

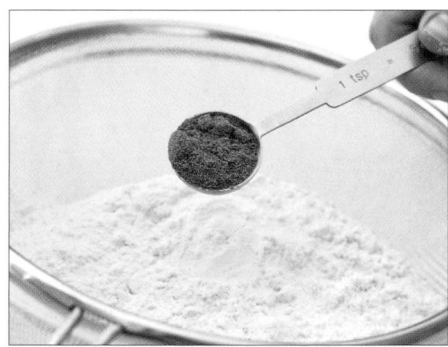

1 All spoon measurements must be level using a recognized set of metric or imperial spoon measures. Never estimate weights, as you will rarely achieve an accurate result.

2 As ingredients must be measured exactly, use good kitchen scales for weighing or graded measuring cups and scoops. These cups should be levelled for accurate measuring unless the recipe calls for a 'generous' cup.

Preparing tins (pans)

When recipes give instructions on how to prepare and line tins, don't be tempted to skip this, or you may ruin the baked cake. If using tins without a non-stick coating, give them a light greasing before use. Line the base of a tin to help the cake turn out easily.

1 Apply a thin film of melted butter with a pastry brush, or rub around the tin with kitchen paper and a little softened margarine.

Lining the sides of the tin

1 Cut a piece of baking parchment or greaseproof (waxed) paper 2.5cm/ 1in wider than the depth of the tin and long enough to fit around the circumference. Make a fold along one long edge of the strip, about 2.5cm/1in deep. Snip this folded edge at regular intervals with sharp scissors.

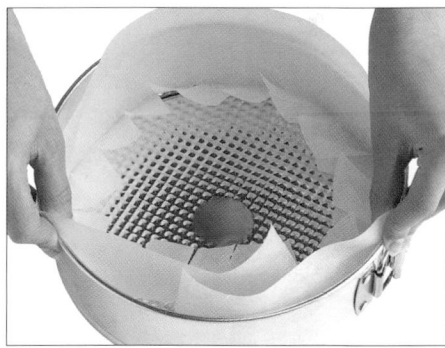

2 Line the sides of the tin using the strip, with the snipped edge at the base, lying flat. The baking parchment should adhere to the greased tin. Lightly grease any overlap of the edges so that it doesn't protrude into the cake batter. If your tin has a loose base this step will stop the baking batter from escaping and burning on the oven base.

Lining the base of a tin

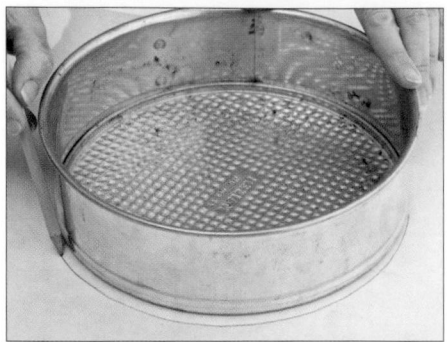

1 Place the tin on a sheet of baking parchment and draw around it with a pencil. Cut out the shape.

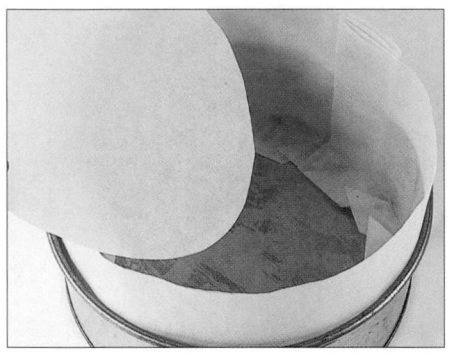

2 Fit the rounds of paper in the base of the tin to cover the snipped edge.

Additional lining for a fruit cake

1 Tins for rich fruit cake batters should be double-lined. Cut a piece of baking parchment large enough to fold double and to stand 5cm/2in higher than the tin sides before continuing as for Lining the Sides of a Tin (above). A layer of brown paper wrapped around the outside will protect the cake.

Lining a baking tray

1 Cut a sheet of paper larger than the tray. Cut into each corner, then press in place.

Coating with flour

1 To coat with flour, tip a spoonful into the greased tin, then tip away the excess. This gives a golden edge.

Filling a cake tin (pan) with batter

1 Pour cake batter into the centre of the cake tin and spread it out to the edges. The batter should be spread evenly to ensure even baking. Rub off any drips from the cake tin because they will burn.

Checking to see if a cake is cooked

There are several clues to help determine whether a cake is ready. Has it baked for the suggested time? The baking times may need reviewing if you know that your oven temperature is inaccurate, if other items are being cooked at the same time, or if the oven door is opened in the baking process.

1 Cakes should be golden, risen and firm to the touch when pressed lightly in the centre. Lighter sponges and cakes should be a pale golden colour and the sides should shrink away slightly from the sides of the tin (pan).

2 To test a cake, insert a thin warmed skewer into the deepest part of the centre. If the cake is cooked, it should come out perfectly cleanly with no mixture sticking to it. If there is mixture on the skewer, bake the cake for a little longer and test again.

Releasing from the tin (pan) and cooling cakes

As freshly baked cakes are very fragile, they need time to stand in the tin to cool for a short time to firm them. Sponges and delicate cakes need 3–4 minutes standing time, but rich fruit cakes are very soft when freshly baked, so leave these in the tin for longer. To give a good shape to the edges, very rich fruit cakes such as wedding cakes should be left in the tins to go cold.

1 Loosen the cake sides by running a small metal spatula around the inside of the tin between the cake and tin, or lining paper and tin.

2 To turn the cake out on a wire rack, put a wire rack on top of the cake tin, then turn the whole thing over so that the cake is upside down. Peel away the lining papers while the cake is warm. Turn the cake back the right way up. Leave the cake to go completely cold before icing and storing.

Storing cakes

Make sure cakes are completely cold before storing, otherwise condensation will form in the tin and this can cause the cakes to go mouldy. Plastic food containers will help to keep cakes moist, so are ideal for storing richer sponges, but an airtight cake tin is necessary to keep fatless sponge-type cakes dry.

Cakes with fresh cream fillings and decorations need to be kept in the refrigerator and ideally, eaten on the day they are filled with cream.

Fatless sponges such as Swiss rolls (jelly rolls) will keep for only 1–2 days. Sponges with added fat will store for 3–5 days and richer cakes, such as creamed sponges, will keep for up to 1 week. Light fruit cakes will store for 2 weeks in a tin, but rich fruit cakes will keep for up to 3 months after cutting.

If you don't have a large cake container, invert a large mixing bowl over the cake on a plate or flat surface and the cake will stay fresh.

FEEDING A FRUIT CAKE
Fruit cakes fed with alcohol have a mellow flavour.

Prick the surface with a cocktail stick (toothpick) and brush with a little alcohol such as rum, brandy or sweet sherry.

Storing a rich fruit cake

Rich fruit cakes, such as wedding cakes, will mature in flavour and improve in texture if kept for 3 months before being eaten, especially if you feed them with alcohol two or three times during that 3 months. Store undecorated fruit cakes in their baking papers.

1 Wrap the original wrappings of the rich fruit cake with clean baking parchment and seal with tape.

2 Wrap in a double layer of foil and seal tightly, then store in a cool dry place.

Freezing cakes

Most cakes will freeze well, undecorated. Cool each cake completely, then wrap in strong freezer film or foil to exclude as much air as possible. Label and freeze. To use, completely unwrap and thaw at room temperature on racks, allowing plenty of time for larger cakes.

Sugarpaste icing

This soft icing is also sold as roll-out icing, ready-to-roll icing or fondant icing. If you are covering a particularly large cake or a tiered cake, you will need to make the sugarpaste in batches. It is suitable for covering a Madeira cake, or a fruit cake that has first been covered in almond paste, *see page 24–25*.

MAKES 350G/12OZ/2 CUPS

1 egg white
15ml/1 tbsp liquid glucose
350g/12oz/3 cups icing
   (confectioners') sugar, sifted,
   plus extra for dusting
paste food colouring, if required

1 Place the egg white and liquid glucose in a large mixing bowl and stir together with a fork, breaking up the egg white.

2 Add the icing sugar gradually, mixing in with a flat-bladed knife until the mixture binds together, forming a ball.

COOK'S TIP
Always use special paste colours for sugarpaste. Don't use liquid food colour, as this will make the sugarpaste go soft and sticky and be difficult to roll out.

3 Turn the sugarpaste out on to a clean surface dusted with icing sugar and knead for 5 minutes, or until soft but firm enough to roll out. If it is too soft, knead in a little more icing sugar until the paste is pliable.

Colouring sugarpaste

1 Colour the paste gradually and knead well to colour evenly.

Working with sugarpaste

1 Roll out the sugarpaste to a circle or square large enough to cover the top and sides of the cake.

2 If you are covering almond paste, brush it with a little cool boiled water, Kirsch or vodka.

3 If you are covering a sponge cake, apply a layer of buttercream icing to the cake surface. The sugarpaste will adhere to the buttercream.

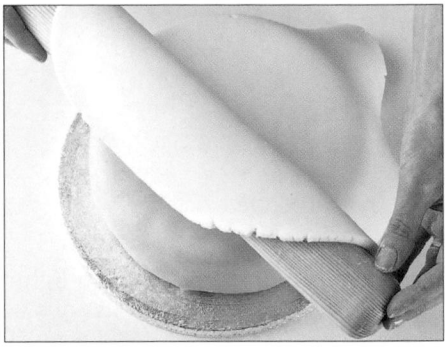

4 Roll the sugarpaste around the rolling pin to hold it. Place the sugarpaste over the cake and sides; avoid pleating the edges.

5 Smooth down over the top and sides, pushing out any air bubbles with your palms. Trim any excess icing away from the base using a metal spatula or sharp knife and smooth the join at the base. Leave to dry out for 24 hours. Work carefully to avoid marking the paste.

DECORATING TIP
Leave sugarpaste-covered cakes to dry out for 24 hours before adding decorations, as this provides a firmer finished surface to work on and one less likely to mark.

Adapting recipes for special diets

Although there are fewer recipes that are suitable to make for people with special diets, it's still possible to adapt some to make gluten-free cakes for people who have an intolerance. Healthier cakes with a lower fat content can be made for anyone who is limiting fats in their diet.

Gluten-free baking

Having an intolerance to gluten does not mean that you have to forego the pleasures of home baking. Gluten is the protein found in wheat that gives the elasticity to cakes and bread, making them light and springy. Gluten is also present in barley, rye and oats. Leaving out wheat flour means that gluten-free cakes will not have the same characteristics as cakes baked with ordinary flours. Gluten-free flours are available, and although these are a little more difficult to work with than regular flours, you will find some recipes can be adapted by following the manufacturer's instructions. A product that aids gluten-free baking is xanthan gum, which is sold in health-food shops. This gum replaces the elastic qualities of gluten lacking in gluten-free flours, and when used in baking will make the cake less crumbly.

Below Sunflower oil is an unsaturated fat. It is useful for making low-fat cakes.

Above clockwise from top left Gluten-free ingredients include ground almonds, cornmeal, xanthan gum and rice flour.

You will find that practice is needed to adapt your favourite recipes for gluten-free flours, but scones, soda breads and banana tea breads are all successful. Replacing wheat flour in a recipe with ground almonds, cornmeal, rice flour, soya flour or a mixture of these flours plus ground almonds can produce light and delicious results.

Lower-fat cakes

Some cakes and bakes are rich in fat and are calorie-laden. Most cakes are based on a mixture of butter, sugar, eggs and flour, with the butter forming a base to help bind and retain moisture in the mixture. It is possible to produce delicious cakes without fat. Meringues, angel cake and a classic fatless sponge, with a filling of fresh fruits instead of lashings of cream, will help cut down your fat intake considerably. You will also find recipes in this

Above Dates, prunes, figs, bananas and sunflower oil provide flavour and moisture to low-fat baking.

book that use oil instead of butter; unsaturated oils such as sunflower are generally healthier than solid fats, and baked goods made with them will appeal to all the family. Choosing recipes that contain less fat and a high percentage of healthy ingredients such as puréed prunes, dates, figs or mashed bananas will also help cut down on your intake of saturated fats. These cakes bake to a deliciously moist texture, usually keep a little longer than others and freeze well.

Low-sugar cakes

Baking for diabetics or those following a low-sugar diet can be a challenge. Diabetics do not need to avoid sugar altogether, but to moderate their intake. Choose recipes with a lower quantity of sugar in them in preference to high-sugar bakes. Sugar substitutes are mostly unsuitable for baking cakes.

Classic cakes

Many cakes are 'classics' and every family has their favourite. This appealing collection includes all of the traditional recipes that have stood the test of time. You will find recipes here for Victoria Sponge, Madeira Cake and Frosted Walnut Layer Cake. There is a Simple Chocolate Cake, light-as-air sponges such as Angel Food Cake, and a delicate Lemon Drizzle Cake. Some of these bakes are super-quick to make, such as the Easy All-in-one Sponge. If you are a novice baker, try a simple recipe such as Carrot Cake with Cream Cheese Icing to impress your friends and family. You will find this chapter contains recipes that you will return to, and they are sure to become your own favourites for years to come.

Left: Cherry Cake and Lemon Roulade with Lemon-curd Cream.

Madeira cake

This fine-textured cake is a good choice for a birthday or celebration cake, as it is firm but light, which makes it the perfect base for decorating. It is ideal to serve with hot drinks, either as it is or split and sandwiched with buttercream. Store for up to one week in an airtight container.

SERVES 8–10

175g/6oz/¾ cup butter, softened,
  plus extra for greasing
175g/6oz/scant 1 cup caster
  (superfine) sugar
3 eggs
15ml/1 tbsp lemon juice
225g/8oz/2 cups plain
  (all-purpose) flour
7.5ml/1½ tsp baking powder

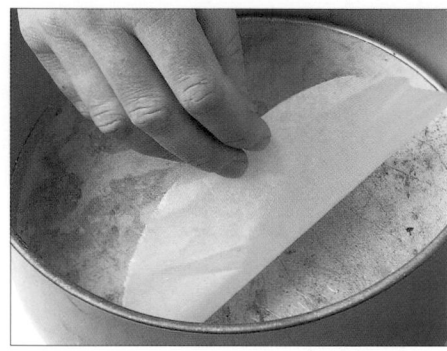

1 Preheat the oven to 160°C/325°F/ Gas 3. Grease and line an 18cm/7in round deep cake tin (pan) with baking parchment.

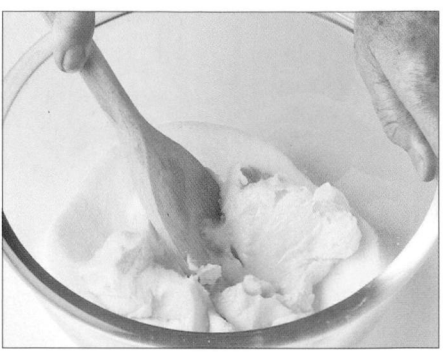

2 In a large bowl, beat the butter and sugar together until light and fluffy, then beat in the eggs one at a time, beating well after each addition. Stir in the lemon juice.

3 Sift in the flour and baking powder and stir to combine.

4 Spoon the mixture into the prepared tin and smooth the top level with the back of the spoon.

5 Bake in the centre of the oven for 1¼–1½ hours, until golden, or until a skewer inserted into the centre comes out clean.

6 Leave the cake to cool in the tin for 45 minutes, then turn out on to a wire rack to go cold. Remove the lining paper.

Energy 453kcal/1894kJ; Protein 6.1g; Carbohydrate 51.4g, of which sugars 30g; Fat 26.3g, of which saturates 15.5g; Cholesterol 155mg; Calcium 74mg; Fibre 0.9g; Sodium 208mg.

Easy all-in-one sponge

This strawberry and 'cream' cake is so quick and easy to make. You'll find this simple topping handy for other cakes too, as you can make it from store-cupboard ingredients. Store for up to three days in an airtight container. Freeze the cakes, undecorated, for up to two months.

SERVES 12

175g/6oz/1½ cups self-raising (self-rising) flour
5ml/1 tsp baking powder
175g/6oz/¾ cup soft tub margarine, plus extra for greasing
175g/6oz/scant 1 cup caster (superfine) sugar
3 eggs
15ml/1 tbsp milk
5ml/1 tsp vanilla extract

For the filling and topping
150g/5oz white chocolate chips
200g/7oz/scant 1 cup cream cheese
25g/1oz/¼ cup icing (confectioners') sugar
30ml/2 tbsp strawberry jam
12 strawberries

1 Preheat the oven to 180°C/350°F/ Gas 4. Grease and line two 20cm/8in round shallow cake tins (pans) with baking parchment.

2 Sift the flour and baking powder into a large bowl, then add all the remaining cake ingredients.

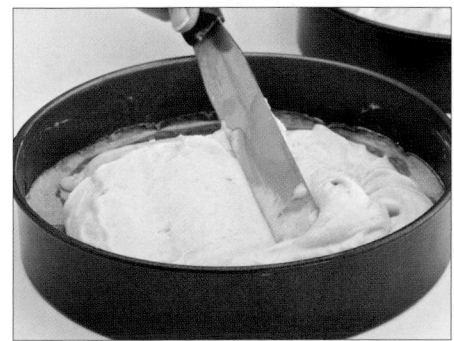

3 Beat until smooth, then divide between the tins and smooth level.

4 Bake for 20 minutes, or until the cakes spring back when pressed. Allow to stand for 5 minutes, then turn out on to a wire rack to go cold. Remove the lining papers.

5 To make the filling and topping, melt the chocolate chips in a heatproof bowl over a pan of gently simmering water. Remove from the heat and cool slightly, then beat in the cream cheese and icing sugar.

6 Spread the top of one sponge with jam. Slice 4 strawberries, then arrange them over the jam.

7 Spread one-third of the filling over the base of the other cake.

8 Put the cakes together. Spread the remaining topping over the cake top. Decorate with strawberries.

Energy 395kcal/1648kJ; Protein 4.7g; Carbohydrate 39.6g, of which sugars 28.5g; Fat 25.3g, of which saturates 15.2g; Cholesterol 94mg; Calcium 90mg; Fibre 0.5g; Sodium 173mg.

Fresh fruit Genoese sponge

Genoese is the original fatless sponge, which can be used for luxury gateaux and Swiss rolls. It has a soft and light texture, but because it is made without fat it should be eaten soon after making, as it does not store well. Decorate with cream and fresh fruit for an indulgent cake.

SERVES 8–10

butter, for greasing
4 eggs
115g/4oz/generous ½ cup caster
   (superfine) sugar
175g/6oz/1½ cups plain
   (all-purpose) flour, sifted

For the filling and topping
90ml/6 tbsp orange-flavoured
   liqueur such as Cointreau
600ml/1 pint/2½ cups double
   (heavy) cream
60ml/4 tbsp vanilla sugar
450g/1lb/4 cups fresh soft fruit,
   such as raspberries, strawberries,
   redcurrants and blueberries
65g/2½oz/½ cup shelled pistachio
   nuts, finely chopped
60ml/4 tbsp apricot jam, warmed
   and sieved (strained)

1 Preheat the oven to 180°C/350°F/ Gas 4. Grease and line a 21cm/ 8½in round deep cake tin (pan) with baking parchment.

2 Put the eggs and sugar in a large bowl and beat with an electric whisk for about 10 minutes, or until the mixture is thick and pale.

3 Sift the pre-sifted flour into the bowl with the egg and sugar mixture, then fold together gently.

4 Transfer the batter to the prepared tin. Bake in the centre of the oven for 30–35 minutes, or until a skewer inserted into the centre of the cake comes out clean.

5 Leave the cake in the tin for 5 minutes, then turn out on to a wire rack to go cold. Peel off the lining paper.

6 Cut the cake in half horizontally to make two layers. Put the bottom layer on to a serving plate.

7 Sprinkle the orange-flavoured liqueur, if using, over the cut side of each cake.

8 To make the filling and topping, put the double cream and vanilla sugar in a large bowl and beat together with an electric whisk until the mixture holds its shape.

9 Spread two-thirds of the cream over the bottom layer of the cake and top with half of the soft fruit.

10 Carefully put the second layer of the cake on top of the first layer and spread the remaining cream over the top.

11 Arrange the rest of the fresh fruit on the top of the cake and sprinkle with the chopped pistachio nuts.

12 Lightly glaze the top layer of fruit by brushing over the warmed apricot jam.

Energy 815kcal/3411kJ; Protein 8.5g; Carbohydrate 99.6g, of which sugars 85.9g; Fat 43g, of which saturates 21.8g; Cholesterol 158mg; Calcium 128mg; Fibre 2g; Sodium 132mg.

Victoria sponge

This light cake was named in honour of Queen Victoria of England. Often referred to as a Victoria sandwich, the mixture is based on equal quantities of fat, sugar and flour. It is usually sandwiched with a layer of jam. Store this cake for up to three days in an airtight container.

4 Sift the flour over the top in two batches and, using a metal spoon, fold in lightly using a figure-of-eight motion until the mixture is smooth.

5 Divide the batter between the prepared tins and smooth out to the edges so that the mixture is level. Bake for 20 minutes, or until golden and firm to the touch in the centre of the cake.

SERVES 6–8

175g/6oz/¾ cup butter, softened, plus extra for greasing
3 large eggs
a few drops of vanilla extract
175g/6oz/scant 1 cup caster (superfine) sugar
175g/6oz/1½ cups self-raising (self-rising) flour
about 60ml/4 tbsp jam
icing (confectioners') sugar, for dusting

1 Preheat the oven to 180°C/350°F/ Gas 4. Grease and line two 20cm/8in round shallow cake tins (pans) with baking parchment.

2 In a small bowl, lightly beat the eggs with the vanilla extract.

3 In a large bowl, beat the butter with the sugar until the mixture is pale, light and fluffy, then beat in the eggs in small quantities, beating well after each addition.

6 Leave the cakes to cool in the tins for a few minutes, then turn out on to a wire rack to go cold. Remove the lining paper.

7 Sandwich the cakes together with jam.

8 Sift a little icing sugar over the top before serving.

Energy 368kcal/1543kJ; Protein 4.6g; Carbohydrate 44.7g, of which sugars 28.5g; Fat 20.3g, of which saturates 12g; Cholesterol 118mg; Calcium 104mg; Fibre 0.7g; Sodium 241mg.

Pound cake

The original pound cake, enjoyed both in the US and Britain for many years, was made using 450g/1lb of each ingredient and having as many as eight eggs to raise it. This recipe is for a smaller variation and is served warm with a delicious, fresh fruit sauce. Keep for up to three days.

SERVES 6–8

175g/6oz/¾ cup butter, softened,
  plus extra for greasing
175g/6oz/¾ cup caster
  (superfine) sugar, plus extra
  for sprinkling
175g/6oz/1½ cups plain
  (all-purpose) flour
10ml/2 tsp baking powder
3 eggs
grated rind of 1 orange
15ml/1 tbsp orange juice

For the sauce
450g/1lb/4 cups fresh raspberries
  or strawberries
25g/1oz/2 tbsp caster
  (superfine) sugar
15ml/1 tbsp lemon juice

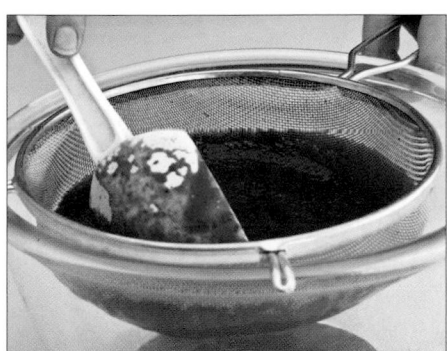

1 To make the sauce, reserve a few fruits for decoration. Process the remaining fruit until smooth in a food processor. Add the sugar and lemon juice, and process to combine. Strain and chill the sauce.

2 Preheat the oven to 180°C/350°F/ Gas 4. Grease a 20cm/8in round ring tin (pan). Sprinkle the base and sides lightly with sugar.

3 Sift the flour with the baking powder into a bowl.

4 In another bowl, beat the butter until creamy. Add the remaining sugar and beat until light and fluffy. Add the eggs, one at a time, beating well after each addition, then beat in the orange rind and juice.

5 Gently fold in the flour mixture in batches, then spoon the batter into the prepared tin and tap gently to release any air bubbles. Bake for 35–40 minutes, or until the top of the cake is golden and springs back when pressed with the fingers.

6 Allow the cake to cool in the tin for 10 minutes, then turn it out on to a wire rack and leave to cool for a further 30 minutes. Serve warm slices with a little of the fruit sauce. Decorate with the reserved fruit.

Energy 366kcal/1533kJ; Protein 5.4g; Carbohydrate 42.7g, of which sugars 26.1g; Fat 20.5g, of which saturates 12.1g; Cholesterol 118mg; Calcium 71mg; Fibre 2.1g; Sodium 163mg.

Cherry cake

Both dried and glacé cherries are used in this elegant cake, partnered with the delicate flavour of almonds and decorated with a drizzle of icing. It is a combination that is perfect for a summer tea party. Store in an airtight container for up to five days. Freeze, undecorated, for two months.

SERVES 10

175g/6oz/¾ cup unsalted butter, softened, plus extra for greasing
175g/6oz/scant 1 cup caster (superfine) sugar
3 eggs, beaten
150g/5oz/1¼ cups self-raising (self-rising) flour
50g/2oz/½ cup plain (all-purpose) flour
75g/3oz/¾ cup ground almonds
75g/3oz/scant ½ cup glacé (candied) cherries, washed, dried and halved, plus extra to decorate
25g/1oz dried cherries
a few drops of almond extract

For the decoration
115g/4oz/1 cup icing (confectioners') sugar, sifted
5ml/1 tsp lemon juice
50g/2oz/½ cup flaked (sliced) almonds, toasted
10 natural glacé (candied) cherries

1 Preheat the oven to 160°C/325°F/ Gas 3. Grease and line a 20cm/8in round deep cake tin (pan).

2 In a bowl, beat the butter with the sugar until light and fluffy, using an electric whisk, if possible. Add the eggs a little at a time, including 5ml/1 tsp of flour with each addition.

3 Sift in the flours, the ground almonds and cherries. Stir well.

4 Add the flour and cherry mixture to the butter and sugar and fold together with the almond extract until smooth. Spoon into the cake tin and smooth level.

5 Bake for 45–50 minutes, or until a skewer inserted into the centre comes out clean. Cool slightly, then turn on to a wire rack to go cold. Remove the lining paper.

6 In a bowl, mix the icing sugar with the lemon juice, and 10–15ml/ 2–3 tsp water, to make a soft icing. Drizzle half over the cake top. Sprinkle the almonds into the centre. Place the cherries around the edge. Drizzle over the remaining icing.

Energy 367kcal/1535kJ; Protein 5g; Carbohydrate 43.7g, of which sugars 26.6g; Fat 20.4g, of which saturates 12g; Cholesterol 118mg; Calcium 75mg; Fibre 0.9g; Sodium 309mg.

Chocolate-orange marble cake

Relive your memories of childhood and make this magical cake with its clever marbled pattern.
Two cake batters are swirled together to give the marbled effect, and, because one is flavoured
with orange and the other with chocolate, the overall taste is wonderful too.

SERVES 10

225g/8oz/1 cup butter, softened,
  plus extra for greasing
225g/8oz/1 generous cup caster
  (superfine) sugar
4 eggs, beaten
225g/8oz/2 cups self-raising
  (self-rising) flour
30ml/2 tbsp unsweetened
  cocoa powder
15ml/1 tbsp milk
grated rind from 1 large orange
15ml/1 tbsp orange juice

For the frosting
115g/4oz plain (semisweet) or milk
  chocolate, melted and cooled
115g/4oz/½ cup unsalted butter
225g/8oz/2 cups icing
  (confectioners') sugar, sifted

1 Preheat the oven to 180°C/350°F/
Gas 4. Grease and line a 20cm/8in
round deep cake tin (pan) with
baking parchment.

2 In a large bowl, beat the butter and
sugar together until pale and fluffy.

3 Beat in the eggs a little at a time.
Fold the flour into the mixture. Put
half of the batter into another bowl.

4 Sift the cocoa into one bowl of
batter and mix well with the milk.

COOK'S TIP
The cake keeps for up to 5 days
in a sealed container.

5 Put the rind and orange juice into
the other bowl and mix well.

6 Spoon alternate tablespoonfuls of
each mixture into the cake tin. Swirl
a knife through the mixture once,
then smooth the top level.

7 Bake for 45 minutes, or until the
centre springs back when pressed.
Leave to cool. Remove the papers.

8 In another bowl, whisk the butter.
Beat in the icing sugar. Stir in the
chocolate. Spread over the cake.

Energy 505kcal/2109kJ; Protein 6.5g; Carbohydrate 48.1g, of which sugars 36.6g; Fat 32.9g, of which saturates 18.8g; Cholesterol 119mg; Calcium 98mg; Fibre 1.5g; Sodium 322mg.

Lady Baltimore cake

This recipe was published in the 19th-century novel *Lady Baltimore* by Owen Wister. The cake usually contains the same basic ingredients: pecan nuts, figs and raisins in a fluffy white frosting. Make it for a special tea-time treat – it looks quite stunning. Store it for up to three days.

SERVES 10–12

250ml/8fl oz/1 cup vegetable oil,
  plus extra for greasing
275g/10oz/2½ cups plain
  (all-purpose) flour
12.5ml/2½tsp baking powder
4 eggs
350g/12oz/1¾ cups caster
  (superfine) sugar
grated rind of 1 large orange
250ml/8fl oz/1 cup fresh
  orange juice

For the frosting
2 egg whites
350g/12oz/1¾ cups caster
  (superfine) sugar
1.25ml/¼ tsp cream of tartar
5ml/1 tsp vanilla extract
50g/2oz/½ cup pecan nuts,
  finely chopped
85g/3oz/generous ½ cup
  raisins, chopped
3 ready-to-eat dried figs,
  finely chopped
18 pecan halves, to decorate

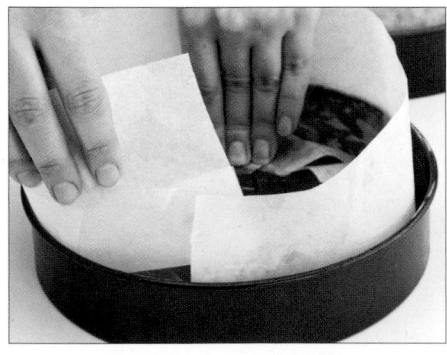

1 Preheat the oven to 180°C/350°F/ Gas 4. Grease and line two 23cm/ 9in round shallow cake tins (pans) with baking parchment.

2 In a bowl, sift together the flour and baking powder. Set aside.

3 Beat the eggs and sugar in another large bowl, using an electric whisk, until thick and pale. Beat in the orange rind and juice, then add the vegetable oil and mix well.

4 On a low speed, beat in the flour mixture in three batches.

5 Divide the cake batter between the tins. Bake for 30 minutes, or until a skewer inserted in to the centre comes out clean.

6 Leave to stand for 15 minutes, then run a knife around the inside of the tins, and transfer the cakes to a rack to go cold. Remove the lining.

7 To make the filling and topping, put the egg whites, sugar, 75ml/ 5 tbsp cold water and the cream of tartar in the top of a double boiler, or in a large heatproof bowl set over a pan of boiling water. Beat the mixture, using an electric whisk, until glossy and thick.

8 Remove the pan from the heat, add the vanilla extract and continue beating until thick.

9 Fold in the nuts, raisins and figs.

10 Spread a layer of the frosting on top of one cake. Sandwich with the second cake.

11 Spread the cake top and sides with the remainder of the frosting. Arrange the pecan halves on top.

Energy 529kcal/2229kJ; Protein 5.9g; Carbohydrate 90.2g, of which sugars 74.3g; Fat 18.6g, of which saturates 2.2g; Cholesterol 63mg; Calcium 107mg; Fibre 1.9g; Sodium 51mg.

Angel food cake

Similar to a whisked sponge cake, the texture of this American classic is springy but slightly sticky, and the colour is snowy white. The cream of tartar helps to aerate the egg whites, and the addition of sugar creates a light meringue mixture. This will keep refrigerated, for up to five days.

SERVES 20

65g/2½oz/9 tbsp plain
  (all-purpose) flour
15ml/1 tbsp cornflour (cornstarch)
225g/8oz/generous 1 cup caster
  (superfine) sugar
10 egg whites
5ml/1 tsp cream of tartar
7.5ml/1½ tsp vanilla extract

For the frosting
2 egg whites
115g/4oz/generous ½ cup caster
  (superfine) sugar
10ml/2 tsp golden (light corn)
  syrup
2.5ml/½ tsp vanilla extract
rind of 1 orange, to decorate

1 Preheat the oven to 180°C/350°F/ Gas 4.

2 In a large bowl, sift together the flour, cornflour and 50g/2oz/¼ cup of the sugar three times, so that the texture is very, very light.

3 Put the egg whites and the cream of tartar into a clean, grease-free bowl and whisk until they form stiff peaks.

4 Gradually whisk in the remaining sugar, 15ml/1 tbsp at a time, until the mixture becomes thick and glossy.

5 Using a metal spoon, gently fold the sifted flour and the vanilla extract into the whisked egg whites until combined. Transfer the mixture to a 25cm/10in non-stick ring mould and smooth out the batter so that it is level.

6 Bake for 35–40 minutes, or until risen and golden. Remove from the oven, invert the cake in its mould on to a wire rack. Leave to go cold.

7 To make the frosting, put the egg whites into a clean, grease-free bowl. Whisk until stiff and dry, then set aside.

8 Heat the sugar and 60ml/4 tbsp water in a small pan, stirring constantly until the sugar dissolves.

9 Increase the heat and boil until the temperature reaches 115°C/240°F on a sugar thermometer. As soon as this temperature is reached, remove the pan from the heat.

10 Pour the syrup into the egg whites, whisking constantly, until the mixture is thick and glossy.

11 Beat in the golden syrup and vanilla, beating for 5 minutes.

12 Lift the mould off the cake and put the cake on a serving plate.

13 Quickly spread the frosting over the cake. Sprinkle with orange rind.

Energy 117kcal/500kJ; Protein 3.1g; Carbohydrate 27.7g, of which sugars 21.4g; Fat 0.1g, of which saturates 0g; Cholesterol 0mg; Calcium 24mg; Fibre 0.3g; Sodium 49mg.

Boston cream pie

Created by chef M. Sanzian at the Parker House Hotel in Boston, in the 1850s, this famous 'pie' is actually a cake. It is unusual, because sandwiched between the two cake layers is a rich custard. With its chocolate glaze it is really very appealing. Keep, refrigerated, for up to three days.

SERVES 8

butter, for greasing
225g/8oz/2 cups plain
   (all-purpose) four
15ml/1 tbsp baking powder
pinch of salt
115g/4oz/½ cup butter, softened,
   plus extra for greasing
200g/7oz/1 cup caster
   (superfine) sugar
2 eggs
5ml/1 tsp vanilla extract
6fl oz/175ml/¾ cup milk

For the filling
8fl oz/250ml/1 cup milk
3 egg yolks
90g/3½oz/½ cup caster
   (superfine) sugar
25g/1oz/¼ cup plain
   (all-purpose) flour
15ml/1 tbsp butter
5ml/1 tsp vanilla extract

For the chocolate glaze
25g/1oz dark (bittersweet)
   chocolate
15g/½oz/1 tbsp butter
50g/2oz/½ cup icing
   (confectioners') sugar, plus extra
   for dusting
2.5ml/½ tsp vanilla extract
15ml/1 tbsp hot water

1 Preheat the oven to 190°C/375°F/Gas 5. Grease and line two 20cm/8in round shallow cake tins (pans) with baking parchment.

2 Sift the flour with the baking powder and salt into a large bowl.

3 In a large bowl, beat the butter and sugar together until light and fluffy. Beat in the eggs one at a time, beating well after each addition. Stir in the vanilla extract.

4 Add the milk and the dry ingredients, alternating the batches and mixing only enough to blend.

5 Divide the cake batter between the prepared tins and spread it out evenly.

6 Bake for 25 minutes, or until a skewer inserted into the centre comes out clean. Allow to stand in the tins for 5 minutes before turning out on to a wire rack to cool completely. Remove the lining.

7 To make the filling, heat the milk to boiling point in a small pan, and remove from the heat.

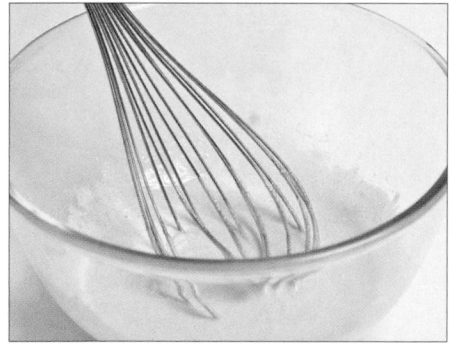

8 In a heatproof bowl, beat the egg yolks until smooth. Gradually add the sugar and continue beating until pale yellow, then beat in the flour.

9 While beating, pour the hot milk into the egg yolk mixture.

10 When all the milk has been added, put the bowl over a pan of boiling water. Heat, stirring constantly, until thickened. Cook for 2 minutes more, then remove from the heat.

11 Stir in the butter and vanilla extract. Leave to cool.

12 Slice off the domed top of each cake to create a flat surface, if necessary. Put one cake on a serving plate and spread on the filling in a thick layer. Set the other cake on top, cut side down. Smooth the edge of the filling layer so that it is flush with the sides of the cake layers.

13 To make the chocolate glaze, melt the chocolate and butter in a heatproof bowl set over a pan of gently simmering water. Stir well.

14 When smooth, remove from the heat and beat in the icing sugar using a wooden spoon. Add the vanilla extract, then beat in a little hot water to give a spreadable consistency. Spread evenly over the top of the cake. When it is set, dust the top with icing sugar.

Energy 499kcal/2100kJ; Protein 6g; Carbohydrate 77.1g, of which sugars 53.1g; Fat 20.3g, of which saturates 12.1g; Cholesterol 146mg; Calcium 112mg; Fibre 1g; Sodium 297mg.

Frosted walnut layer cake

Walnuts go very well in rich cakes, especially when combined with a sweet filling. This moist and nutty cake is layered with vanilla buttercream and then topped with swirls of light and fluffy frosting. It is ideal for a special party. Keep the cake for five days in an airtight container.

SERVES 12

225g/8oz/1 cup butter, softened,
    plus extra for greasing
225g/8oz/2 cups self-raising
    (self-rising) flour
5ml/1 tsp baking powder
225g/8oz/1 cup soft light
    brown sugar
75g/3oz/³⁄4 cup walnuts,
    finely chopped
4 eggs
15ml/1 tbsp treacle (molasses)

For the buttercream
75g/3oz/6 tbsp unsalted butter
5ml/1 tsp vanilla extract
175g/6oz/1½ cups icing
    (confectioners') sugar

For the meringue frosting
2 large (US extra large) egg whites
350g/12oz/1³⁄4 cups golden caster
    (superfine) sugar
pinch of salt
pinch of cream of tartar
15ml/1 tbsp warm water
whole walnut halves, to decorate

1 Preheat the oven to 160°C/325°F/ Gas 3. Grease and line two 20cm/8in round shallow cake tins (pans) with baking parchment.

2 Sift the flour and baking powder into a large bowl, then add all the remaining ingredients.

3 Beat together for 2 minutes, or until smooth, then divide between the tins and spread level.

4 Bake for 25 minutes, or until golden and springy to the touch in the centre.

5 Allow to stand for 5 minutes, then turn out on to a wire rack to go cold. Remove the lining papers. Cut each cake in half horizontally using a long-bladed sharp knife.

6 To make the buttercream, in a large bowl, beat the butter, vanilla extract and icing sugar together until light and fluffy.

7 Spread a third thinly over one sponge half and place a sponge layer on top, then continue layering the sponges with the buttercream. Put the cake on to a serving plate.

8 To make the frosting, put the egg whites in a large heatproof bowl and add the caster sugar, salt, cream of tartar and water. Put the bowl over a pan of hot water and whisk with an electric mixer for 7 minutes, or until the mixture is thick and stands in peaks.

9 Immediately, use a metal spatula to swirl the frosting over the top and sides of the cake.

10 Arrange the walnut halves on top and leave to set for 10 minutes before serving.

Energy 563kcal/2349kJ; Protein 8.5g; Carbohydrate 50.6g, of which sugars 39.2g; Fat 35.3g, of which saturates 10.1g; Cholesterol 108mg; Calcium 114mg; Fibre 1.5g; Sodium 177mg.

Simple chocolate cake

Make this easy, everyday chocolate cake and fill it with chocolate buttercream for a sweet afternoon treat that will be popular with all the family. Use a good quality chocolate with more than 70 per cent cocoa solids for the best flavour. Store this cake for up to three days.

SERVES 6–8

150g/5oz/10 tbsp unsalted butter, softened, plus extra for greasing
115g/4oz plain (semisweet) chocolate, broken into pieces
45ml/3 tbsp milk
150g/5oz/generous ½ cup light muscovado (brown) sugar
3 eggs
200g/7oz/1¾ cups self-raising (self-rising) flour
15ml/1 tbsp unsweetened cocoa powder

For the buttercream
75g/3oz/6 tbsp unsalted butter, softened
175g/6oz/1½ cups icing (confectioners') sugar, plus extra for dusting
15ml/1 tbsp unsweetened cocoa powder, plus extra for dusting
2.5ml/½ tsp vanilla extract

1 Preheat the oven to 180°C/350°F/ Gas 4. Grease and line two 18cm/ 7in round shallow cake tins (pans).

2 Melt the chocolate with the milk in a heatproof bowl set over a pan of simmering water. Cool.

3 In a bowl, beat the butter with the sugar until fluffy, then beat in the eggs. Stir in the chocolate mixture.

4 Sift the flour and cocoa over the mixture and fold in until evenly mixed. Spoon into the tins and smooth level. Bake for 35–40 minutes, or until risen and firm. Turn out on to wire racks to cool. Remove the lining papers.

5 To make the buttercream, put all the ingredients into a large bowl. Beat well to a smooth, spreadable consistency. Sandwich the cake layers together with the buttercream. Dust with cocoa and icing sugar.

Energy 427kcal/1776kJ; Protein 6.1g; Carbohydrate 29.2g, of which sugars 9.8g; Fat 32.6g, of which saturates 19.6g; Cholesterol 139mg; Calcium 65mg; Fibre 1.4g; Sodium 238mg.

Mississippi mud cake

This rich chocolate cake is a variation of Mississippi mud pie, a gooey dessert baked in a pie shell. The cake tastes good served, as you would serve the pie, with a scoop of vanilla ice cream or a dollop of whipped cream – or even both. This cake will keep refrigerated for two days.

SERVES 8–10

225g/8oz/1 cup butter, plus extra
  for greasing
unsweetened cocoa powder,
  for dusting
150g/5oz plain (semisweet)
  chocolate, broken into pieces
300ml/½ pint/1¼ cups strong,
  brewed coffee
50ml/2fl oz/¼ cup bourbon
400g/14oz/2 cups caster
  (superfine) sugar
225g/8oz/2 cups plain
  (all-purpose) flour
5ml/1 tsp baking powder
2 eggs
7.5ml/1½ tsp vanilla extract

1 Preheat the oven to 140°C/275°F/ Gas 1. Grease a 25cm/10in round deep cake tin (pan), then dust it lightly with cocoa powder.

2 Put the chocolate in a heatproof bowl with the coffee, bourbon and butter. Set the bowl over a pan of gently simmering water. Stir the mixture with a wooden spoon until melted and smooth. Remove the bowl from the heat and set aside to cool slightly.

3 Using an electric whisk on low speed, gradually beat the sugar into the chocolate. Continue beating until the sugar dissolves.

4 Increase the speed to medium and add the flour and baking powder. Mix well, then beat in the eggs and vanilla extract.

5 Pour the batter into the tin. Bake for 1 hour 20 minutes, or until a skewer inserted into the centre comes out clean. Leave to cool in the tin for 15 minutes, then turn out on to a wire rack to go cold.

6 Place on a serving plate and dust the cake with cocoa powder.

Energy 534kcal/2227kJ; Protein 6.3g; Carbohydrate 49.5g, of which sugars 38.5g; Fat 35.2g, of which saturates 19.6g; Cholesterol 87mg; Calcium 110mg; Fibre 2.1g; Sodium 142mg.

Lemon roulade with lemon-curd cream

This feather-light roulade is flavoured with almonds and filled with a rich lemon-curd cream. It makes a marvellous dessert or a tea-time treat. Use best-quality or home-made lemon curd for that perfect touch. Eat this cake fresh for the best taste. It will store chilled for 1–2 days.

SERVES 8

butter, for greasing
4 eggs, separated
115g/4oz/generous ½ cup caster
  (superfine) sugar
finely grated rind of 2 lemons,
  plus extra to decorate
5ml/1 tsp vanilla extract
40g/1½oz/⅓ cup plain
  (all-purpose) flour
25g/1oz/¼ cup ground almonds

For the lemon-curd cream
300ml/½ pint/1¼ cups double
  (heavy) cream
60ml/4 tbsp lemon curd
45ml/3 tbsp icing (confectioners')
  sugar, for dusting

1 Preheat the oven to 190°C/375°F/ Gas 5. Grease and line a 33 × 23cm/ 13 × 9in Swiss roll tin (jelly roll pan) with baking parchment.

2 In a large bowl, beat the egg yolks with half the sugar until foamy. Beat in the lemon rind and vanilla extract.

3 Sift the flour over the egg mixture and lightly fold in with the ground almonds, using a metal spoon.

4 Put the egg whites into a clean, grease-free bowl and whisk until they form stiff, glossy peaks.

5 Gradually whisk in the remaining sugar to form a stiff meringue.

6 Stir half the meringue mixture into the egg yolk mixture to slacken it. When combined, fold in the remainder of the meringue mixture.

7 Pour the batter into the prepared tin and smooth level.

8 Bake for 10 minutes, or until risen and spongy to the touch.

9 Put the tin on a wire rack and cover loosely with a sheet of baking parchment and a damp dish towel. Leave to cool.

10 To make the lemon curd-cream, whip the cream until it holds its shape, then fold in the lemon cream.

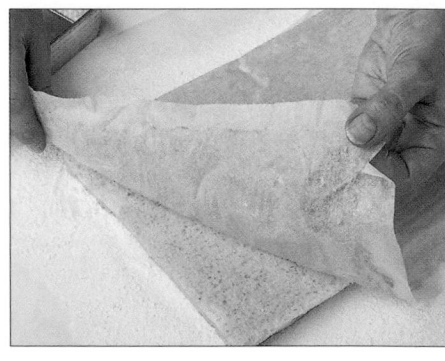

11 Sift the icing sugar over a piece of baking parchment. Turn the sponge out on to it. Peel off the lining paper and spread over the filling.

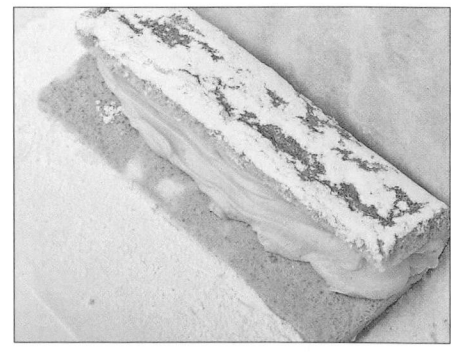

12 Using the paper, roll up the sponge from one long side. Sprinkle with lemon rind.

Energy 337kcal/1401kJ; Protein 5g; Carbohydrate 24.5g, of which sugars 18.9g; Fat 25.1g, of which saturates 13.6g; Cholesterol 148mg; Calcium 55mg; Fibre 0.4g; Sodium 50mg.

Lemon drizzle cake

Wonderfully moist and lemony, this cake is a favourite at coffee mornings and for afternoon tea. A lemon and sugar syrup is poured over the cooked cake and allowed to soak through, so that the whole cake is sweet and tangy. It will store in an airtight container for up to five days.

3 In a large bowl, beat the butter with the lemon and sugar mixture until light and fluffy, then beat in the eggs one at a time.

4 Sift the flour and baking powder into the mixture in three batches and beat well.

5 Turn the batter into the prepared tin and smooth the top level. Bake for 1½ hours, or until golden brown and springy to the touch.

6 To make the syrup, slowly heat the juice with the sugar until dissolved.

7 Prick the cake top with a skewer and pour over the syrup. Sprinkle over the shredded lemon rind and 5ml/1 tsp sugar, then leave to cool. Remove the lining paper.

SERVES 6–8

225g/8oz/1 cup unsalted butter, softened, plus extra for greasing
finely grated rind of 2 lemons
175g/6oz/scant 1 cup caster (superfine) sugar, plus 5ml/1 tsp
4 eggs
225g/8oz/2 cups self-raising (self-rising) flour
5ml/1 tsp baking powder
shredded rind of 1 lemon, to decorate

For the syrup
juice of 1 lemon
150g/5oz/¾ cup caster (superfine) sugar

1 Preheat the oven to 160°C/ 325°F/Gas 3. Grease and line the base and sides of an 18–20cm/ 7–8in round deep cake tin (pan) with baking parchment.

2 Mix the lemon rind and sugar together in a bowl.

Energy 659kcal/2765kJ; Protein 8g; Carbohydrate 84.1g, of which sugars 56.2g; Fat 34.8g, of which saturates 21.4g; Cholesterol 213mg; Calcium 184mg; Fibre 1.2g; Sodium 466mg.

Almond and raspberry-filled roll

This light and airy whisked sponge cake is rolled up with a gorgeous filling of fresh raspberries and cream, making it a perfect treat with tea in the garden in summer. It is also excellent filled with other soft fruits, such as small or sliced strawberries, or blackcurrants. Eat fresh.

SERVES 8

butter, for greasing
4 eggs
115g/4oz/generous ½ cup caster
   (superfine) sugar, plus extra
   for dusting
150g/5oz/1¼ cups plain
   (all-purpose) flour, sifted
25g/1oz/¼ cup ground almonds

For the filling
250ml/8fl oz/1 cup double
   (heavy) cream
275g/10oz/1⅔ cups fresh
   raspberries
toasted flaked (sliced) almonds,
   to decorate

1 Preheat the oven to 200°C/400°F/ Gas 6. Grease and line a 33 × 23cm/ 13 × 9in Swiss roll tin (jelly roll pan) with baking parchment.

2 Put the eggs and sugar in a large bowl and beat with an electric whisk for about 10 minutes, or until the mixture is thick and pale.

3 Sift the flour over the mixture and gently fold in with the ground almonds, using a metal spoon.

4 Spoon the batter into the tin and smooth level. Bake for 10–12 minutes, or until the sponge is well risen and springy to the touch.

5 Dust a sheet of baking parchment liberally with caster sugar. Turn out the cake on to the paper, and leave to cool with the tin still in place.

6 Lift the tin off the cooled cake and carefully peel away the lining paper.

7 To make the filling, whip the cream until it holds its shape. Fold in 250g/8oz/1¼ cups of the raspberries, and spread over the cooled cake, leaving a border.

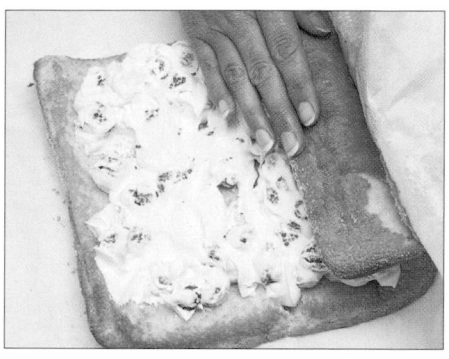

8 Carefully roll up the cake from a narrow end, using the paper to lift the sponge.

9 Dust with caster sugar. Serve decorated with the remaining raspberries and the toasted flaked almonds.

Energy 271kcal/1127kJ; Protein 4.7g; Carbohydrate 16.7g, of which sugars 11.9g; Fat 21.1g, of which saturates 11.2g; Cholesterol 114mg; Calcium 56mg; Fibre 1.2g; Sodium 35mg.

Old-fashioned treacle cake

Just a little treacle gives this cake a rich colour and a deep flavour. Mixed fruit and warm spices make it a traditional tea-time cake. The cake is made using what is known as the rubbing-in method, where the fat is rubbed into the flour rather than beaten with the sugar.

SERVES 8–10

75g/3oz/6 tbsp butter, diced, plus
  extra for greasing
250g/9oz/2¼ cups self-raising
  (self-rising) flour
2.5ml/½ tsp mixed (apple pie)
  spice
25g/1oz/2 tbsp caster (superfine)
  sugar
150g/5oz/scant 1 cup mixed
  dried fruit
1 egg
15ml/1 tbsp treacle (molasses)
about 100ml/3½fl oz/
  scant ½ cup milk

1 Preheat the oven to 180°C/350°F/ Gas 4. Grease and line a 20–23cm/ 8–9in round deep tin (pan).

2 Sift the flour and spice into a large bowl.

3 Add the butter and rub in until the mixture resembles fine breadcrumbs. Stir in the sugar and mixed dried fruit.

4 Beat the egg in a jug (pitcher), then stir in the treacle using a small whisk, followed by the milk.

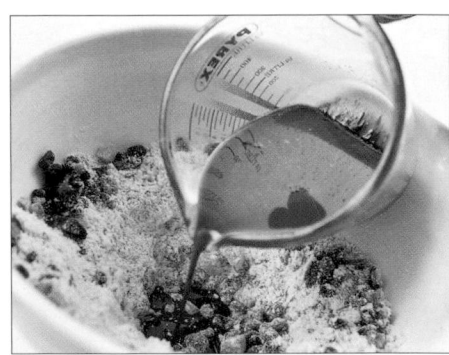

5 Stir the liquid into the flour and fruit mixture to make a fairly stiff but moist consistency, adding a little extra milk, if necessary.

6 Spoon the cake batter into the prepared tin and smooth the top level. Bake for 1 hour, or until the cake is firm to the touch and a skewer inserted into the centre comes out clean.

7 Leave to cool in the tin for 5 minutes, then turn out on to a wire rack to go cold. Remove the lining paper.

COOK'S TIP
Keep for up to 5 days in an airtight container, or wrap tightly in foil.

Energy 208kcal/880kJ; Protein 3.7g; Carbohydrate 34g, of which sugars 15.2g; Fat 7.2g, of which saturates 4.2g; Cholesterol 35.6mg; Calcium 72mg; Fibre 1.1g; Sodium 67mg.

Lemon-and-lime cake

Here's a quick all-in-one moist citrus cake that has a lime syrup poured over the baked lemon sponge. It's a perfect recipe for busy cooks, and the tangy topping transforms it without the need for icing. Keep this cake for up to three days in an airtight container.

SERVES 8

225g/8oz/1 cup butter, softened, plus extra for greasing
225g/8oz/2 cups self-raising (self-rising) flour
5ml/1 tsp baking powder
225g/8oz/generous 1 cup caster (superfine) sugar
4 eggs, beaten
grated rind of 2 lemons
30ml/2 tbsp lemon juice

For the topping
finely pared rind of 1 lime
juice of 2 limes
150g/5oz/³⁄₄ cup caster (superfine) sugar

1 Preheat the oven to 160°C/325°F/ Gas 3. Grease and line a 20cm/8in round deep cake tin (pan) with baking parchment.

2 Sift the flour and baking powder into a large bowl.

3 Add the sugar, butter and eggs, then beat together for 2 minutes until the mixture is smooth and fluffy. Use an electric mixer for speed, if you like.

4 Beat in the lemon rind and juice. Turn the mixture into the prepared tin, smooth the top and make a shallow indentation in the centre.

5 Bake for 1¼–1½ hours, or until the cake is golden on top, and a skewer inserted into the centre comes out clean.

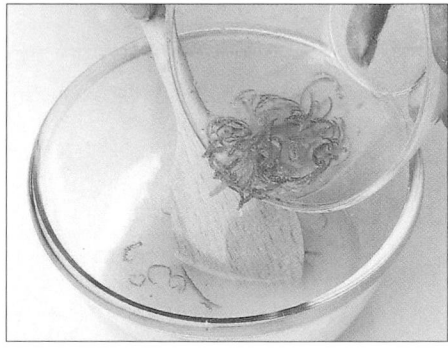

6 Meanwhile, make the topping by mixing all the ingredients together in a bowl.

7 As soon as the cake is baked, pour the topping over the surface. Leave to stand on a wire rack and allow the cake to cool in the tin. Remove the lining paper when cold.

Energy 527kcal/2209kJ; Protein 6.2g; Carbohydrate 71g, of which sugars 49.6g; Fat 26.3g, of which saturates 15.5g; Cholesterol 155mg; Calcium 84mg; Fibre 0.9g; Sodium 209mg.

Spice, nut and seed cakes

The simplest of bakes can be transformed by the addition of spices, as the volatile oils in the spices give their characteristic flavour and aroma. You may be familiar with ground cinnamon, allspice and ginger as the basic spices used in baking, but it is also fun to experiment with new flavours, so – a taste of the exotic in Cardamom Cake. Baking with seeds emphasizes their aromatic qualities, as found in Caraway Seed Cake, with its warm hues, a hint of lemon and delicious buttery flavour. Ginger adds heat and piquancy to baking. Its rich, sweet flavour blends beautifully in Pineapple and Ginger Upside-down Cake. It is always worth keeping a few oranges and lemons in your kitchen, as well as a lime, to add extra zest to your baking. Citrus fans will find plenty of zest packed into Date and Walnut Spice Cake, as well as tangy Rich Lemon Poppy Seed Cake.

Left: Pear and Cardamom Spice Cake and Lavender Cake.

Cardamom cake

Warm-flavoured cardamom is a favourite spice among all the Scandinavian countries and it is used in a variety of cakes, buns and other dishes. Here is a traditional tea- or coffee-time treat that tastes good without being too rich. Keep this for up to five days in an airtight container.

SERVES 10

250g/9oz/generous 1 cup butter, softened, plus extra for greasing
375g/13oz/3¼ cups plain (all-purpose) flour
45ml/3 tbsp baking powder
10 cardamom pods, seeds removed and finely crushed
250g/9oz/1¼ cups caster (superfine) sugar
3 large (US extra large) eggs, lightly beaten
150ml/¼ pint/⅔ cup milk
45ml/3 tbsp raisins
45ml/3 tbsp candied peel
15ml/1 tbsp flaked (sliced) almonds

1 Preheat the oven to 190°C/375°F/Gas 5. Grease and line a 1kg/2¼lb loaf tin (pan) with baking parchment.

2 Sift the flour, baking powder and crushed cardamom seeds together.

4 Add the milk, a little at a time, folding in well after each addition.

6 Bake for 50 minutes, or until risen and firm to the touch. Turn out and cool on a wire rack. Remove the lining paper.

3 In a large bowl, cream together the butter and sugar until light and fluffy. Beat in the eggs one at a time, adding a teaspoon of the flour with each egg. Fold in the remaining flour.

5 Add the raisins, candied peel and almonds, and fold in well. Turn the mixture into the tin and smooth the top level.

Energy 389kcal/1619kJ; Protein 4.6g; Carbohydrate 34.9g, of which sugars 17.7g; Fat 26.6g, of which saturates 14.8g; Cholesterol 97mg; Calcium 61mg; Fibre 2g; Sodium 201mg.

Caraway seed cake

Just a few caraway seeds give this cake a delicately warm and spicy flavour that blends well with the tang of the citrus peel. It's a simple and traditional tea-time cake, ideal with a cup of tea on a chilly afternoon. This cake will keep for up to two days in an airtight container.

SERVES 8

175g/6oz/¾ cup butter, softened, plus extra for greasing
175g/6oz/scant 1 cup caster (superfine) sugar
3 eggs
225g/8oz/2 cups plain (all-purpose) flour
5ml/1 tsp baking powder
10ml/2 tsp caraway seeds
50g/2oz/⅓ cup finely chopped mixed (candied) peel
milk

1 Preheat the oven to 180°C/ 350°F/Gas 4. Grease and line a 20cm/8in round deep cake tin (pan) with baking parchment.

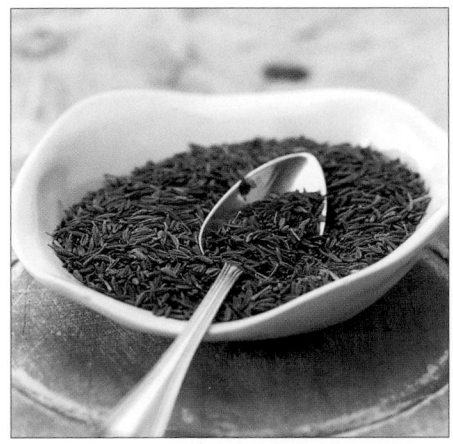

2 In a bowl, beat the butter and sugar until fluffy, then beat in the eggs one at a time. Sift the flour with the baking powder into the bowl. Add the caraway seeds. Beat well.

3 Using a metal spoon, fold in the remaining ingredients.

4 Spoon the batter into the prepared tin and smooth the top level. Bake for 1–1¼ hours, or until a skewer comes out clean when inserted.

5 Cool for 15 minutes in the tin, then turn out on to a wire rack to go cold. Remove the lining paper.

Energy 281kcal/1181kJ; Protein 4.6g; Carbohydrate 36.9g, of which sugars 15.5g; Fat 13.8g, of which saturates 8g; Cholesterol 87mg; Calcium 58mg; Fibre 0.8g; Sodium 109mg.

Lavender cake

The delicate flavour and fragrance of lavender makes a delightful addition to cooking and is most suitable for sweet baking. Make this scented moist cake for tea on a summer's day using fresh lavender, or dried culinary lavender. This cake will keep for up to three days in an airtight container.

2 In a large bowl, cream the butter and sugar together until light and fluffy. Add the eggs one at a time, beating thoroughly between each addition, until a skewer comes out clean when inserted.

3 Sift in the flour, then fold in with the lavender, vanilla and milk.

4 Spoon the mixture into the tin and smooth the top level. Bake for 1 hour, until golden.

5 Leave to cool for 5 minutes before turning out on to a wire rack to go cold.

SERVES 8

175g/6oz/¾ cup unsalted butter, softened, plus extra for greasing
175g/6oz/scant 1 cup caster (superfine) sugar
3 eggs
175g/6oz/1½ cups self-raising (self-rising) flour
15ml/1 tbsp fresh lavender florets or dried culinary lavender, roughly chopped (see Tip)
2.5ml/½ tsp vanilla extract
30ml/2 tbsp milk

For the topping
50g/2oz/½ cup icing (confectioners') sugar, sifted
fresh lavender florets, to decorate

1 Preheat the oven to 180°C/350°F/ Gas 4. Grease and flour a 20cm/8in round deep cake tin (pan).

COOK'S TIP
Dried lavender is stronger in flavour than fresh florets, so use half the amount.

6 To make the topping, mix the icing sugar with a few drops of water until smooth. Pour over the cake. Decorate with lavender florets.

Energy 375kcal/1572kJ; Protein 4.7g; Carbohydrate 46.2g, of which sugars 30g; Fat 20.4g, of which saturates 12.1g; Cholesterol 118mg; Calcium 111mg; Fibre 0.7g; Sodium 241mg.

Spice cake

Cardamom, cloves and allspice join the more usual cake spices to give this cake a heady blend that smells so good as you take it out of the oven. The flavour will improve after a few days, so make the cake in advance and wrap well. This will keep for up to five days in an airtight container.

SERVES 20

butter, for greasing
breadcrumbs, for sprinkling
500g/1¼lb/5 cups plain
   (all-purpose) flour
20ml/4 tsp baking powder
pinch of salt
350g/12oz/1½ cups light
   muscovado (brown) sugar
10ml/2 tsp ground cinnamon
1.5ml/¼ tsp ground allspice
1.5ml/¼ tsp ground cloves
2.5ml/½ tsp freshly grated nutmeg
1.5ml/¼ tsp ground cardamom
400–450ml/14–15fl oz/
   1⅔–2 cups milk

1 Preheat the oven to 150°C/300°F/ Gas 2. Grease a 20–23cm/8–9in round deep cake tin (pan) and sprinkle with breadcrumbs. Remove the excess crumbs.

2 Sift the flour, baking powder and salt into a large bowl. Stir in the sugar, cinnamon, allspice, cloves, nutmeg and cardamom.

3 Gradually stir the milk into the mixture, then whisk until smooth and with a pourable consistency.

4 Pour the mixture into the prepared tin and bake for 1½ hours, or until a skewer inserted into the centre comes out clean. Leave to stand in the tin for 5 minutes.

5 Turn out on to a wire rack to go cold. Wrap the cake in foil and store for at least 3 days before eating to allow the flavour of the spices to develop fully.

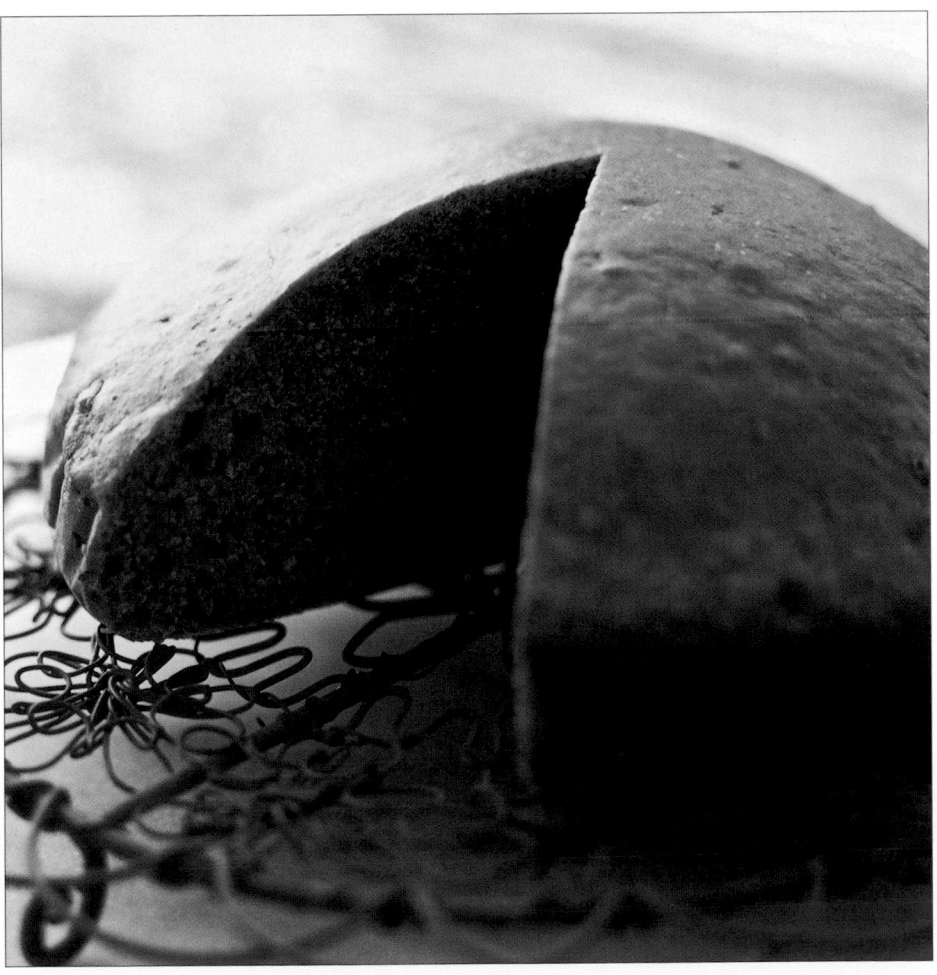

Energy 166kcal/708kJ; Protein 3.2g; Carbohydrate 39.2g, of which sugars 19.6g; Fat 0.7g, of which saturates 0.3g; Cholesterol 1.2mg; Calcium 80mg; Fibre 0.7g; Sodium 227mg.

Coffee and mint cream cake

Ground almonds give this buttery coffee-flavoured sponge a moist texture and delicate flavour. It is sandwiched together with a generous filling of mint buttercream, which contrasts wonderfully with the coffee. Keep this cake for up to three days in a cool place.

2 Put the butter, sugar, flour, almonds, eggs and infused ground coffee in a large bowl. Beat well for 1 minute until blended.

3 Divide the mixture evenly between the tins and smooth the top level. Bake for 25 minutes, or until well risen and firm to the touch. Leave in the tins for 5 minutes, then turn out on to a wire rack to go cold.

4 To make the filling, cream the butter, icing sugar, peppermint extract and milk together in a bowl until light and fluffy.

5 Remove the lining paper from the sponges and sandwich together with the filling. Generously dust the top with icing sugar. Top with the fresh mint leaves just before serving.

SERVES 8

175g/6oz/¾ cup unsalted butter, softened, plus extra for greasing
15ml/1 tbsp ground coffee infused (steeped) in 25ml/1½ tbsp near-boiling water for 4 minutes, then strained and cooled
175g/6oz/scant 1 cup caster (superfine) sugar
225g/8oz/2 cups self-raising (self-rising) flour, sifted
50g/2oz/½ cup ground almonds
3 eggs
small sprigs of fresh mint, to decorate

For the filling
50g/2oz/¼ cup unsalted butter
115g/4oz/1 cup icing (confectioners') sugar, sifted, plus extra for dusting
2 drops of peppermint extract plus 15ml/1 tbsp milk

1 Preheat the oven to 180°C/350°F/ Gas 4. Grease and line two 18cm/ 7in round shallow cake tins (pans).

> **COOK'S TIP**
> Freeze, unfilled, for 2 months.

Energy 508kcal/2127kJ; Protein 6.5g; Carbohydrate 59.6g, of which sugars 38.5g; Fat 28.8g, of which saturates 16.1g; Cholesterol 136mg; Calcium 148mg; Fibre 1.3g; Sodium 341mg.

Coconut and coffee cake

Some flavours work particularly well together and make natural partners, such as coconut and coffee, and the combination is at its best here. Ground coffee has a good strong flavour that is perfect for this cake. It will keep for up to five days in an airtight container.

SERVES 9

75g/3oz/6 tbsp butter, plus extra
  for greasing
25g/1oz/2 tbsp caster (superfine)
  sugar
175g/6oz/¾ cup golden (light
  corn) syrup
40g/1½oz/½ cup desiccated (dry
  unsweetened shredded) coconut
175g/6oz/1½ cups plain
  (all-purpose) flour
2.5ml/½ tsp bicarbonate of soda
  (baking soda)
2 eggs, lightly beaten
45ml/3 tbsp ground coffee infused
  (steeped) in 75ml/5 tbsp
  near-boiling milk for 4 minutes,
  then strained

For the icing
115g/4oz/½ cup butter, softened
225g/8oz/2 cups icing
  (confectioners') sugar, sifted
25g/1oz/⅓ cup shredded or flaked
  coconut, toasted

1 Preheat the oven to 160°C/325°F/ Gas 3. Grease and line a 20cm/8in square deep cake tin (pan) with baking parchment.

2 Heat the caster sugar, golden syrup, butter and desiccated coconut in a pan, stirring with a wooden spoon, until completely melted.

3 Sift the flour and bicarbonate of soda into the butter mixture. Add the eggs and 45ml/3 tbsp of the coffee-flavoured milk. Stir well to combine.

4 Spoon the mixture into the prepared tin and smooth it level.

5 Bake for 40–50 minutes, or until well risen and firm.

6 Allow the cake to cool in the tin for 10 minutes. Turn out on to a wire rack to go cold. Remove the lining papers.

7 To make the icing, beat the softened butter until smooth, then gradually beat in the icing sugar and remaining coffee-flavoured milk to give a soft consistency.

8 Spread over the top of the cake with a flat-bladed knife and decorate with toasted coconut. Cut into 5cm/2in squares to serve.

Energy 418kcal/1756kJ; Protein 3.7g; Carbohydrate 59.7g, of which sugars 44.9g; Fat 20g, of which saturates 13g; Cholesterol 90mg; Calcium 57mg; Fibre 1g; Sodium 225mg.

Coffee and walnut roll

There's something about coffee and walnuts together in a cake that gives it such a delicious taste. Here they appear together in a light and fluffy sponge enclosing a smooth and creamy filling that is luxuriously flavoured with Cointreau. Eat this roll fresh for the best flavour.

SERVES 8

butter, for greasing
3 eggs
75g/3oz/6 tbsp caster (superfine) sugar, plus extra for dusting
75g/3oz/¾ cup self-raising (self-rising) flour
10ml/2 tsp ground coffee infused (steeped) in 15ml/1 tbsp near-boiling water for 4 minutes, then strained
50g/2oz/½ cup toasted walnuts, finely chopped

For the filling

115g/4oz/generous ½ cup caster (superfine) sugar, plus extra for dusting
50ml/2fl oz/¼ cup cold water
2 egg yolks
115g/4oz/½ cup unsalted butter, softened
15ml/1 tbsp Cointreau or orange liqueur

1 Preheat the oven to 200°C/400°F/ Gas 6. Grease and line a 33 × 23cm/13 × 9in Swiss roll tin (jelly roll pan) with baking parchment.

2 Whisk the eggs and sugar together in a large bowl until pale and thick.

3 Sift the flour over the egg and sugar mixture and fold in with the coffee and walnuts.

4 Pour into the tin and bake for 10–12 minutes, until golden.

5 Turn out on to a piece of baking parchment sprinkled with caster sugar, peel off the lining paper and cool for about 2 minutes. Trim the edges.

> **COOK'S TIP**
> Try this decorated with swirls of piped whipped cream and walnuts, if you like.

6 Roll up from one of the short ends, using the baking parchment. Leave to cool, still rolled up.

7 To make the filling, put the sugar in a pan with the water over a low heat until dissolved. Boil rapidly until the syrup reaches 105°/220°F on a sugar thermometer.

8 Pour the syrup over the egg yolks, whisking all the time, until thick and mousse-like. Gradually add the butter, then whisk in the orange liqueur. Leave to cool and thicken.

9 Unroll the sponge and spread with filling. Re-roll and place on a serving plate, seam-side down.

10 Dust with extra caster sugar and chill until ready to serve.

Energy 357kcal/1489kJ; Protein 4.1g; Carbohydrate 31.9g, of which sugars 28.7g; Fat 24.6g, of which saturates 11.9g; Cholesterol 125mg; Calcium 43mg; Fibre 0.4g; Sodium 153mg.

Rich lemon poppy-seed cake

The classic combination of poppy seeds and lemon is used for this light cake. Luxurious lemon curd adds richness to both the cake and the creamy filling, making it very moreish. Eat this cake fresh for best flavour, or freeze without filling, wrapped in foil for up to two months.

4 Put the egg whites into a clean, grease-free bowl and whisk until they form soft peaks. Carefully fold them into the cake mixture until just combined.

5 Divide the cake mixture between the prepared tins. Bake for 40–45 minutes, or until golden and a skewer inserted into the centre of the cakes comes out clean.

6 Leave to cool in the tins for 5 minutes, then turn out on to wire racks to go cold. Remove the lining.

SERVES 10–12

350g/12oz/1½ cups unsalted
   butter, plus extra for greasing
350g/12oz/1¾ cups golden caster
   (superfine) sugar
45ml/3 tbsp poppy seeds
20ml/4 tsp finely grated lemon rind
60ml/4 heaped tbsp lemon curd
6 eggs, separated
120ml/4fl oz/½ cup milk
350g/12oz/3 cups self-raising
   (self-rising) flour
icing (confectioners') sugar,
   for dusting

For the filling
150g/5oz/½ lemon curd
150ml/¼ pint/⅔ cup mascarpone

1 Preheat the oven to 180°C/350°F/ Gas 4. Grease and line two 23cm/ 9in round shallow cake tins (pans) with baking parchment.

2 Beat together the butter and sugar until light and fluffy. Add the poppy seeds, lemon rind, lemon curd and egg yolks. Beat well, then add the milk and mix well.

3 Sift the flour over the mixture and gently fold in until combined.

7 To finish, spread one cake with lemon curd and spoon the mascarpone evenly over the top. Put the second cake on top, press down gently, then dust with icing sugar before serving.

Energy 805kcal/3374kJ; Protein 10.7g; Carbohydrate 99.6g, of which sugars 60.9g; Fat 43.3g, of which saturates 25.3g; Cholesterol 246mg; Calcium 242mg; Fibre 1.4g; Sodium 509mg.

Yogurt cake with pistachio nuts

Flavoured with vanilla seeds and pistachio nuts, this unusual cake contains very little flour.
The texture is lightened with whisked egg whites. Serve it with crème fraîche and passion fruit or
summer berries to make a soft and sweet summer dessert. Eat fresh for the best taste.

SERVES 8–12

butter, for greasing
3 eggs, separated
75g/3oz/scant ½ cup caster
   (superfine) sugar
seeds from 2 vanilla pods (beans)
300ml/½ pint/1¼ cup Greek (US
   strained plain) yogurt
grated rind and juice of 1 lemon
15ml/1 tbsp plain
   (all-purpose) flour
handful of pistachio nuts,
   roughly chopped
90ml/6 tbsp crème fraîche, to serve
4–6 fresh passion fruit, or
   50g/2oz/½ cup summer berries,
   to serve

1 Preheat the oven to 180°C/350°F/
Gas 4. Grease and line a 25cm/10in
square shallow tin (pan) with
baking parchment.

2 In a mixing bowl, beat the egg
yolks with 50g/2oz/¼ cup sugar
until pale and fluffy.

3 Beat in the vanilla seeds and stir in
the yogurt, lemon rind and juice.
Sift in the flour and beat well until
light and airy.

4 Put the egg whites into a clean,
grease-free bowl and whisk until
they form stiff peaks, then gradually
whisk in the rest of the sugar to
form soft peaks.

5 Fold the whisked whites into the
yogurt mixture. Turn the batter into
the cake tin.

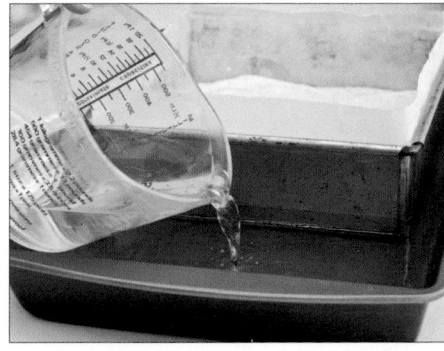

6 Put the tin in a roasting pan and
pour water in the pan to come
halfway up the cake tin. Bake for 20
minutes, or until risen and just set.

7 Sprinkle the nuts over the cake
and bake for another 20 minutes.
Serve warm or cold with crème
fraîche and a spoonful of fruit.

Energy 152kcal/638kJ; Protein 6.6g; Carbohydrate 16g, of which sugars 14.1g; Fat 7.9g, of which saturates 3.4g; Cholesterol 95mg; Calcium 99mg; Fibre 0.1g; Sodium 71mg.

Moist orange and almond cake

There are many techniques for adding moisture and flavour to cake batters. Here a whole orange is cooked slowly until completely tender and then blended to a purée. Ground almonds that add richness make the perfect partner. Eat fresh, served with orange slices and whipped cream.

SERVES 8

1 large orange, washed
butter, for greasing
3 eggs
225g/8oz/generous 1 cup caster
    (superfine) sugar
5ml/1 tsp baking powder
25g/1oz/¼ cup plain
    (all-purpose) flour
225g/8oz/2 cups ground almonds
icing (confectioners') sugar,
    for dusting
whipped cream and orange slices
    (optional), to serve

COOK'S TIP
Do not use a microwave to cook the orange.

1 Pierce the orange with a skewer. Put it in a deep pan and cover with water. Bring to the boil, lower the heat, cover and simmer for 1 hour, until soft. Drain, then cool.

2 Preheat the oven to 180°C/350°F/Gas 4. Grease and line a 20cm/8in round deep cake tin (pan).

3 Cut the orange in half and discard the pips. Put the orange, skin and all, in a blender or food processor and purée until smooth and pulpy.

4 In a bowl, whisk the eggs and sugar. Fold in the baking powder, flour and almonds, then the purée.

5 Pour into the prepared tin, level the surface and bake for 1 hour, or until a skewer inserted into the middle comes out clean.

6 Allow to cool for 10 minutes, then turn out on to a wire rack to go cold. Peel off the lining paper.

7 Dust the cake with icing sugar and serve with whipped cream. Tuck thick orange slices under the cake just before serving, if you like.

Energy 187kcal/783kJ; Protein 5.1g; Carbohydrate 20g, of which sugars 18.2g; Fat 10.2g, of which saturates 1.1g; Cholesterol 41mg; Calcium 60mg; Fibre 1.4g; Sodium 19mg.

Apple and cinnamon cake

Dates and grated apples bring lots of fruitiness and moisture to this spicy cake mix. It also includes gram flour (made from ground chickpeas) and coconut milk, giving it an Asian touch. It is a good cake to add to packed lunches. Keep this for up to five days in an airtight container.

SERVES 8–10

115g/4oz/½ cup butter, plus extra
  for greasing
200g/7oz/generous 1 cup dried,
  stoned (pitted) dates
1–2 tart eating apples or 1 cooking
  apple, about 225g/8oz
12.5ml/2½ tsp mixed (apple pie)
  spice
pinch of salt
150g/5oz/1¼ cups wholemeal
  (whole-wheat) flour
115g/4oz/ 1 cup gram flour
10ml/2 tsp baking powder
75g/3oz/generous ½ cup raisins
2 eggs, beaten
175ml/6fl oz/¾ cup unsweetened
  coconut milk

1 Preheat the oven to 180°C/350°F/ Gas 4. Grease and line a 20cm/8in deep square cake tin (pan) with baking parchment.

2 Combine the butter and dates in a food processor.

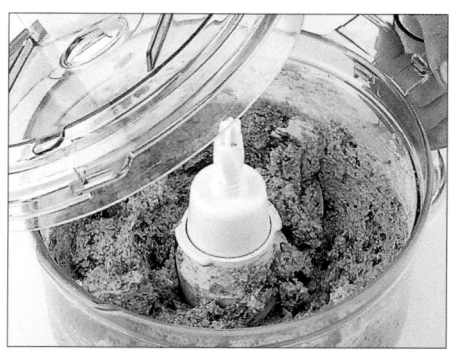

3 Peel, core and grate the apple and add to the butter and date mixture with the mixed spice and salt. Process until thoroughly blended.

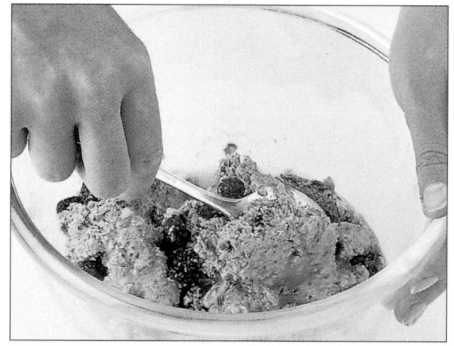

4 Spoon the apple and date mixture into a bowl. In batches, sift and fold in the flours and baking powder, alternating with the raisins, beaten eggs and coconut milk. Transfer to the prepared tin and smooth the top level.

5 Bake for 30–40 minutes, or until dark golden and firm to the touch, and a skewer inserted into the centre comes out clean. Allow the cake to cool in the tin for 15 minutes before turning out on to a wire rack to go completely cold. Remove the lining.

Energy 587kcal/2472kJ; Protein 5.5g; Carbohydrate 92g, of which sugars 69.7g; Fat 24.5g, of which saturates 10.6g; Cholesterol 40mg; Calcium 95mg; Fibre 2.5g; Sodium 129mg.

Pecan cake

Ground pecan nuts give this light cake a mellow flavour, which is further enriched with butter and honey drizzled over the cake once cooked. Serve with a dollop of whipped cream to make an unusual dessert. Keep refrigerated for up to three days.

6 Fold the beaten whites into the butter mixture, then gently fold in the flour and nut mixture.

7 Spoon the batter into the prepared tin and bake for 30 minutes, or until a skewer inserted in the centre comes out clean.

SERVES 8

115g/4oz/½ cup butter, softened, plus extra for greasing
115g/4oz/1 cup pecan nuts
75g/3oz/¾ cup plain (all-purpose) flour
115g/4oz/½ cup soft light brown sugar
5ml/1 tsp vanilla extract
4 large (US extra large) eggs, separated
pinch of salt
12 whole pecan nuts, to decorate
whipped cream, to serve

For drizzling
50g/2oz/¼ cup butter
120ml/4fl oz/scant ½ cup clear (runny) honey

1 Preheat the oven to 180°C/350°F/Gas 4. Grease and line a 20cm/8in round shallow cake tin (pan) with baking parchment.

2 Toast the pecan nuts in a dry frying pan for 5 minutes, shaking frequently.

3 Grind the nuts finely in a blender or food processor. Stir in the flour.

4 In a mixing bowl, beat the butter and sugar together until light and fluffy, then beat in the vanilla extract and egg yolks.

5 Put the egg whites and salt into a clean, grease-free bowl and whisk until they form soft peaks.

8 Allow the cake to cool in the tin for 5 minutes, then turn out on to a wire rack to go cold. Remove the lining paper. Arrange the pecan nuts on top of the cake. Transfer to a serving plate.

9 Melt the butter for drizzling in a small pan, add the honey and bring to the boil, stirring. Lower the heat and simmer for 3 minutes. Pour over the cake. Serve with whipped cream.

Energy 428kcal/1785kJ; Protein 6.2g; Carbohydrate 34.7g, of which sugars 27.4g; Fat 30.5g, of which saturates 12.5g; Cholesterol 158mg; Calcium 51mg; Fibre 1g; Sodium 170mg.

Almond cake

Toasted almonds are the main ingredient in this light cake, giving it a nutty flavour and an excellent texture. It is best served warm, and a scoop of vanilla or good-quality chocolate ice cream would also go well with it. Eat this fresh, or keep it for one day in an airtight container.

SERVES 4–6

25g/1oz/2 tbsp butter, plus extra
  for greasing
225/8oz/2 cups blanched
  whole almonds
75g/3oz/¾ cup icing (confectioners')
  sugar, plus extra for dusting
3 eggs
2.5ml/½ tsp almond extract
25g/1oz/¼ cup plain
  (all-purpose) flour
3 egg whites
15ml/1 tbsp caster (superfine)
  sugar

4 Add the whole eggs and the remaining icing sugar to the bowl. With an electric whisk, beat until the mixture forms a trail when the beaters are lifted away.

5 In a small pan, melt the butter, then mix into the nut and egg mixture with the almond extract.

6 Sift over the flour and fold in.

7 Whisk the egg whites into a clean, grease-free bowl until they form soft peaks. Add the sugar. Beat until stiff.

8 Fold the egg whites into the batter. Spoon into the cake tin. Bake for 15–20 minutes, until golden. Turn out of the tin. Remove the papers.

9 Decorate with the toasted almonds and dust with icing sugar.

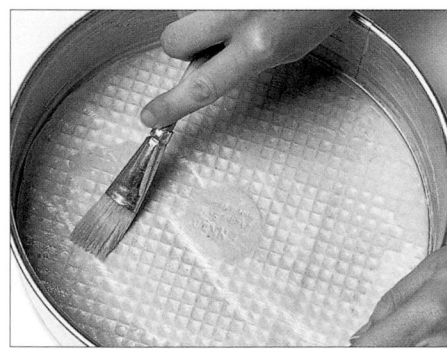

1 Preheat the oven to 160°C/325°F/ Gas 3. Grease and line a 23cm/9in round shallow cake tin (pan) with baking parchment.

2 Spread the almonds in an even layer in a baking tray and bake for 10 minutes. Allow the almonds to cool. Set aside a few of the almonds for decoration. Chop the rest, then grind them with half of the icing sugar in a food processor. Transfer to a large bowl.

3 Increase the oven temperature to 200°C/400°F/Gas 6.

Energy 376kcal/1568kJ; Protein 13g; Carbohydrate 21.5g, of which sugars 17.3g; Fat 27.2g, of which saturates 4.6g; Cholesterol 104mg; Calcium 120mg; Fibre 2.9g; Sodium 97mg.

Walnut cake

Brandy, orange and cinnamon warmed in a sugar syrup are poured over this baked walnut cake, making it superbly moist and full of complementary flavours. This technique is an excellent way to add flavour and moisture to a cake. Keep this cake, refrigerated, for three days.

SERVES 10–12

150g/5oz/10 tbsp unsalted butter, plus extra for greasing
115g/4oz/generous ½ cup caster (superfine) sugar
4 eggs, separated
60ml/4 tbsp brandy
2.5ml/½ tsp ground cinnamon
300g/11oz/2¾ cups walnuts
150g/5oz/1¼ cups self-raising (self-rising) flour
5ml/1 tsp baking powder
pinch of salt

For the syrup
250g/9oz/1¼ cups caster (superfine) sugar
30ml/2 tbsp brandy
2 or 3 strips of pared orange rind
2 cinnamon sticks

1 Preheat the oven to 190°C/375°F/ Gas 5. Grease and line a 35 × 23cm/ 14 × 9in shallow cake tin (pan).

2 In a bowl, beat the butter and sugar together until light and fluffy. Beat in the egg yolks one at a time. Stir in the brandy and cinnamon.

3 Coarsely chop the walnuts, using a food processor, and stir them in.

4 Sift the flour with the baking powder and set aside.

5 Put the egg whites and salt into a clean, grease-free bowl and whisk until they form stiff peaks.

6 Fold the egg whites into the butter and sugar mixture, alternating with tablespoons of flour.

7 Spread the batter evenly in the prepared tin. Bake for about 40 minutes, or until the top is golden and a skewer inserted into the centre comes out clean. Set on a wire rack in the tin.

8 To make the syrup, mix the sugar and 300ml/½ pint/1¼ cups water in a small pan. Heat gently, stirring, until the sugar has dissolved. Bring to the boil, lower the heat and add the brandy, orange rind and cinnamon sticks. Simmer for 10 minutes.

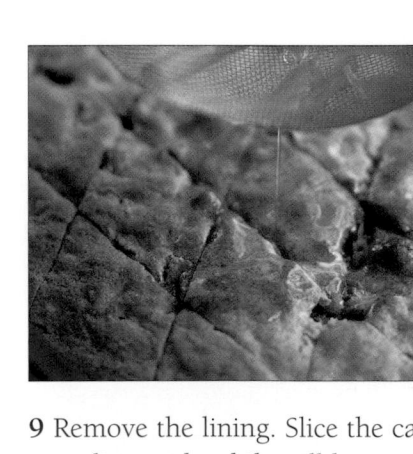

9 Remove the lining. Slice the cake into diamonds while still hot and strain the syrup over it. Let it stand for 10–20 minutes, then turn out on to a wire rack to go cold.

Energy 563kcal/2349kJ; Protein 8.5g; Carbohydrate 50.6g, of which sugars 39.2g; Fat 35.3g, of which saturates 10.1g; Cholesterol 108mg; Calcium 114mg; Fibre 1.5g; Sodium 177mg.

Pine nut and almond cake

This unusual recipe uses olive oil, toasted semolina and nuts to give the cake a rich flavour and a dense, grainy texture. It is also incredibly moist because it is soaked in a cinnamon and sugar syrup. Unlike traditional cakes it is not baked in the oven, but heated in a pan. Eat fresh.

SERVES 6–8

500g/1¼lb/2¾ cups caster
    (superfine) sugar
1 cinnamon stick
250ml/8fl oz/1 cup olive oil
350g/12oz/2 cups coarse semolina
50g/2oz/½ cup blanched almonds
30ml/2 tbsp pine nuts
5ml/1 tsp ground cinnamon

1 Put the sugar in a heavy pan with 1 litre/1¾ pints/4 cups cold water and the cinnamon stick. Bring to the boil, stirring until the sugar dissolves, then boil without stirring for 4 minutes to make a syrup.

2 Meanwhile, heat the oil in a separate, heavy pan. When it is almost smoking, add the semolina gradually and stir constantly until it turns light brown.

3 Lower the heat, add the almonds and pine nuts, and brown together for 2–3 minutes, stirring constantly.

4 Take the semolina mixture off the heat and set aside. Remove the cinnamon stick from the hot syrup using a slotted spoon and discard it.

5 Carefully add the hot syrup to the semolina mixture, stirring all the time. The mixture will hiss and spit at this point, so stand well away from it.

6 Return the pan to a gentle heat and stir until the syrup has been absorbed and the mixture is smooth.

7 Remove the pan from the heat, cover it with a clean dish towel and leave it to stand for 10 minutes so that any remaining moisture is absorbed.

8 Spoon the mixture into a 20–23cm/ 8–9in round non-stick cake tin (pan), and set it aside. When cold, unmould it on to a platter and dust it all over with the cinnamon.

Energy 643kcal/2706kJ; Protein 6.8g; Carbohydrate 99.8g, of which sugars 65.7g; Fat 26.8g, of which saturates 3.3g; Cholesterol 0mg; Calcium 56mg; Fibre 1.5g; Sodium 10mg.

Poppy seed cake

This plain and simple cake is flavoured with lemon and vanilla and is packed with black poppy seeds – a popular ingredient for speciality breads. As well as giving the cake a good crunch, poppy seeds add a nutty and distinctive taste. Serve it with cream, and keep for up to three days.

3 Sift and fold the flour and baking powder into the egg and poppy seed mixture, in three batches, alternating with the milk.

4 Add the cooled, melted butter and the sunflower oil, and stir in.

5 Pour the mixture into the tin and bake for 40 minutes, or until firm. Cool in the tin for 15 minutes, then invert on to a wire rack. Leave until cold, dust with icing sugar and serve with cream.

SERVES 8

130g/4½oz/generous ½ cup
  unsalted butter, melted, plus
  extra for greasing
2 eggs
225g/8oz/generous 1 cup caster
  (superfine) sugar
5–10ml/1–2 tsp vanilla extract
200g/7oz/scant 1½ cups poppy
  seeds, ground
15ml/1 tbsp grated lemon rind
130g/4½oz/generous 1 cup
  self-raising (self-rising) flour
5ml/1 tsp baking powder
120ml/4fl oz/½ cup milk
30ml/2 tbsp sunflower oil
icing (confectioners') sugar, sifted,
  for dusting
whipped cream, to serve

1 Preheat the oven to 180°C/350°F/ Gas 4. Grease a 23cm/9in round deep cake tin (pan).

2 In a large bowl, beat together the eggs, sugar and vanilla extract, using an electric whisk, for 4–5 minutes, or by hand until pale and fluffy. Stir in the poppy seeds and the lemon rind.

COOK'S TIP
Culinary poppy seeds have a distinctive nutty taste. To enhance the aroma and flavour, lightly toast them first.

Energy 485kcal/2023kJ; Protein 8.3g; Carbohydrate 42.7g, of which sugars 30.5g; Fat 32.4g, of which saturates 11.4g; Cholesterol 83mg; Calcium 267mg; Fibre 2.5g; Sodium 188mg.

Date and walnut spice cake

This deliciously moist and rich spiced cake is topped with a sticky honey and orange glaze.
Serve it as a dessert with a generous spoonful of natural yogurt, or crème fraîche, flavoured with
grated orange rind. Keep this cake, refrigerated, for up to three days.

SERVES 8

115g/4oz/½ cup unsalted butter,
  plus extra for greasing
175g/6oz/¾ cup soft dark
  brown sugar
2 eggs
175g/6oz/1½ cups self-raising
  (self-rising) flour, plus extra
  for dusting
5ml/1 tsp bicarbonate of soda
  (baking soda)
2.5ml/½ tsp freshly grated nutmeg
5ml/1 tsp mixed spice
pinch of salt
175ml/6fl oz/¾ cup buttermilk
50g/2oz/⅓ cup ready-to-eat stoned
  (pitted) dates, chopped
25g/1oz/¼ cup walnuts, chopped

For the topping
60ml/4 tbsp clear honey
45ml/3 tbsp fresh orange juice
15ml/1 tbsp coarsely grated
  orange rind

1 Preheat the oven to 180°C/350°F/
Gas 4. Grease and lightly flour a
23cm/9in round deep cake tin (pan).

2 In a bowl, beat the butter and
sugar until light and fluffy, then beat
in the eggs one at a time.

3 Sift together the flour, bicarbonate
of soda, spices and salt into a bowl.

4 Add the flour mixture to the egg
and sugar mixture, alternating with
the buttermilk, and stir well to
combine. Add the dates and
walnuts, and mix in.

 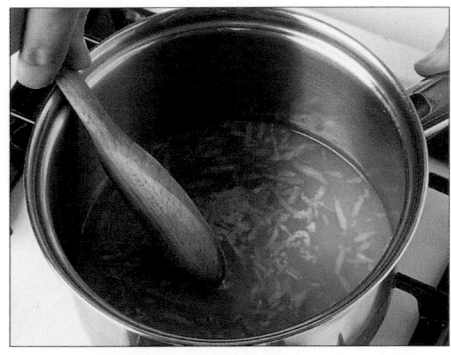

5 Spoon the batter into the prepared
cake tin and smooth the top level.

6 Bake for 50 minutes, or until a
skewer inserted into the centre
comes out clean. Leave to cool for
5 minutes. Turn out on to a wire
rack to go cold.

7 To make the topping, heat the
honey, orange juice and rind in a
pan. Bring to the boil. Boil rapidly,
without stirring, for 3 minutes, or
until syrupy.

8 Prick holes in the top of the cake
and pour over the hot syrup.

Energy 350kcal/1472kJ; Protein 5.1g; Carbohydrate 50.3g, of which sugars 34.1g; Fat 15.7g, of which saturates 8.1g; Cholesterol 79mg; Calcium 131mg; Fibre 1g; Sodium 196mg.

Chocolate cakes

Most people love chocolate, and this luxurious ingredient makes cakes rich and delectable. The flavour of chocolate varies according to the brand but, as a general rule, the higher the cocoa content, the better the quality. However, it is more important to find a chocolate that you enjoy. Melted block chocolate has many uses in baking, such as for toppings, frostings and sauces. Cocoa powder, with its concentrated flavour, will add a deep chocolate richness to cakes, icings and buttercreams.

It is amazing how many ingredients work well with chocolate, and what a variety of combinations you can make by adding nuts, fruit, orange, ginger, mint, coffee, cinnamon and spirits such as rum and brandy. Who could resist juicy dark cherries with chocolate in Black Forest Gateau? Or try a sophisticated Chocolate Orange Marquise – ideal for a dessert. You may be surprised by the Chocolate and Beetroot Layer Cake and the Chocolate Potato Cake, but just try a slice to experience their sweet, rich notes and moist textures.

Left: Black Forest Gateau and Sachertorte.

Chocolate sandwich cake

A light chocolate sponge cake has lots of appeal, especially when filled and topped with a rich, chocolatey frosting. It also works as a celebration cake, topped with small squares of fudge and white chocolate buttons, or flaked chocolate. Keep it for up to three days in an airtight container.

SERVES 10–12

130g/4½oz/generous ½ cup
   butter, softened, plus extra
   for greasing
250g/9oz/1¼ cups caster
   (superfine) sugar
3 eggs, beaten
225g/8oz/2 cups plain
   (all-purpose) flour
5ml/1 tsp bicarbonate of soda
   (baking soda)
50g/2oz/½ cup unsweetened
   cocoa power
250ml/8fl oz/1 cup buttermilk

For the chocolate buttercream
50g/2oz dark (bittersweet)
   chocolate
175g/6oz/1½ cups icing
   (confectioners') sugar, sifted
115g/4oz/½ cup unsalted
   butter, softened
few drops of vanilla extract

1 Preheat the oven to 180°C/350°F/ Gas 4. Grease and line two 20cm/8in round shallow cake tins (pans) with baking parchment.

2 In a mixing bowl, cream the butter and sugar until light and fluffy.

3 Gradually beat in the eggs. Sift the flour, bicarbonate of soda and cocoa over in batches and beat well to combine. Add the buttermilk and mix well.

4 Spoon into the prepared tins and bake for 30–35 minutes, or until firm to the touch.

5 Let stand for 5 minutes, then turn out of the tins, peel off the papers and leave on a wire rack to go cold.

6 To make the buttercream, melt the chocolate in a heatproof bowl set over a pan of gently simmering water. Stir occasionally. Allow to cool slightly.

7 In another bowl, beat the icing sugar with the butter until soft and creamy. Mix in the melted chocolate.

8 Use half of the buttercream to sandwich the cakes together, and spread the remainder on the top of the cake. Store refrigerated to keep the buttercream firm.

Energy 430kcal/1790kJ; Protein 7.8g; Carbohydrate 29.5g, of which sugars 28.8g; Fat 32.1g, of which saturates 13.6g; Cholesterol 96mg; Calcium 92mg; Fibre 1.9g; Sodium 125mg.

Chocolate, almond and coffee cake

This easy all-in-one cake recipe is a favourite because it is so quick to make. Add a lovely coffee buttercream for the filling and topping, and the chocolate cake is transformed into something extra special. Keep this cake for up to three days, refrigerated, in an airtight container.

SERVES 8

175g/6oz/¾ cup butter, softened, plus extra for greasing
175g/6oz/1½ cups self-raising (self-rising) flour
25ml/1½ tbsp unsweetened cocoa powder
pinch of salt
175g/6oz/¾ cup soft dark brown sugar
50g/2oz/½ cup ground almonds
3 large (US extra large) eggs, lightly beaten

For the coffee buttercream
175g/6oz/¾ cup unsalted butter
350g/12oz/3 cups icing (confectioners') sugar, sifted
30ml/2 tbsp coffee extract
whole hazelnuts or pecan nuts, to decorate (optional)

1 Preheat the oven to 180°C/350°F/ Gas 4. Grease and line two 18cm/ 7in round shallow cake tins (pans).

2 Sift the flour, cocoa and salt into a large bowl.

3 In another bowl, cream the butter with the sugar until light and fluffy.

4 Add the ground almonds, eggs, flour and cocoa, and beat well. Divide the batter between the tins.

5 Bake for 25–30 minutes. Turn out on a wire rack to go cold. Remove the paper lining.

6 To make the buttercream, beat the butter, then gradually beat in the icing sugar and coffee extract.

7 Put one quarter of the buttercream into a small piping (pastry) bag fitted with a star nozzle.

8 Sandwich the cakes together with some of the buttercream. Cover the top and sides with the rest.

9 Pipe rosettes around the top of the cake and decorate with whole hazelnuts or pecan nuts, if you like.

Energy 737kcal/3085kJ; Protein 7g; Carbohydrate 86.4g, of which sugars 69.6g; Fat 43g, of which saturates 24g; Cholesterol 1.4mg; Calcium 1.06mg; Fibre 12.2g; Sodium 3.28mg.

Devilish chocolate roulade

This decadent roulade can be made a day ahead and then filled and rolled before serving. It has a rich brandy, chocolate and mascarpone filling and is decorated with chocolate-dipped strawberries to make it extra special. Once filled, keep it, refrigerated, for up to two days.

SERVES 6–8

butter, for greasing
175g/6oz plain (semisweet)
   chocolate, broken into pieces
4 eggs, separated
115g/4oz/generous ½ cup caster
   (superfine) sugar
unsweetened cocoa powder,
   for dusting

For the filling
225g/8oz plain (semisweet)
   chocolate, broken into pieces
45ml/3 tbsp brandy
2 eggs, separated
250g/9oz/generous 1 cup
   mascarpone
chocolate-dipped strawberries

1 Preheat the oven to 180°C/350°F/ Gas 4. Grease and line a 33 × 23cm/ 13 × 9in Swiss roll tin (jelly roll pan) with baking parchment.

2 Melt the chocolate in a heatproof bowl over a pan of gently simmering water, then remove from the heat.

3 Whisk the egg yolks and sugar in a bowl until pale and thick, then stir in the melted chocolate.

4 Put the egg whites into a clean, grease-free bowl and whisk until they form soft peaks, then fold lightly and evenly into the egg and chocolate mixture.

5 Pour the mixture into the prepared tin and smooth level. Bake for 15–20 minutes, or until well risen and firm to the touch.

6 Dust a sheet of baking parchment with cocoa. Turn the sponge out on to the paper, cover with a clean dish towel and leave to cool.

7 To make the filling, melt the chocolate with the brandy in a heatproof bowl set over a pan of gently simmering water. Remove from the heat.

8 Beat the egg yolks together, then beat into the warm chocolate mixture until smooth.

9 Put the egg whites into a clean, grease-free bowl and whisk until they form soft peaks. Fold them lightly and evenly into the filling in three batches until the mixture is light and smooth. Cool completely.

10 Uncover the roulade, remove the lining paper and spread with most of the mascarpone.

11 Spread the chocolate mixture over the top, then roll up from a long side to enclose the filling.

12 Transfer to a serving plate, top with mascarpone, fresh chocolate-dipped strawberries, and dust with cocoa powder.

CHOCOLATE-DIPPED STRAWBERRIES
Dip the lower half of each strawberry into some good quality melted chocolate. Leave to set on a baking sheet lined with baking parchment.

Energy 486kcal/2022kJ; Protein 10.2g; Carbohydrate 32.8g, of which sugars 32.4g; Fat 34.5g, of which saturates 19.9g; Cholesterol 189mg; Calcium 41mg; Fibre 1.3g; Sodium 143mg.

Black Forest gateau

Perhaps the most famous chocolate cake of all, this Kirsch-flavoured gateau is layered with fresh cream containing chopped black cherries, and is decorated with chocolate curls. It is the perfect gateau for a special-occasion party. This will keep, refrigerated, for up to three days.

SERVES 10–12

75g/3oz/6 tbsp butter, melted, plus extra for greasing
5 eggs
175g/6oz/scant 1 cup caster (superfine) sugar
50g/2oz/½ cup plain (all-purpose) flour, sifted
50g/2oz/½ cup unsweetened cocoa powder, sifted

For the filling and topping
75–90ml/5–6 tbsp Kirsch
600ml/1 pint/2½ cups double (heavy) cream
425g/15oz can black cherries, drained, pitted and chopped

For the decoration
225g/8oz plain (semisweet) chocolate, to make chocolate curls, *see page 84*
15–20 fresh cherries, preferably with stems
sifted icing (confectioners') sugar (optional)

1 Preheat the oven to 180°C/350°F/ Gas 4. Grease and line two 20cm/ 8in round deep cake tins (pans) with baking parchment.

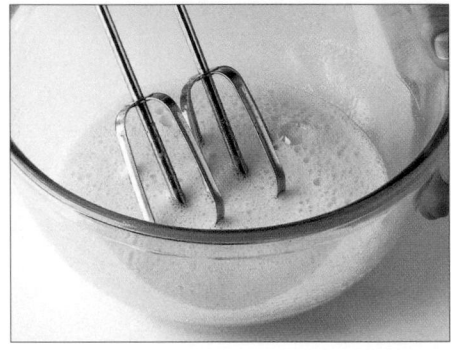

2 Put the eggs and sugar in a large bowl and beat with an electric whisk for about 10 minutes, or until the mixture is thick and pale and leaves a trail when the beaters are lifted.

3 Sift together the flour and cocoa powder, then sift again into the whisked mixture. Fold in gently using a metal spoon and a figure-of-eight motion.

4 Slowly trickle in the cooled melted butter and fold in gently.

5 Divide the batter between the tins and smooth level. Bake for 30 minutes, until springy to the touch.

6 Leave in the tin for 5 minutes, then turn out on to a wire rack to cool. Peel off the lining paper.

7 Cut each cake in half horizontally. Sprinkle the four layers evenly with the Kirsch.

8 In a large bowl, whip the cream until it holds soft peaks.

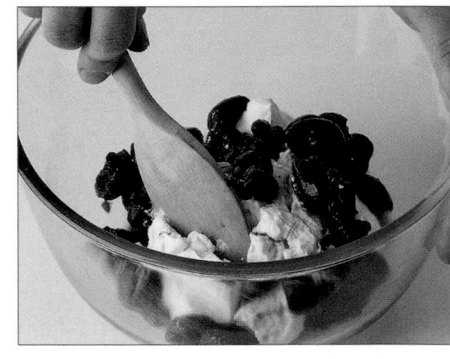

9 Transfer two-thirds of the cream to another bowl and stir in the chopped cherries.

10 Place a layer of cake on a serving plate and spread over one-third of the filling. Top with another portion of cake and continue layering, finishing with the cake top.

11 Use the remaining whipped cream to cover the top and sides of the gateau. Decorate with chocolate curls, cherries and a dusting of icing sugar.

Energy 448kcal/1864kJ; Protein 4.8g; Carbohydrate 26.4g, of which sugars 22.7g; Fat 35.2g, of which saturates 21.1g; Cholesterol 161mg; Calcium 61.8mg; Fibre 0.8g; Sodium 121mg.

Death by chocolate

One of the richest chocolate cakes ever, this amazing confection has layers of jam and brandy-flavoured chocolate filling between layers of light cake. It is covered with chocolate ganache – a rich chocolate-truffle topping. Serve this in thin slices, and store, refrigerated, for up to three days.

SERVES 16–20

115g/4oz/½ cup unsalted butter, plus extra for greasing
225g/8oz plain (semisweet) chocolate, broken into pieces
150ml/¼ pint/⅔ cup milk
225g/8oz/1 cup light muscovado (brown) sugar
10ml/2 tsp vanilla extract
2 eggs, separated
150ml/¼ pint/⅔ cup sour cream
225g/8oz/2 cups self-raising (self-rising) flour
5ml/1 tsp baking powder

For the filling
60ml/4 tbsp seedless raspberry jam
60ml/4 tbsp brandy
400g/14oz plain (semisweet) chocolate, broken into pieces
200g/7oz/scant 1 cup unsalted butter
plain and white chocolate curls, *see page 84*, and chocolate-dipped physalis, to decorate

For the ganache
250ml/8fl oz/1 cup double (heavy) cream
225g/8oz plain (semisweet) chocolate, broken into pieces

1 Preheat the oven to 180°C/350°F/Gas 4. Grease and line a 23cm/9in round deep cake tin (pan) with baking parchment.

2 Put the chocolate, butter and milk in a pan. Stir over a very low heat until the chocolate melts. Remove from the heat.

3 Beat in the sugar and vanilla.

4 Beat the egg yolks and cream in a bowl, then beat into the chocolate mixture. Sift the flour and baking powder over the mixture and fold in.

5 Spoon into the cake tin and bake for 45–55 minutes. Turn on to a wire rack to go cold. Remove the lining papers. Slice into three even layers.

6 To make the filling, warm the jam with 15ml/1 tbsp of the brandy in a small pan. Brush over one side of two cake layers, then leave to set.

7 Put the remaining brandy in the pan with the chocolate and butter. Melt gently over a low heat, stirring until smooth. Cool until the filling is just beginning to thicken.

8 Spread one layer of the cake with half of the chocolate filling. Top with a second layer of cake, jam side up, and the remaining filling. Top with the final cake and leave to set.

9 To make the ganache, heat the cream and chocolate together in a pan over a low heat, stirring until the chocolate melts. Pour into a bowl, leave to cool, then whisk until the mixture begins to hold its shape.

10 Spread the cake top and sides with ganache.

11 Decorate with chocolate curls and chocolate-dipped physalis. Store, chilled, until ready to serve.

CHOCOLATE-DIPPED PHYSALIS
Melt chocolate in a heatproof bowl over a pan of gently simmering water. Peel back the papery leaves from the physalis. Holding the leaves, dip each physalis into the chocolate. Leave to set on a baking sheet lined with baking parchment.

Energy 432kcal/1809kJ; Protein 4.7g; Carbohydrate 49.9g, of which sugars 38.4g; Fat 24.7g, of which saturates 14.9g; Cholesterol 57mg; Calcium 99mg; Fibre 1.4g; Sodium 120mg.

Chocolate gooey cake

For perfect results it is essential to undercook this cake so that it is soft in the middle, so it is unsuitable for children and the elderly. It is made with almonds instead of flour, and so has a superb nutty flavour and is also gluten-free. Serve as a dessert with whipped cream. Eat fresh.

SERVES 8

115g/4oz/½ cup unsalted butter,
  diced, plus extra for greasing
115g/4oz dark (bittersweet)
  chocolate, broken into pieces
2 eggs, separated
175g/6oz/1½ cups ground almonds
5ml/1 tsp vanilla sugar
whipped double (heavy) cream,
  to serve

1 Preheat the oven to 180°C/350°F/
Gas 4. Grease and line a 20cm/8in
round shallow cake tin (pan).

2 Put the chocolate into a pan.
Add 5ml/1 tsp water and heat
very gently until the chocolate
has melted, stirring occasionally.
Remove from the heat.

3 Add the butter to the chocolate
and stir until melted.

4 Add the egg yolks, ground
almonds and vanilla sugar, and stir
together. Turn the mixture into a
large bowl.

5 Put the egg whites into a clean,
grease-free bowl and whisk until
they form stiff peaks, then fold in
batches into the chocolate mixture.

6 Put the mixture into the prepared
tin and bake for 15–17 minutes, or
until just set. The mixture should
still be soft in the centre. Remove
the lining paper.

7 Leave to cool in the tin, then
carefully turn out on to a serving
plate. Serve with whipped cream.

Energy 311kcal/1288kJ; Protein 6.8g; Carbohydrate 10g, of which sugars 9.3g; Fat 27.4g, of which saturates 9.9g; Cholesterol 75mg; Calcium 66.2mg; Fibre 1.9g; Sodium 97mg.

Devil's food cake

Originating in the US and dating back to 1905, this cake is always made using cocoa powder rather than melted chocolate. The chocolate cake is layered and covered with a fine white frosting flavoured with orange. It tastes very good indeed, and will keep for four days.

SERVES 10–12

175g/6oz/¾ cup butter, at room temperature, plus extra for greasing
50g/2oz/½ cup unsweetened cocoa powder
350g/12oz/scant 2 cups soft dark brown sugar
3 eggs
275g/10oz/1½ cups plain (all-purpose) flour
7.5ml/1½ tsp bicarbonate of soda (baking soda)
1.5ml/¼ tsp baking powder
120ml/4fl oz/½ cup sour cream
shreds of orange rind, to decorate

For the frosting
300g/11oz/1½ cups caster (superfine) sugar
2 egg whites
60ml/4 tbsp orange juice concentrate
15ml/1 tbsp lemon juice
grated rind of 1 orange

1 Preheat the oven to 180°C/350°F/ Gas 4. Grease and line two 23cm/9in round shallow cake tins (pans) with baking parchment.

2 In a bowl, mix the cocoa powder with 175ml/6fl oz/¾ cup boiling water until smooth. Leave to cool.

3 Beat the butter and sugar until light and fluffy, then beat in the eggs one at a time.

4 When the cocoa mixture is luke-warm, add it to the butter mixture.

5 Sift the flour, bicarbonate of soda and baking powder into the cocoa mixture in three batches, alternating with the soured cream.

6 Pour into the tins and bake for 30–35 minutes, or until the cake pulls away from the sides.

7 Leave to cool in the tins for 15 minutes, then turn out to cool on a wire rack to go cold. Remove the lining papers.

8 To make the frosting, put all the ingredients into a heatproof bowl set over a pan of gently simmering water. With an electric whisk, beat until the mixture holds soft peaks. Remove from the heat and continue beating until thick enough to spread.

9 Quickly sandwich the cake layers with frosting, then spread over the top and sides. Decorate with orange rind shreds.

Energy 455kcal/1916kJ; Protein 5.7g; Carbohydrate 75.5g, of which sugars 57.6g; Fat 16.6g, of which saturates 9.6g; Cholesterol 84.6mg; Calcium 86.5mg; Fibre 1.2g; Sodium 165mg.

Chocolate drizzle party cake

Make this moist chocolate and hazelnut cake to celebrate almost any family occasion. The decoration couldn't be simpler, but it looks effective. The cake is easy to make, children and adults love it, and it can even be served with fresh summer fruits or a scoop of ice cream.

SERVES 10

115g/4oz/½ cup butter, softened, plus extra for greasing
175g/6oz/scant 1 cup natural caster (superfine) sugar
4 large (US extra large) eggs, separated
175g/6oz/1½ cups self-raising (self-rising) flour, sifted
115g/4oz plain (semisweet) chocolate, grated
90ml/6 tbsp milk
115g/4oz/1 cup ground hazelnuts

For the filling and topping
60ml/4 tbsp chocolate and hazelnut spread, warmed
200g/7oz milk chocolate
150g/5oz white chocolate
edible gold or silver balls
Materials: wired silver ribbon

1 Preheat the oven to 220°C/425°F/Gas 7. Grease and line a 20cm/8in deep round cake tin (pan) with baking parchment.

2 Beat the butter and sugar together until light and fluffy, then whisk in the egg yolks gradually, adding 5ml/1 tsp flour with each addition to prevent the mixture from curdling.

COOK'S TIP
The cake keeps for 4 days in an airtight container. Freeze the base, undecorated and wrapped in foil, for up to 2 months.

3 Fold in the grated chocolate, milk and ground hazelnuts until smooth.

4 Whisk the egg whites in a clean, grease-free bowl until they form soft peaks. Fold them into the mixture, alternating with the remaining flour.

5 Spoon into the tin and smooth level. Reduce the oven temperature to 170C/350F/Gas 3. Bake in the centre of the oven for about 1 hour 10 minutes, or until the centre springs back when pressed.

6 Cool in the tin for 5 minutes, then turn out to cool on a wire rack and peel away the lining paper.

7 Cut the cake in half, and cover one half with warmed chocolate spread.

8 Sandwich the other half on top and put them on to a serving plate.

9 Melt the chocolates in two separate heatproof bowls set over pans of gently simmering water, then spoon into two separate small paper piping (pastry) bags. Alternatively, melt in two heatproof bowls in the microwave oven.

10 Snip off the end of each bag and drizzle each chocolate over the top and side of the cake in a random pattern.

11 Sprinkle the edible gold or silver balls over the top and leave to set for 1 hour. Finish with a large wired bow in the centre of the cake, or add candles if made for a birthday celebration.

Energy 430kcal/1790kJ; Protein 7.8g; Carbohydrate 29.5g, of which sugars 28.8g; Fat 32.1g, of which saturates 13.6g; Cholesterol 96mg; Calcium 92mg; Fibre 1.9g; Sodium 125mg.

Chocolate, cherry and polenta cake

Almonds and polenta give this richly flavoured chocolate cake a nutty and dense texture, which is lightened with whisked egg whites. Crisp glacé cherries and a hint of orange make a delicious contrast. This cake will keep for up to three days in an airtight container.

3 Melt the chocolate in a heatproof bowl over a pan of simmering water.

4 Whisk the egg yolks with the sugar in a bowl until thick and pale.

5 Beat in the chocolate. Fold in the polenta, almonds, flour and orange.

6 Put the egg whites into a clean, grease-free bowl and whisk until they form stiff peaks.

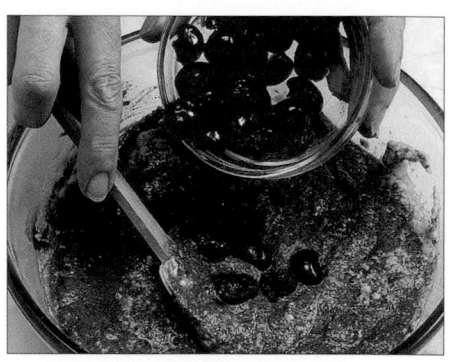

7 Stir 15ml/1 tbsp of the whites into the chocolate mixture, then fold in the rest. Finally, fold in the cherries.

SERVES 8

50g/2oz/½ cup quick-cook polenta
butter, for greasing
200g/7oz plain (semisweet)
   chocolate, broken into pieces
5 eggs, separated
175g/6oz/scant 1 cup caster
   (superfine) sugar
115g/4oz/1 cup ground almonds
60ml/4 tbsp plain
   (all-purpose) flour
finely grated rind of 1 orange
115g/4oz/½ cup glacé (candied)
   cherries, halved
icing (confectioners') sugar,
   for dusting

1 Put the polenta in a bowl and add 120ml/4fl oz/½ cup boiling water, cover and leave for 30 minutes.

2 Preheat the oven to 190°C/375°F/ Gas 5. Grease and line a 20cm/8in round deep cake tin (pan).

8 Turn the mixture into the prepared tin and bake for 45–55 minutes, or until firm to the touch. Turn out and cool on a wire rack. Remove the lining paper. Dust with icing sugar.

Energy 420kcal/1764kJ; Protein 9.6g; Carbohydrate 56.4g, of which sugars 45.5g; Fat 18.8g, of which saturates 5.8; Cholesterol 120mg; Calcium 89mg; Fibre 2.2g; Sodium 53mg.

Chocolate and prune cake

Ready-to-eat prunes add moisture and a depth of flavour that complements chocolate in this cake. The rich mixture also includes gram flour, made from chickpeas, which has no gluten and is higher in carbohydrates than ordinary flour. Keep for up to five days in an airtight container.

SERVES 8–10

150g/5oz/10 tbsp butter, plus extra
   for greasing
300g/11oz dark (bittersweet)
   chocolate
150g/5oz/1¼ cups gram flour
10ml/2 tsp baking powder
200g/7oz/generous 1 cup
   ready-to-eat stoned (pitted)
   prunes, quartered
3 eggs, beaten
120ml/4fl oz/½ cup coconut
   milk

1 Preheat the oven to 180°C/350°F/Gas 4. Grease and line a 20cm/8in round deep cake tin (pan) with baking parchment.

5 Gradually fold the melted chocolate and eggs into the prunes, alternating with the flour mixture.

6 Beat in the coconut milk, then spoon into the prepared tin and smooth the top level.

7 Bake for 20–30 minutes, or until the cake is firm to the touch and a skewer inserted into the centre comes out clean. Remove the lining.

8 Leave to cool on a wire rack before serving.

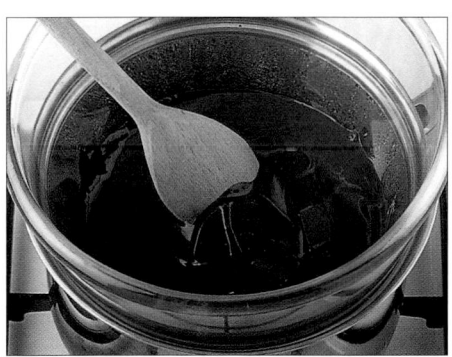

2 Melt the chocolate in a heatproof bowl set over a pan of gently simmering water. Remove from the heat to cool.

3 Sift the flour and baking powder into a bowl.

4 Place the butter and prunes in a food processor fitted with a flat blade. Process until light and fluffy, then scrape into a large bowl.

Energy 317kcal/1329kJ; Protein 6.5g; Carbohydrate 37.7g, of which sugars 26g; Fat 16.6g, of which saturates 7.3g; Cholesterol 60mg; Calcium 54mg; Fibre 2.4g; Sodium 127mg.

Chocolate orange marquise

This fabulous cake has very little flour, but is rich with butter, eggs and chocolate, and flavoured with orange rind and juice. Enjoy this special cake with coffee, or with cream as a dessert. Store chilled in an airtight container for up to three days.

SERVES 6–8

225g/8oz/1 cup unsalted butter, diced, at room temperature, plus extra for greasing
200g/7oz/1 cup caster (superfine) sugar
60ml/4 tbsp freshly squeezed orange juice
350g/12oz plain (semisweet) chocolate, broken into pieces
5 eggs
finely grated rind of 1 orange
45ml/3 tbsp plain (all-purpose) flour
icing (confectioners') sugar, to decorate
finely pared strips of orange rind, to decorate

1 Preheat the oven to 180°C/350°F/ Gas 4. Grease and line a 23cm/9in round deep cake tin (pan) with baking parchment.

2 Put 115g/4oz/generous ½ cup of the caster sugar in a heavy pan with the fresh orange juice. Place over a low heat until all the sugar has dissolved. Stir constantly so that the sugar does not catch and burn. Do not allow to boil.

3 Remove from the heat and stir in the chocolate until melted, then add the butter, stirring, until melted and evenly mixed. Cool.

4 Put the eggs with the remaining sugar in a large bowl and whisk until pale and very thick. Add the orange rind.

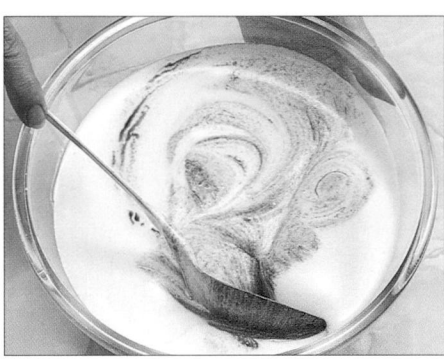

5 Using a metal spoon, fold the chocolate mixture lightly and evenly into the egg mixture using a metal spoon and a figure-of-eight motion. Sift the flour over and fold in evenly.

COOK'S TIP
Make the marquise ahead of time and freeze for up to 3 months in a freezerproof box.

6 Scrape the mixture into the prepared tin. Put the tin into a roasting pan, then pour hot water into the roasting pan to reach halfway up the outside of the cake tin.

7 Bake for 1 hour, or until the cake is firm to the touch. Carefully remove the cake tin from the roasting pan and cool for 15–20 minutes.

8 Invert the cake on a baking sheet. Lift away the tin and lining paper. Place a serving plate over the cake, then turn the baking sheet and plate over as one so that the cake is transferred to the plate.

9 Dust with icing sugar, decorate with strips of pared orange rind and serve slightly warm or cold.

Energy 553kcal/2309kJ; Protein 3.1g; Carbohydrate 59.1g, of which sugars 54.4g; Fat 35.5g, of which saturates 22g; Cholesterol 63mg; Calcium 41mg; Fibre 1.3g; Sodium 176mg.

Sachertorte

This glorious gateau has a pedigree going back to 1832, when it was created by Franz Sacher, a chef of the royal household in Vienna. It is rich and dark, with a flavour that contrasts with the apricot glaze – and it's topped with a rich, glossy icing. Keep, refrigerated, for up to three days.

SERVES 10–12

150g/5oz/10 tbsp unsalted butter,
   plus extra for greasing
115g/4oz/generous ½ cup caster
   (superfine) sugar
8 eggs, separated
225g/8oz dark (bittersweet)
   chocolate, melted and cooled
115g/4oz/1 cup plain
   (all-purpose) flour

For the glaze
225g/8oz/1 cup apricot jam
15ml/1 tbsp lemon juice

For the icing
225g/8oz dark (bittersweet)
   chocolate, broken into pieces
200g/7oz/1 cup caster
   (superfine) sugar
15ml/1 tbsp golden
   (light corn) syrup
250ml/8fl oz/1 cup double
   (heavy) cream
5ml/1 tsp vanilla extract
chocolate curls, to decorate,
   see page 84

1 Preheat the oven to 180°C/350°F/ Gas 4. Grease and line a 23cm/9in round deep cake tin (pan).

2 In a bowl, beat the butter with the sugar until pale and fluffy, then add the egg yolks, one at a time, beating well after each addition.

3 Beat in the melted chocolate, then sift the flour over the mixture and fold it in evenly with a large metal spoon.

4 Put the egg whites into a clean, grease-free bowl and whisk until they form stiff peaks.

5 Stir about a quarter of the whites into the chocolate mixture to lighten it, then fold in the remaining whites.

6 Tip the mixture into the prepared tin and smooth the top level. Bake for 50–55 minutes, or until firm.

7 Leave to stand in the tin for 5 minutes, then turn out on to a wire rack to go cold. Remove the lining paper. Slice in half across the middle to make two even layers.

8 To make the glaze, heat the apricot jam with the lemon juice in a small pan until melted, then strain through a sieve (strainer) into a bowl.

9 Brush the top and sides of each layer with the apricot glaze, then sandwich them together. Put the cake on a wire rack.

10 To make the icing, put the chocolate, sugar, golden syrup, cream and vanilla extract in a pan. Heat gently, stirring constantly, until the mixture is thick and smooth.

11 Simmer gently for 3–4 minutes, without stirring, until the mixture registers 95°C/200°F on a sugar thermometer.

12 Pour the icing quickly over the cake, spreading to cover the top and sides completely.

13 Leave to set, then decorate with chocolate curls.

Energy 625kcal/2618kJ; Protein 7.6g; Carbohydrate 73.1g, of which sugars 65.5g; Fat 35.8g, of which saturates 20.8g; Cholesterol 184mg; Calcium 73mg; Fibre 1.2g; Sodium 143mg.

Individual cakes

Miniature cakes are attractive and fun to make, and are always popular. They are visually appealing and make a focal point at parties. Muffins and cupcakes have good keeping qualities and are ideal to prepare ahead, so you can bake them the day before and store them in an airtight tin. You can also freeze them undecorated (although you will need to replace the paper cases). Fun cakes for children to help decorate include Novelty Party Cupcakes and the scary Hallowe'en Horrors. Make up a selection of little cakes for a coffee morning or a tea party and include some light and delicate cakes such as Simple Coconut Cakes and French Madeleines, which will make a beautiful display alongside richer cakes such as Rich Chocolate Ruffles. Some plainer bakes, such as Rock Buns and Buttermilk Scones, are best freshly made and eaten on the same day. Bake a tray for a brunch party and serve them warm from the oven – you'll find they will soon disappear.

Left: Marshmallow Daisy Cakes, Snowballs and Buttermilk Scones.

Fondant fancies

A classic fondant coating is light and shiny, and ideal to finish these delicate little cakes. These fancies are extra special, so serve them for a classic celebration such as a christening. They will keep for two days in an airtight container. Freeze the undecorated base for up to three months.

MAKES 28

50g/2oz/½ cup unsalted butter
  oil, for greasing
3 large (US extra large) eggs
100g/3¾oz/generous ½ cup caster
  (superfine) sugar
100g/3¾oz/scant 1 cup plain
  (all-purpose) flour
15ml/1 tbsp cornflour (cornstarch)
pinch of salt

For the icing and decoration
500g/1lb/5 cups fondant icing
  sugar, sifted
food colourings

1 Melt the butter in a small pan over a gentle heat and allow to cool.

2 Preheat the oven to 180°C/ 350°F/Gas 4. Oil and line a 28 × 18cm/11 × 7in baking tin with baking parchment.

3 In a large bowl, whisk the eggs and sugar together, using an electric mixer, until pale, thick and creamy, and the mixture leaves a trail when the beaters are lifted away.

4 Sift the flour, cornflour and salt over the surface and pour the melted butter around the sides of the bowl. Gently fold together, taking care not to knock out the air, then pour into the lined tin.

5 Bake for 20 minutes, or until light golden and just firm to the touch.

6 Cool in the tin for 5 minutes, then turn out, peel away the lining paper and leave on a wire rack until cold.

7 Stamp out rounds using a 3.5cm/ 1½in pastry (cookie) cutter, fancy shapes or small squares, and put on a wire rack standing over a tray.

8 Put the sifted fondant icing sugar into a bowl and add enough cold water to give a coating consistency. Divide the icing among several bowls and colour it delicately with a few drops of food colouring. Keep each bowl covered with a damp cloth until needed.

9 Working quickly, spoon the icing over each cake and smooth down to cover the tops and sides. Put in paper cases to serve.

Energy 259kcal/1094kJ; Protein 2.7g; Carbohydrate 49.7g, of which sugars 41.4g; Fat 6.9g, of which saturates 4g; Cholesterol 40mg; Calcium 50mg; Fibre 0.3g; Sodium 66mg.

Marshmallow daisy cakes

These lemony cakes are as fresh as a daisy; they are quick and very simple to make and bake. The marshmallow flowers take moments to create – all you need is a pair of scissors. They are sure to be a hit, especially with children, and will keep for two days in an airtight container.

MAKES 12

115g/4oz/1 cup self-raising
  (self-rising) flour
5ml/1 tsp baking powder
115g/4oz/generous ½ cup caster
  (superfine) sugar
115g/4oz/½ cup soft tub margarine
2 large (US extra large)
  eggs, beaten
15ml/1 tbsp lemon juice
finely grated rind of 1 lemon

For the decoration
½ quantity buttercream, *see*
  page 22
12 pink and white marshmallows
caster (superfine) sugar, for dusting
small sweets (candies)

1 Preheat the oven to 180°C/350°F/ Gas 4. Line a 12-cup muffin tin (pan) with paper cases.

2 Sift the flour, baking powder and sugar into a large bowl, then add the remaining ingredients. Beat until light and creamy, then place heaped spoonfuls into the paper cases.

3 Bake for about 20 minutes, or until golden and firm to the touch.

4 Allow to cool for 2 minutes, then turn out on to a wire rack to go cold.

5 When cold, spread the top of each cake with a little buttercream.

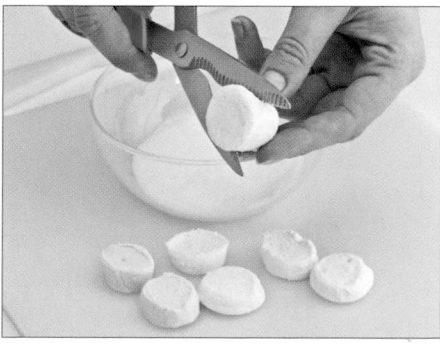

6 Use kitchen scissors to cut each marshmallow in half horizontally.

7 Dip the cut marshmallow edges in caster sugar to prevent sticking. Repeat, cutting the marshmallows in half again, and dipping the cut edge in caster sugar.

8 Press the tips of four halves together to form four petals of a flower. Arrange them on top of a cupcake and press a small sweet into the centre.

COOK'S TIP
Freeze undecorated. You may have to replace the paper cases, as these tend to peel away.

Energy 115kcal/483kJ; Protein 1.3g; Carbohydrate 16.5g, of which sugars 12.1g; Fat 5.4g, of which saturates 3.2g; Cholesterol 31mg; Calcium 18mg; Fibre 0.2g; Sodium 43mg.

Buttermilk scones

Plain scones filled with jam and cream make a delicious addition to afternoon tea. Baking them with buttermilk instead of plain milk gives them additional flavour. Serve with a good bought or home-made jam and clotted cream to make them a little special. They are best eaten fresh.

MAKES 12

75g/3oz/6 tbsp butter, diced, plus extra for greasing
350g/12oz/3 cups self-raising (self-rising) flour, plus extra for dusting
115g/4oz/generous ½ cup caster (superfine) sugar
175ml/6fl oz/¾ cup buttermilk or natural (plain) low-fat yogurt
raspberry jam, to serve
clotted cream, to serve

1 Preheat the oven to 200°C/ 400°F/Gas 6 and lightly grease a baking sheet.

2 Sift the flour into a large bowl and add the diced butter.

3 Rub together with your fingertips until the mixture resembles fine breadcrumbs. Stir in the sugar and mix, then make a well in the centre.

4 Add the buttermilk or yogurt. Stir in lightly with a flat-bladed knife until the mixture forms a soft dough.

5 Turn the dough out on to a lightly floured surface and knead lightly.

6 Roll out to a 2.5cm/1in thickness. Stamp out rounds using a 5cm/2in round pastry (cookie) cutter, then gather up the trimmings, re-knead and stamp out more rounds.

7 Put the rounds on the baking sheet and bake for 12–14 minutes, or until risen and light golden.

8 Allow to cool on a wire rack and serve split open with jam and cream. Home-made scones are best eaten fresh on the day of baking.

Energy 74kcal/311kJ; Protein 1.7g; Carbohydrate 10.9g, of which sugars 0.7g; Fat 3g, of which saturates 1.8g; Cholesterol 8mg; Calcium 34mg; Fibre 0.4g; Sodium 26mg.

Madeleines

These small shell-shaped sponge cakes are light as a feather and traditionally served with a cup of tea. In France on Christmas Eve, however, you'll find them coloured a delicate pink and accompanied by a glass of champagne. Eat these fresh on the day they are made. Do not freeze.

MAKES 15

50g/2oz/¼ cup unsalted butter,
  melted, plus extra melted butter
  for greasing
2 eggs
50g/2oz/¼ cup vanilla caster
  (superfine) sugar
50g/2oz/½ cup plain (all-purpose)
  flour, plus extra for dusting
a few drops of orange flower water
pink food colouring (optional)
icing (confectioners') sugar,
  for dusting

1 Preheat the oven to 200°C/400°F/ Gas 6. Lightly grease a scalloped madeleine mould with a little melted butter, making sure all the indentations are greased well, so the cakes are released easily. Dust with a little flour, shake the tin, then tap out any excess.

2 Put the eggs and sugar in a heatproof bowl set over a pan of hot water. Whisk until very thick and mousse-like, and the mixture leaves a thick ribbon trail when the beaters are lifted away. Remove from the heat and continue whisking for 2 minutes.

3 Sift half the flour over the surface and fold in gently with a large metal spoon, then repeat with the remaining flour.

4 Gently fold in the cooled melted butter and the orange flower water.

5 Divide the mixture in half, if you like, and colour half a delicate pink with a few drops of food colour.

6 Spoon into the moulds to just level with the top. Smooth level and bake for 10 minutes, or until firm and pale golden.

7 Cool in the tin for a few minutes, then turn out to cool on a wire rack.

8 Re-grease and flour the tins, then use up the remaining batter.

9 Serve with the shell sides upward, dusted with icing sugar.

Energy 130kcal/547kJ; Protein 2.4g; Carbohydrate 17.3g, of which sugars 6.8g; Fat 6.2g, of which saturates 3.5g; Cholesterol 45mg; Calcium 28mg; Fibre 0.4g; Sodium 50mg.

Novelty party cupcakes

One of the easiest ways to keep children happy is to let them bake and decorate their own party cakes. You can use sweets or bought decorations – or even make your own from sugarpaste. This simple all-in-one batter can be mixed together in a food processor, if you like. Eat fresh.

MAKES 12

115g/4oz/1 cup self-raising
 (self-rising) flour
5ml/1 tsp baking powder
115g/4oz/generous ½ cup caster
 (superfine) sugar
115g/4oz/1 cup soft tub margarine
2 large (US extra large) eggs
5ml/1 tsp vanilla extract

For the decoration
1 quantity glacé icing, *see page 24*
food colourings
small coloured sweets (candies),
 jellies or piped decorations

COOK'S TIP
Freeze the cakes undecorated for up to 1 month. You may need to replace the paper cases when the cakes have thawed as these can peel away from the cakes.

1 Preheat the oven to 160°C/325°F/ Gas 3. Line a 12-cup muffin tin (pan) with cupcake cases.

2 Sift the flour and baking powder into a bowl, or food processor, and add all the remaining ingredients.

3 Beat with an electric mixer, or process until smooth, then divide among the paper cases.

4 Bake for 20 minutes, or until firm to the touch. Cool on a wire rack.

5 To decorate, colour the glacé icing in batches and spoon a little over each cake. Decorate with sweets while the icing is wet. Leave to set.

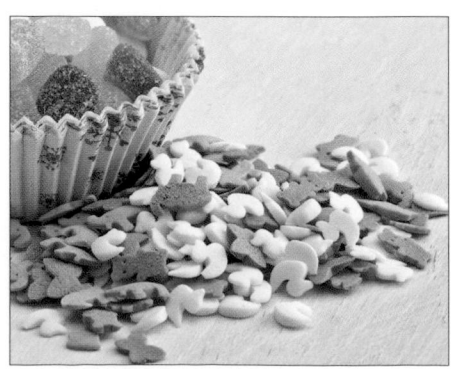

Energy 228kcal/957kJ; Protein 2.5g; Carbohydrate 27.9g, of which sugars 20.5g; Fat 12.7g, of which saturates 7.9g; Cholesterol 74mg; Calcium 32mg; Fibre 0.3g; Sodium 121mg.

Cinnamon meringues

These meringues have a hint of cinnamon and almond, which gives them a delicate flavour. They have a slightly chewy texture that goes particularly well with luscious summer fruits and amaretto-flavoured cream. Eat fresh, or store, undecorated, in an airtight container for two weeks.

MAKES 10

4 egg whites
1.25ml/¼ tsp cream of tartar
225g/8oz/generous 1 cup caster
   (superfine) sugar
2.5ml/½ tsp ground cinnamon
a few drops of almond extract
40g/1½oz/generous ⅓ cup
   ground almonds

For the filling
300ml/½ pint/1¼ cups double
   (heavy) cream
15ml/1 tbsp amaretto liqueur
   (optional)
350g/12oz/3 cups fresh redcurrants
   and raspberries
tiny sprigs of fresh mint

1 Preheat the oven to 110°C/225°F/
Gas ¼. Line two baking sheets with
baking parchment.

2 Rinse out a clean mixing bowl
with boiling water, then dry with
kitchen paper to make sure it is
totally grease-free.

3 Put the egg whites into the bowl
and whisk until they form stiff
peaks. Add the cream of tartar.
Gradually whisk in the sugar with
the cinnamon and almond extract in
small batches until the mixture is
thick and stiff. Fold in the almonds.

COOK'S TIP
These cakes are not suitable
for freezing.

4 Spoon 20 rough dessertspoonfuls
on to the baking sheets, then bake
for 2 hours, or until crisp and dry,
swapping over the position of the
baking sheets halfway through.
Cool, then peel off from the papers.

5 Whip the cream until soft peaks
form. Fold in the liqueur, if using,
then fill a piping (pastry) bag.
Pipe cream on to 10 meringue
bases. Arrange the fruits, mint and
meringue lid and serve immediately.

Energy 193kcal/821kJ; Protein 2.7g; Carbohydrate 40g, of which sugars 40g; Fat 1.6g, of which saturates 0.1g; Cholesterol 0mg; Calcium 31mg; Fibre 1.4g; Sodium 26mg.

Snowballs

These snowy muffins prove that variations on this simple theme appear to be endless. They have the tastiest topping ever, white chocolate mixed with coconut liqueur and cream, then sprinkled with coconut strands. They make an irresistible winter's treat. Keep for up to two days.

MAKES 12

175g/6oz/12 tbsp caster (superfine) sugar
2.5ml/½ tsp baking powder
200g/7oz/1¾ cups self-raising (self-rising) flour
15ml/2 tbsp desiccated (dry unsweetened shredded) coconut
175g/6oz/¾ cup soft tub margarine
3 eggs, beaten
15ml/1 tbsp milk

For the topping
175g/6oz white chocolate, chopped
15ml/1 tbsp coconut liqueur
75ml/5 tbsp double (heavy) cream
175g/6oz/2 cups large shredded coconut strands or curls

1 Preheat the oven to 180°C/350°F/ Gas 4. Line a 12-cup deep muffin tin (pan) with paper cases.

2 Sift the sugar, baking powder, flour and coconut into a large bowl.

3 Add the margarine, eggs and milk and beat until smooth and creamy.

4 Divide the batter evenly among the paper cases.

5 Bake for 18–20 minutes, or until risen, golden and firm to the touch. Leave in the tin for 2 minutes, then turn out to cool on a wire rack.

6 To make the topping, put the chocolate and liqueur in a bowl. Put the cream in a pan and bring to the boil, then pour it over the chocolate and liqueur. Stir until smooth, then cool and chill for 30 minutes.

7 Whisk with an electric mixer for a few minutes, or until light and fluffy.

8 Spread the icing over the top of each muffin, then sprinkle coconut strands liberally over the icing to cover completely.

Energy 481kcal/2005kJ; Protein 5.9g; Carbohydrate 39.6g, of which sugars 35.2g; Fat 34.3g, of which saturates 23.9g; Cholesterol 12mg; Calcium 137mg; Fibre 3g; Sodium 167mg.

Rich chocolate ruffles

These glossy chocolate cakes are a class act, decorated with ruffles of chocolate and glinting with gold leaf. Each one is contained in a gold foil case to make them perfect individual cakes for a special occasion. The attractive ruffle is a useful technique for using on other cakes.

MAKES 12

65g/2½oz/9 tbsp self-raising (self-rising) flour
25g/1oz/¼ cup unsweetened cocoa powder
75g/3oz/⅓ cup soft dark brown sugar
75g/3oz/6 tbsp butter, softened
3 eggs
30ml/2 tbsp milk

For the ruffles
125g/4oz plain (semisweet) chocolate, grated
37.5ml/2½ tbsp liquid glucose (clear corn syrup)

For the topping
100ml/3½fl oz/scant ½ cup double (heavy) cream
15ml/1 tbsp liquid glucose (clear corn syrup)
200g/7oz dark (bittersweet) chocolate, melted
scraps of edible gold leaf (optional)

1 Preheat the oven to 190°C/375°F/ Gas 5. Line a 12-cup muffin tray with gold foil cases.

2 Sift the flour and cocoa into a bowl, add the sugar, butter, eggs and milk, and beat for about 2 minutes, or until smooth.

3 Divide the batter among the cases and bake for 15 minutes, or until just firm to the touch in the centre.

4 Remove from the tray and leave to cool on a wire rack.

5 To make the ruffles, melt the chocolate in a heatproof bowl set over a pan of warm water. Remove from the heat. Beat in the glucose until a paste forms that comes away from the sides of the bowl. Chill in a plastic bag for 1 hour.

6 Break off pieces and knead until pliable. Roll out between sheets of non-stick paper until 5mm/¼in thick. Mould into delicate fans.

7 To make the topping, bring the cream to the boil in a pan.

8 Remove from the heat, add the liquid glucose and the melted chocolate, and stir.

9 Spoon the mixture over the top of each cake, top with a chocolate ruffle and tiny scraps of gold leaf, if you like, then leave to set. Eat fresh for the best taste.

Energy 392kcal/1641kJ; Protein 5g; Carbohydrate 42.2g, of which sugars 30.5g; Fat 23.8g, of which saturates 14.8g; Cholesterol 111mg; Calcium 110mg; Fibre 0.7g; Sodium 235mg.

Sugar sparkle cupcakes

These delicate rose-flavoured cakes are pretty in pink and perfect for a girls-only party.
Make the cakes ahead, if you like, and have fun decorating them with sugar sprinkles, sugar
flowers or shapes in your choice of colours. Keep for up to two days in an airtight container.

MAKES 12

115g/4oz/1 cup self-raising
  (self-rising) flour
115g/4oz/generous ½ cup caster
  (superfine) sugar
115g/4oz/½ cup unsalted
  butter, softened
2 eggs
15ml/1 tbsp rose water
15ml/1 tbsp milk
pink food colouring, optional

For the topping and decoration
225g/8oz/2 cups icing
  (confectioners') sugar, sifted
15ml/1 tbsp rose water
pink sugar sprinkles, or sugar
  flowers or shapes

1 Preheat the oven to 190°C/375°F/
Gas 5. Line a 12-cup muffin tin
(pan) with paper cases.

2 Put the flour, sugar, butter and
eggs into a large bowl with the rose
water and beat until smooth. Add
the milk and a few drops of pink
food colouring.

3 Divide among the paper cases.

4 Bake for 15–20 minutes, or until
the cakes are risen and golden,
and are just firm to the touch.
Remove them from the tray and put
on a wire rack to cool.

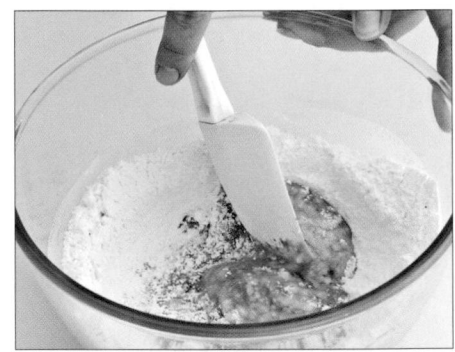

5 To make the topping, sift the icing
sugar into a bowl. Add the rose
water with a few drops of pink
food colouring and 5ml/1 tsp cold
water, or enough to mix to a
spreadable icing.

6 Spoon a little icing over the top of
each cake, then top with sugar
sprinkles, flowers or shapes.

COOK'S TIP
Freeze, undecorated, for up to
3 months.

Energy 249kcal/1041kJ; Protein 2.4g; Carbohydrate 27g, of which sugars 20.4g; Fat 16.5g, of which saturates 9.5g; Cholesterol 76mg; Calcium 35mg; Fibre 0.3g; Sodium 89mg.

Autumn passionettes

Moist and moreish, these sweet carrot and apple bakes are guaranteed to be a winner with children and adults alike. They are perfect for autumn snacks, with their warming mixed spice flavouring and walnut topping. These cakes will keep for up to four days in an airtight container.

MAKES 24

150g/5oz/scant ¾ cup
  butter, melted
200g/7oz/1 cup soft light
  brown sugar
115g/4oz/1 cup carrots, peeled
  and finely grated
50g/2oz/1 cup dessert apples,
  peeled and finely grated
pinch of salt
1–2 tsp/5–10ml mixed (apple
  pie) spice
2 eggs
200g/7oz/1¾ cups self-raising
  (self-rising) flour
10ml/2 tsp baking powder
115g/4oz/1 cup walnuts,
  finely chopped

For the topping
175g/6oz/¾ cup cream cheese
75ml/5 tbsp single (light) cream
50g/2oz/½ cup icing
  (confectioners') sugar
24 walnut halves
10ml/2 tsp unsweetened cocoa
  powder, sifted

1 Preheat the oven to 180°C/350°F/Gas 4. Arrange 24 paper cases in muffin trays.

2 Put the butter, sugar, carrots, apples, salt, mixed spice and eggs in a mixing bowl and beat well to combine.

3 Sift together the flour and baking powder into the butter and sugar mixture. Add the chopped walnuts and fold in until evenly blended.

4 Half-fill the paper cases with the batter, then bake for 20–25 minutes, until golden, or until they spring back when pressed lightly with a finger.

5 Leave the cakes in the tins for about 5 minutes, before transferring them to a wire rack to cool completely.

6 To make the topping, put the cream cheese in a mixing bowl and beat in the cream and icing sugar until smooth.

7 Put a spoonful of the topping in the centre of each cake, then decorate with the walnuts. Dust with sifted cocoa powder and allow the icing to set before serving.

Energy 194kcal/808kJ; Protein 3.1g; Carbohydrate 18.3g, of which sugars 11.8g; Fat 12.6g, of which saturates 5.5g; Cholesterol 37mg; Calcium 38mg; Fibre 0.7g; Sodium 75mg.

Hallowe'en horrors

Children will love decorating these little chocolate cupcakes with ghostly shapes, pumpkins, witches' hats, or they can think up their own scary creations to celebrate this fun and spooky festival. Keep these for two days in an airtight container or freeze, undecorated, for three months.

MAKES 24

175g/6oz/scant 1 cup caster (superfine) sugar
175g/6oz/¾ cup soft tub margarine
3 eggs, beaten
150g/5oz/1¼ cups self-raising (self-rising) flour
5ml/1 tsp baking powder
25g/1oz/¼ cup unsweetened cocoa powder

For the icing and decoration
50g/2oz/¼ cup unsalted butter
25g/1oz/¼ cup unsweetened cocoa powder
30ml/2 tbsp milk
225g/8oz/2 cups natural icing (confectioners') sugar
500g/1¼lb sugarpaste (fondant)
orange, green, red and black paste food colourings
tubes of coloured writing icing

1 Preheat the oven to 180°C/350°F/ Gas 4. Line two 12-cup muffin tins (pans) with paper cases.

2 Put the sugar, margarine and eggs in a bowl, then sift in the flour, baking powder and cocoa. Beat for 2 minutes, or until smooth and creamy.

3 Spoon the mixture into the paper cases and bake for 15–20 minutes, or until well risen and the tops spring back when lightly touched with a finger. Transfer to a wire rack to cool completely.

4 To make the icing, melt the butter with the cocoa in a small pan over low heat. Remove from the heat and add the milk, then beat in the icing sugar until smooth and glossy. Spread thickly on top of each cake.

5 Thinly roll out one third of the white sugarpaste. Cut out circles using a pastry cutter. Hold the centre and ruche up the circle to look like a ghost. Pipe black dots for eyes and a circle for the mouth using a tube of black writing icing. Make seven more.

6 Colour half of the remaining paste orange and the rest black.

7 Roll the orange paste into eight balls. Gently press a skewer at regular intervals into the side of each. Mould a green fondant stalk.

8 To make eight witches' hats, roll the black icing into equal balls, then taper into a cone. Flute the larger end. Decorate with white icing. Stick one decoration to each cake.

Energy 203kcal/859kJ; Protein 2g; Carbohydrate 42.8g, of which sugars 32.5g; Fat 3.8g, of which saturates 0.6g; Cholesterol 10mg; Calcium 72mg; Fibre 0.7g; Sodium 60mg.

Chocolate and strawberry-filled palmiers

Who could resist sweet and crisp puff pastry, with layers of chocolate, whipped cream and fresh strawberries, as a summer treat? These traditional little pastries, formed into rounded swirls, may look complicated but are actually easy to make, and they look delightful. Eat fresh.

MAKES 8

butter, for greasing
15g/¹⁄₂oz/2 tbsp unsweetened
　cocoa powder
375g/13oz puff pastry, thawed,
　if frozen
25g/1oz/2 tbsp golden caster
　(superfine) sugar

For the filling
300ml/¹⁄₂ pint/1¹⁄₄ cups whipping
　cream, whipped
45ml/3 tbsp dark (bittersweet)
　chocolate spread
175g/6oz/generous 1 cup sliced
　strawberries
icing (confectioners') sugar,
　for dusting

1 Preheat the oven to 220°C/425°F/Gas 7. Grease two large baking sheets.

2 Dust a clean, dry working surface lightly with 15ml/1 tbsp cocoa powder.

3 Keeping the long side of pastry towards you, roll it out on half the cocoa powder to a rectangle 35 × 23cm/14 × 9in. Lightly brush the top of the pastry with cold water, then sprinkle over the caster sugar and remaining cocoa.

4 Measure and mark the centre of the pastry. Roll up each of the short sides like a Swiss roll (jelly roll) so that they both meet in the centre. Brush the join with a little water and press the rolls together to secure.

5 Mark and then cut the roll into 16 slices. Arrange on the baking sheets, spacing them well apart.

6 Bake for 8–10 minutes, or until risen, puffy and golden brown. Transfer to a wire rack to cool.

7 Lightly spread half the pastries with the chocolate spread.

8 To make the filling, put the cream in a piping (pastry) bag fitted with a small plain nozzle. Pipe the cream on top of the chocolate spread, then top with a few strawberry slices.

9 Top each chocolate spread cream and strawberry layer with a pastry. Dust lightly with icing sugar and serve immediately.

Energy 368kcal/1533kJ; Protein 4.2g; Carbohydrate 27g, of which sugars 9.7g; Fat 28.3g, of which saturates 10.4g; Cholesterol 40mg; Calcium 60mg; Fibre 0.5g; Sodium 180mg.

Traybakes

Versatile traybakes can be simple and plain or elaborately decorated. They are baked in square or rectangular shallow tins and the texture can be firm like a cookie or soft like a cake. Add a topping to make them even more tasty – sweet icing, a crumble or crunchy layer, or rich chocolate – and cut them into portions. Indulgent traybakes such as Millionaire's Shortbread are a special treat, but healthier slices such as Granola Squares or Marmalade Flapjacks are great to pack for school lunches or to take to the office. Traybakes are just right for feeding a large number, so they are the ideal cakes for bazaars, fêtes, coffee mornings, cake stalls, picnics and children's parties. They require little effort to prepare and are easy to transport if you leave them in the tins in which they have been baked. They usually freeze well undecorated, so you can make and freeze them ahead or bake and store them in sealed flat containers for one to two days.

Left: Almond Slices and Blueberry Coffee Cake.

Vanilla streusel bars

The crumbly topping on this cake makes a crunchy contrast to the moist vanilla-flavoured sponge underneath. A full flavour is achieved by using vanilla extract as well as vanilla sugar, which is easy to make at home. These will keep for up to four days in an airtight container.

MAKES 25 BARS

175g/6oz/¾ cup butter, softened,
  plus extra for greasing
175g/6oz/1½ cups self-raising
  (self-rising) flour
5ml/1 tsp baking powder
175g/6oz/scant 1 cup vanilla sugar
3 eggs, beaten
7.5ml/1½ tsp vanilla extract
15–30ml/1–2 tbsp milk

For the topping
115g/4oz/1 cup self-raising
  (self-rising) flour
75g/3oz/6 tbsp butter
75g/3oz/6 tbsp vanilla sugar
icing (confectioners') sugar,
  for dusting

1 Preheat the oven to 180°C/350°F/Gas 4. Lightly grease and line a 23 × 18cm/9 × 7in shallow tin (pan) with baking parchment.

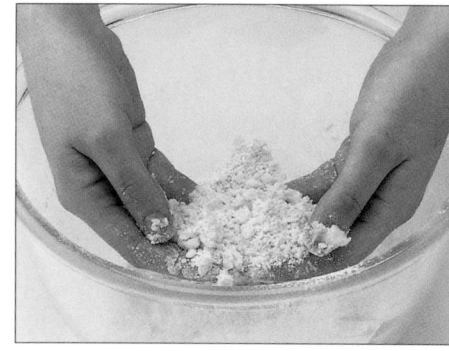

2 To make the topping, sift the flour into a bowl and rub in the butter until the mixture resembles crumbs. Stir in the vanilla sugar. Set aside.

3 To make the base, sift the flour and baking powder into a bowl. Add the butter, vanilla sugar and eggs. Beat well until smooth, adding the vanilla extract and just enough milk to give a soft dropping consistency.

4 Spoon the mixture into the prepared tin and smooth level.

5 Sprinkle the streusel topping over the surface and press down to cover the cake batter. Bake for 45–60 minutes, or until browned and firm.

6 Cool in the tin for 5 minutes, then turn out on to a wire rack to go cold. Remove the lining paper.

7 Place on a board and dust with icing sugar. Cut into 25 bars with a sharp knife.

Energy 162kcal/680kJ; Protein 2g; Carbohydrate 19.5g, of which sugars 10.7g; Fat 9g, of which saturates 5.4g; Cholesterol 44mg; Calcium 27mg; Fibre 0.4g; Sodium 70mg.

Honey cake

The earliest form of sweetener, honey has always been an important ingredient in cooking. It adds its own distinctive aroma to foods, but there is no need to use an expensive honey for cakes, as the flavour changes slightly with baking. Keep for up to five days in an airtight container.

MAKES 16 SQUARES

175g/6oz/¾ cup butter, plus extra
    for greasing
175g/6oz/¾ cup clear honey
115g/4oz/½ cup soft light
    brown sugar
2 eggs, lightly beaten
15–30ml/1–2 tbsp milk
225g/8oz/2 cups self-raising
    (self-rising) flour

1 Grease and line a 23cm/9in square tin (pan) with baking parchment.

2 In a pan, gently heat the butter, honey and sugar, stirring until the sugar has dissolved and the butter has melted. Set aside to cool slightly.

3 Preheat the oven to180°C/ 350°F/Gas 4.

4 In two batches, beat the eggs and milk into the cooled mixture in the pan, using a wooden spoon.

5 Sift the flour over the top, stir in and beat well. The batter should have a smooth pouring consistency.

6 Pour the mixture into the tin. Bake for 30 minutes, or until well risen, golden brown and firm to the touch.

7 Cool for 20 minutes, then turn on to a wire rack to go cold. Remove the paper lining and cut into squares.

Energy 152kcal/639kJ; Protein 1.9g; Carbohydrate 23.5g, of which sugars 13g; Fat 6.3g, of which saturates 3.8g; Cholesterol 26mg; Calcium 30mg; Fibre 0.4g; Sodium 49mg.

Cherry batter cake

This simple traybake is made with three contrasting layers: a cake batter, drained black cherries from a jar and a speedy brown sugar topping. It tastes lovely with a little whipped cream. This cake can be kept for up to two days in an airtight container.

3 Drain the fruit and evenly distribute it over the base.

4 Mix the remaining topping ingredients together and spoon evenly over the fruit. Bake for 40 minutes, or until golden brown and firm to the touch.

5 Leave to cool in the tin. Dust with icing sugar, cut into slices, then remove from the tin.

MAKES 12 SLICES

75g/3oz/6 tbsp butter, softened, plus extra for greasing
225g/8oz/2 cups self-raising (self-rising) flour
5ml/1 tsp baking powder
150g/5oz/⅔ cup soft light brown sugar
1 egg, lightly beaten
15–30ml/1–2 tbsp milk

For the topping
675g/1½lb jar black cherries
175g/6oz/¾ cup soft light brown sugar
50g/2oz/½ cup self-raising (self-rising) flour
50g/2oz/¼ cup butter, melted
icing (confectioners') sugar, for dusting
whipped cream, to serve (optional)

1 Preheat the oven to 190°C/375°F/Gas 5. Grease a 33 × 23cm/13 × 9in Swiss roll tin (jelly roll pan). Line the base and sides with baking parchment.

2 To make the base, sift the flour and baking powder into a large bowl. Add the butter, sugar, egg and milk. Beat the mixture until smooth, then turn into the prepared tin and smooth the surface.

Energy 314kcal/1327kJ; Protein 3.6g; Carbohydrate 57g, of which sugars 39.7g; Fat 9.5g, of which saturates 5.7g; Cholesterol 38.8mg; Calcium 74mg; Fibre 1.5g; Sodium 81mg.

Blueberry cake

This cake is studded with blueberries and has a hint of lemon zest, giving it a lovely fruity flavour and texture. It is a perfect accompaniment to a morning cup of coffee. It will keep for up to two days in an airtight container.

MAKES 12 SLICES

65g/2½oz/5 tbsp butter, at room
   temperature, plus extra
   for greasing
225g/8oz/2 cups plain
   (all-purpose) flour
15ml/1 tbsp baking powder
5ml/1 tsp salt
150g/5oz/¾ cup caster
   (superfine) sugar
1 egg
250ml/8fl oz/1 cup milk
2.5ml/½ tsp grated lemon rind
225g/8oz/2 cups fresh or frozen
   blueberries, well drained
115g/4oz/1 cup icing
   (confectioners') sugar
30ml/2 tbsp fresh lemon juice

1 Preheat the oven to 180°C/350°F/ Gas 4. Grease and line a 33 × 9cm/ 13 × 9in shallow tin (pan).

2 Sift the flour with the baking powder and salt.

3 In a large bowl, beat the butter and sugar until light and fluffy. Beat in the egg and milk. Fold in the flour mixture, then mix in the lemon rind.

4 Scrape half of the batter into the cake tin, spreading it to the edges.

5 Sprinkle with half the blueberries. Top with the remaining batter and then the remaining blueberries.

6 Bake for 35–45 minutes, or until golden brown and a skewer inserted into the centre comes out clean.

7 Allow to stand for 5 minutes in the tin, then turn out on to a wire rack to go cold. Remove the lining.

8 To make the topping, mix the icing sugar with the lemon juice to make a smooth glaze with a pouring consistency.

9 Drizzle the glaze over the top of the warm cake. Allow to set before cutting into slices and serving.

Energy 217kcal/918kJ; Protein 3.3g; Carbohydrate 41.3g, of which sugars 26.3g; Fat 5.5g, of which saturates 3.3g; Cholesterol 30mg; Calcium 66mg; Fibre 1g; Sodium 60mg.

Sticky gingerbread

The secret of this gingerbread's rich stickiness lies in the huge amount of treacle used, as well as storing the cake for two or three days to mature. Serve spread with butter or cream cheese, to contrast with the cake's taste and texture. This will keep for a week in an airtight container.

MAKES 12 SLICES

115g/4oz/½ cup butter, softened,
  plus extra for greasing
225g/8oz/2 cups plain
  (all-purpose) flour
10ml/2 tsp ground ginger
5ml/1 tsp mixed (apple pie) spice
pinch of salt
2 pieces preserved stem ginger,
  drained and chopped
115g/4oz/½ cup muscovado
  (molasses) sugar, sifted
275g/10oz/generous ⅔ cup
  treacle (molasses)
2 eggs, beaten
2.5ml/½ tsp bicarbonate of soda
  (baking soda)
30ml/2 tbsp milk, warmed
butter or cream cheese, to serve

1 Preheat the oven to 160°C/325°F/ Gas 3. Grease and line an 18cm/7in square deep cake tin (pan) with baking parchment.

2 Sift the flour, ground ginger, mixed spice and salt together into a large bowl. Add the chopped preserved ginger and toss it in the flour to coat all the pieces.

3 In a large bowl, cream the butter and sugar together until fluffy, then gradually beat in the treacle. Beat in the eggs, then the flour mixture.

4 Dissolve the bicarbonate of soda in the milk and gradually beat this into the mixture.

5 Pour the batter into the prepared tin and smooth the top level. Bake for 45 minutes. Reduce the oven temperature to 150°C/300°F/Gas 2 and bake for a further 30 minutes. The gingerbread should be dark and slightly risen. A skewer inserted into the centre should come out clean.

6 Allow to cool in the tin for 5 minutes, then turn out on to a wire rack to go cold. Remove the paper lining and slice the cake.

Energy 373kcal/1572kJ; Protein 5.2g; Carbohydrate 60.9g, of which sugars 38.7g; Fat 13.9g, of which saturates 8.1g; Cholesterol 78.5mg; Calcium 253.6mg; Fibre 0.9g; Sodium 170.5mg.

Parkin

From the north of England, parkin contains oatmeal and lots of syrup and treacle. This exceptionally moist ginger cake improves in flavour and texture when stored in a tin for several days. It is perfect for autumnal days, and will keep for up to a week in an airtight container.

MAKES 16–20 SQUARES

115g/4oz/½ cup butter, plus extra
   for greasing
300ml/½ pint/1¼ cups milk
225g/8oz/1 cup golden
   (light corn) syrup
225g/8oz/scant ¾ cup
   treacle (molasses)
50g/2oz/¼ cup soft dark
   brown sugar
450g/1lb/4 cups plain
   (all-purpose) flour
2.5ml/½ tsp bicarbonate of soda
   (baking soda)
7.5ml/1½ tsp ground ginger
350g/12oz/3 cups medium oatmeal
1 egg, beaten
icing (confectioners') sugar,
   for dusting

1 Preheat the oven to 180°C/350°F/ Gas 4. Grease and line a 20cm/8in square deep cake tin (pan).

2 Gently heat together the milk, syrup, treacle, butter and sugar, stirring until smooth; do not boil.

3 Sift the flour into a bowl, add the bicarbonate of soda, ginger and oatmeal. Make a well in the centre.

4 Allow the treacle mixture to cool in the pan slightly so that it is just warm. Add the mixture to the bowl with the egg, stirring to make a smooth batter.

5 Pour the batter into the tin and bake for 45 minutes, or until firm to the touch.

6 Cool slightly in the tin, then turn out on to a wire rack to go cold. Remove the lining paper. Dust with icing sugar and cut into squares.

COOK'S TIP
Parkin freezes well, wrapped in foil, for up to 3 months. After this the spices lose their power.

Energy 273kcal/1152kJ; Protein 5.3g; Carbohydrate 50g, of which sugars 20.1g; Fat 7.1g, of which saturates 3.3g; Cholesterol 23mg; Calcium 127mg; Fibre 1.9g; Sodium 102mg.

Marmalade flapjacks

Everyone enjoys making flapjacks because they take so little time to prepare. You don't even need a bowl – just weigh out the ingredients and mix them in the pan. These ones are fruity and tangy with orange and cranberries. Store them in an airtight container for up to five days.

5 Add the oats, sultanas and cranberries. Stir together.

6 Turn into the tin and smooth the top level. Bake for 25–30 minutes, or until firm and golden, then put the tin on a wire rack to cool. Remove the lining paper.

MAKES 16 SLICES

115g/4oz/½ cup butter or block margarine, plus extra for greasing
1 small orange
115g/4oz/scant ⅓ cup golden (light corn) syrup
50g/2oz/½ cup soft light brown sugar
175g/6oz/scant 2 cups rolled oats
50g/2oz/⅓ cup sultanas (golden raisins)
25g/1oz/¼ cup dried cranberries
75ml/3 tbsp orange marmalade

1 Preheat the oven to 180°C/350°F/Gas 4. Grease and line a 20cm/8in square shallow tin (pan) with baking parchment.

2 Finely grate the rind from the orange. Squeeze the juice into a separate container and set aside.

3 Melt the butter or margarine, syrup and sugar together in a heavy pan over a medium heat.

4 Add the orange rind and 15ml/1 tbsp orange juice to the pan.

7 Brush the marmalade over the top of the hot flapjack, then mark into 16 slices. Leave to go cold in the tin.

Energy 154kcal/646kJ; Protein 1.5g; Carbohydrate 23g, of which sugars 15g; Fat 6.8g, of which saturates 3.9g; Cholesterol 17mg; Calcium 14mg; Fibre 0.8g; Sodium 80mg.

Granola squares

These chewy treats are packed with flavour as well as lots of healthy ingredients: nuts, seeds and dried fruits. They make great lunchbox additions to keep tummies from rumbling in the afternoon. These squares keep for four days in an airtight container.

MAKES 9 SQUARES

175g/6oz/¾ cup butter, plus extra
  for greasing
150g/5oz/scant ⅔ cup clear honey
250g/9oz/generous 1 cup demerara
  (raw) sugar
350g/12oz/scant 4 cups rolled oats
5ml/1 tsp ground cinnamon
75g/3oz/¾ cup chopped pecan nuts
75g/3oz/generous ½ cup raisins
75g/3oz/½ cup dried mango,
  chopped
75g/3oz/scant ½ cup ready-to-eat
  dried apricots, chopped
50g/2oz/4 tbsp sesame seeds
75g/3oz/6 tbsp pumpkin seeds
50g/2oz/½ cup ground almonds

1 Preheat the oven to 190°C/375°F/
Gas 5. Grease and line a 23cm/9in
square shallow tin (pan) with
baking parchment.

2 Put the honey, butter and sugar in
a heavy pan and heat gently until
the sugar is dissolved.

3 Bring to the boil, then boil for
2 minutes, stirring, until a thick
caramel sauce has formed.
Remove from the heat.

4 Add all the remaining ingredients
and stir well.

5 Spoon into the tin, then smooth
the top level.

6 Bake for 15 minutes, or until just
pale golden. Cool in the tin for 10
minutes, then turn out on to a wire
rack. Remove the lining and mark
into nine squares. Leave to go cold.

Energy 522kcal/2189kJ; Protein 8.4g; Carbohydrate 63.8g, of which sugars 40.9g; Fat 27.7g, of which saturates 8.9g; Cholesterol 31mg; Calcium 93mg; Fibre 4.3g; Sodium 108mg.

Cranberry brownies

Gooey chocolate brownies are an all-time favourite, and these are packed with cranberries and crunchy nuts. Keep some dried cranberries in the store cupboard, as they will add interest to cakes and traybakes. Keep these for up to five days in an airtight container.

3 Add the beaten eggs, and sift in the flour and spice. Add the cranberries and mix well.

4 Spread half the mixture into the tin, sprinkle over the nuts, then spread the rest of the mixture on top.

MAKES 18 SLICES

225g/8oz/1 cup butter, plus extra
  for greasing
300g/11oz plain (semisweet)
  chocolate, broken into squares
275g/10oz/1¼ cups soft dark
  brown sugar
60ml/4 tbsp milk
4 eggs, beaten
225g/8oz/2 cups plain
  (all-purpose) flour
2.5ml/½ tsp ground cinnamon
75g/3oz/¾ cup dried cranberries
50g/2oz/½ cup chopped
  mixed nuts
icing (confectioners') sugar,
  for dusting

1 Preheat the oven to 180°C/350°F/
Gas 4. Grease and line a 28 × 18cm/
7 × 11in shallow tin (pan) with
baking parchment.

2 Put the chocolate, butter, sugar
and milk in a pan and heat gently,
stirring constantly, until melted.
Leave to cool for 5 minutes.

5 Bake for 25 minutes, or until
springy to the touch. Mark into
squares while warm. Leave to cool
in the tin on a wire rack.

Energy 290kcal/1208kJ; Protein 3.1g; Carbohydrate 20.6g, of which sugars 18.3g; Fat 22.3g, of which saturates 11.5g; Cholesterol 68mg; Calcium 35mg; Fibre 0.9g; Sodium 180mg.

Florentine slices

If you're looking for a popular cake for a cake sale or coffee morning, you'll find the colourful jewel-like topping on these fruity slices makes them a great seller – and they'll also be snapped up at home in no time. These cakes keep in an airtight container for up to four days.

MAKES 12 SLICES

150g/5oz/10 tbsp butter, plus extra
   for greasing
150g/5oz/²⁄₃ cup golden caster
   (superfine) sugar
3 eggs
175g/6oz/1½ cups self-raising
   (self-rising) flour
275g/10oz/1²⁄₃ cups mixed
   dried fruit
90g/3½oz/generous ½ cup glacé
   (candied) cherries, halved
a few drops of almond extract

For the topping
100g/4oz/½ cup glacé (candied)
   cherries, chopped
15ml/1 tbsp golden
   (light corn) syrup
50g/2oz/½ cup flaked
   (sliced) almonds
25g/1oz/2 tbsp angelica, chopped

1 Preheat the oven to 190°C/375°F/ Gas 5. Grease and line a 28 × 18cm/ 11 × 7in shallow cake tin (pan) with baking parchment.

2 Whisk the butter and sugar together until light and fluffy. Whisk in the eggs one at a time.

3 Fold in the flour, then set aside 30ml/2 tbsp of the mixture in a bowl.

4 Fold the dried fruit, cherries and almond extract into the remaining cake mixture, then spoon into the tin and smooth the top level.

5 Bake for 20 minutes, reduce the heat to 180°C/350°F/Gas 4. Bake for a further 15 minutes, until just set.

6 To make the topping, stir the chopped cherries into the reserved cake mixture with the syrup, almonds and angelica, and mix well.

7 Spread evenly over the cake top using a wetted spoon. Bake for 15 minutes. Leave to cool in the tin.

8 Loosen the lining papers. Cut into 12 fingers when cold.

Energy 340kcal/1429kJ; Protein 4.6g; Carbohydrate 51.7g, of which sugars 40.8g; Fat 14.2g, of which saturates 7.4g; Cholesterol 76mg; Calcium 101mg; Fibre 1.4g; Sodium 177mg.

Lamingtons

Cake that is a day old is best for coating with the chocolate icing and coconut for these tasty little squares. Bake the base the day before, then it will cut more easily into squares. Keep a slab in the deep freeze, ready for thawing, cutting and coating. Eat them fresh once decorated.

MAKES 24 SQUARES

150g/5oz/generous ½ cup butter, softened, plus extra for greasing
300g/11oz/2¾ cups self-raising (self-rising) flour, plus extra for dusting
200g/7oz/1 cup caster (superfine) sugar
3 eggs, beaten
5ml/1 tsp vanilla extract
150ml/¼ pint/⅔ cup milk

For the icing and decoration
675g/1½lb/3½ cups caster (superfine) sugar
30ml/2 tbsp unsweetened cocoa powder
150g/5oz/1⅔ cups desiccated (dry unsweetened shredded) coconut

1 Preheat the oven to 180°C/350°F/ Gas 4. Grease a 20 × 30cm/8 × 12in deep cake tin (pan) and dust it lightly with a little flour. Tap the tin and shake out any excess flour.

2 Beat the butter and sugar together until light and fluffy. Beat in the eggs in batches, adding 5ml/1 tsp flour with each addition to prevent the mixture from curdling.

3 Sift in the remaining flour, then fold into the mixture. Add the vanilla and milk, and mix to a soft, dropping consistency.

4 Spoon into the tin and smooth level, then bake for 30 minutes, or until golden and firm in the centre.

5 Cool in the tin for 5 minutes, then turn out on to a wire rack to go cold. Store, wrapped in foil, for 1 day.

6 To make the icing, put the sugar, cocoa and 250ml/8fl oz/1 cup water in a large pan. Heat over a low heat until the sugar has dissolved. Bring to the boil, then simmer, without stirring, for about 12 minutes, or until thickened into a syrup.

7 Put the coconut into a large bowl.

8 Cut the cake into 5cm/2in cubes.

9 Stab a cake cube with a fork and dip into the chocolate icing to coat all over. Coat the cube in the coconut and put on a tray to dry. Repeat with the remaining cake until all the cubes are coated.

Energy 273kcal/1140kJ; Protein 3.1g; Carbohydrate 28.7g, of which sugars 22.4g; Fat 17g, of which saturates 12.2g; Cholesterol 44mg; Calcium 59mg; Fibre 2.3g; Sodium 160mg.

Grated berry bake

Pastry layers envelop a delicious and sticky fruit filling for this traybake. If your pastry skills are zero, never fear, as the pastry is grated into the tin, so you'll still be able to make this a success. Serve this with a spoonful of cream, if you like, and keep for two days in an airtight container.

MAKES 12 BARS

275g/10oz/2½ cups plain
   (all-purpose) flour
2.5ml/½ tsp ground cinnamon
175g/6oz/¾ cup butter, diced, plus
   extra for greasing
115g/4oz/generous ½ cup golden
   caster (superfine) sugar
1 egg, beaten
icing (confectioners') sugar,
   for dusting

For the filling
350g/12oz/3 cups fresh or frozen
   fruits of the forest (mixed
   blackcurrants, redcurrants,
   raspberries, blackberries)
150g/5oz/¾ cup sugar

1 Sift the flour and cinnamon into a bowl or food processor, add the butter, then rub together.

2 Stir in the sugar and beaten egg, and mix together to form a firm dough. Put in a plastic bag and chill for 2 hours or freeze for 20 minutes, or until the pastry forms a firm block.

3 To make the filling, put the fruit in a pan with 30ml/2 tbsp water and simmer for 5 minutes to soften. Add the sugar and stir until it dissolves, then boil for 5 minutes, or until syrupy and thick. Leave to cool.

4 Preheat the oven to 200°C/400°F/ Gas 6. Grease and line a 28 × 18cm/ 11 × 7in shallow tin (pan) with baking parchment.

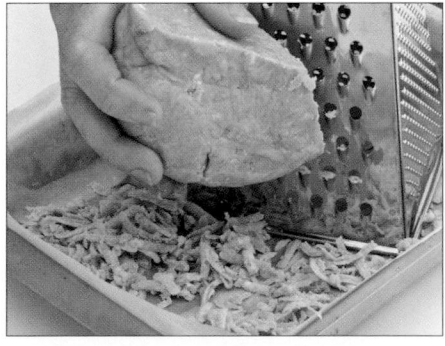

5 Cut the chilled dough in half and, using a coarse grater, grate one half into the tin. Spread out evenly and press down lightly.

6 Spoon the cooled fruit over the pastry. Coarsely grate the rest of the pastry over the fruit to cover completely, but do not flatten it.

7 Bake for 35 minutes, or until golden brown and firm. When cool, remove the lining paper and cut into 12 bars. Dust with icing sugar.

COOK'S TIP
Freeze baked or unbaked in the tin, foil-wrapped, for 2 months.

Energy 286kcal/1203kJ; Protein 3.3g; Carbohydrate 42.2g, of which sugars 24.8g; Fat 12.8g, of which saturates 8.1g; Cholesterol 49mg; Calcium 56mg; Fibre 1.4g; Sodium 118mg.

American apple-sauce traybake

When apples are plentiful, cook them into a purée and mix them into this delicious fruit cake mixture to make it wonderfully moist. Top it with a vanilla frosting and decorate with walnuts for a very moreish treat. These squares will keep for five days in the refrigerator.

MAKES 15 SQUARES

450g/1lb dessert apples, peeled, cored and sliced
75g/3oz/6 tbsp butter, plus extra for greasing
115g/4oz/generous ½ cup golden caster (superfine) sugar
2 eggs
175g/6oz/1½ cups plain (all-purpose) flour
10ml/2 tsp baking powder
5ml/1 tsp mixed (apple pie) spice
50g/2oz/½ cup walnut pieces, chopped
115g/4oz/scant 1 cup raisins

For the frosting
175g/6oz/1½ cups icing (confectioners') sugar
75g/3oz/6 tbsp unsalted butter, softened
1 egg white
a few drops of vanilla extract
15 walnut halves, to decorate

1 Put the sliced apples into a pan with 15ml/1 tbsp water. Cook until thick and pulpy, stirring, then pour into a bowl and leave to cool.

2 Preheat the oven to 180°C/350°F/ Gas 4. Grease and line a 28 × 18cm/ 11 × 7in shallow tin (pan) with baking parchment.

3 In a large bowl, beat the butter and sugar together until light and fluffy. Gradually beat in the eggs.

4 Stir in the cold apple purée and mix well. Sift the flour, baking powder and mixed spice into the bowl, then add the walnuts and raisins. Mix well.

5 Spoon into the tin and smooth the top level. Bake for 45 minutes, or until a skewer inserted into the centre comes out clean. Cool for 5 minutes, then turn out on to a wire rack. Peel away the lining paper.

6 Put all the frosting ingredients except the walnuts into a bowl, and beat together until fluffy. Spread on top of the cake. Cut into squares and decorate each with a walnut.

Energy 255kcal/1070kJ; Protein 3g; Carbohydrate 37.4g, of which sugars 28.4g; Fat 11.4g, of which saturates 5.8g; Cholesterol 48mg; Calcium 40mg; Fibre 1.1g; Sodium 95mg.

Cornflake crunch-nut traybake

These squares have a moist, cranberry sponge base topped with a fruity and crunchy layer made with cornflakes. The combination of contrasting textures in one cake makes it hard to resist. These cakes will keep for up to two days in an airtight container.

MAKES 15 SQUARES

175g/6oz/¾ cup butter, softened,
  plus extra for greasing
175g/6oz/1½ cups self-raising
  (self-rising) flour
5ml/1 tsp baking powder
175g/6oz/scant 1 cup caster
  (superfine) sugar
3 eggs, beaten
75ml/5 tbsp cranberry sauce

For the topping
45ml/3 tbsp golden (light corn)
  syrup
75g/3oz/¾ cup dried cranberries
115g/4oz/4 cups cornflakes

1 Preheat the oven to 180°C/350°F/
Gas 4. Grease and line a 28 × 18cm/
11 × 7in shallow tin (pan) with
baking parchment.

2 Sift the flour and baking powder
into a bowl and add the remaining
ingredients, then beat until smooth.

COOK'S TIP
This traybake is not suitable
for freezing.

3 Spoon into the tin and smooth the
top level. Bake for 30 minutes, or
until golden and firm in the centre.

4 To make the topping, heat the
syrup and cranberries in a large pan
over a low heat, then simmer for
2 minutes.

5 Add the cornflakes and gently
fold in. Spoon over the cake layer
and return to the oven. Bake for
10 minutes, or until lightly brown.

6 Cool in the tin for 5 minutes, then
turn out on a wire rack to go cold.
Remove the lining paper.

Energy 237kcal/994kJ; Protein 3.2g; Carbohydrate 33.7g, of which sugars 18.8g; Fat 10.9g, of which saturates 6.6g; Cholesterol 65mg; Calcium 35mg; Fibre 0.5g; Sodium 197mg.

Mincemeat and marzipan traybake

This easy fruit cake is mixed all in one go, then a crunchy almond-paste topping is added. It is ideal for Christmas parties or to make for cake sales at that time of the year. Home-made almond paste adds an edge when it comes to flavour. Keep this for up to five days in an airtight container.

MAKES 15 SQUARES

115g/4oz/½ cup butter, softened, plus extra for greasing
225g/8oz/2 cups self-raising (self-rising) flour
400g/14oz jar fruit mincemeat
115g/4oz/⅔ cup mixed dried fruit
115g/4oz/½ cup muscovado (molasses) sugar
finely grated rind of ½ lemon
5ml/1 tsp mixed (apple pie) spice
2 eggs, beaten

For the topping and icing
250g/9oz almond paste, *see page 24*
115g/4oz/1 cup icing (confectioners') sugar
15ml/1 tbsp lemon juice

1 Preheat the oven to 160°C/ 325°F/Gas 3. Grease and line a 28 × 18cm/11 × 7in shallow tin (pan) with baking parchment.

2 Put all the cake ingredients in a mixing bowl and beat for about 3 minutes, or until smooth. Spoon into the prepared tin and smooth the top level. Bake for 50 minutes, or until golden.

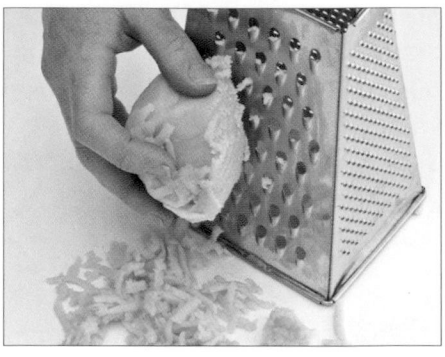

3 To make the topping, grate the almond paste using a coarse grater.

4 Sprinkle the almond paste on top of the hot cake in an even layer. Return to the oven and bake for 10 minutes, or until the almond paste is light golden. Cool in the tin for 5 minutes, then turn out on to a wire rack to go cold. Remove the lining paper.

5 To make the icing, mix the icing sugar with the lemon juice and 5–10ml/1–2 tsp water to make a drizzling consistency.

6 Fill a small paper piping (pastry) bag with icing, snip off the end, then drizzle lines over the cooled cake in a random pattern. When set, cut into 15 squares.

Energy 290kcal/1230kJ; Protein 3.6g; Carbohydrate 60.8g, of which sugars 49.4g; Fat 5g, of which saturates 1.6g; Cholesterol 29mg; Calcium 57mg; Fibre 1.3g; Sodium 60mg.

Almond slices

A light pastry base is spread with raspberry jam, topped with almond cake and a layer of flaked almonds to make elegant old-fashioned pastry slices. They are the quintessential summer tea-party cake. These cakes keep for up to three days in an airtight container.

MAKES 16

butter, for greasing
225g/8oz shortcrust or sweet
    shortcrust pastry, thawed
    if frozen
flour, for dusting
60ml/4 tbsp raspberry jam
4 egg whites
175g/6oz/1½ cups ground almonds
175g/6oz/scant 1 cup golden caster
    (superfine) sugar
a few drops of almond extract
75g/3oz/¾ cup flaked
    (sliced) almonds
15ml/1 tbsp icing (confectioners')
    sugar, for dusting (optional)

1 Preheat the oven to 180°C/350°F/ Gas 4. Grease a 28 × 18cm/11 × 7in shallow tin (pan).

2 Roll out the pastry on a lightly floured surface to a rectangle large enough to line the base and sides of the tin.

3 Lower the pastry into the tin, using a rolling pin. Press into all the corners, then trim the edges.

4 Spread the jam over the pastry.

5 Put the egg whites into a clean, grease-free bowl and whisk until they form stiff peaks.

6 Fold in the ground almonds, sugar and almond extract. Spoon into the tin, then spread the top level. Sprinkle over the flaked almonds.

7 Bake for 30–35 minutes, or until the pastry is crisp and the topping is golden and firm to the touch. Leave to cool completely in the tin.

8 Mark into 16 slices, then cut these out with a sharp knife. Dust with icing sugar, if you like.

Energy 204kcal/850kJ; Protein 4.7g; Carbohydrate 18.7g, of which sugars 12.2g; Fat 12.7g, of which saturates 0.7g; Cholesterol 0mg; Calcium 50mg; Fibre 1.4g; Sodium 41mg.

Loaf cakes

Teabreads are one of the oldest of family cakes, originally baked in a rectangular tin that fitted into the small side oven of a range cooker or wood-burning stove. There are many regional variations of loaf cakes and teabreads, such as Bara Brith, which add up to a wealth of traditional recipes. These cakes are so simple and quick to make that it's a good idea to double up the mixture and bake two at a time, then keep one in the freezer until needed. Teabreads usually keep longer if they are enriched with fruit and nuts. As they remain moist, they are useful for adding to lunch boxes: Fruit Malt Loaf, Gingerbread or Banana Bread are great for this, or for taking on a picnic. Serve them at tea time, in generously buttered slices, or if they begin to go stale, they are still delicious toasted.

Left: Raspberry and Almond Teabread and Lemon and Walnut Teabread.

Chickpea cake

Although an unusual ingredient for a cake, chickpeas add moisture and give a texture rather like Christmas pudding. Flavoured with orange and cinnamon, it tastes wonderful; try it with fresh mango or pineapple and a spoonful of yogurt. It will keep up to three days in an airtight container.

SERVES 8–10

butter, for greasing
2 × 275g/10oz cans chickpeas,
  drained and rinsed
5ml/1 tsp baking powder
grated rind and juice of 1 orange
225g/8oz/generous 1 cup caster
  (superfine) sugar
10ml/2 tsp ground cinnamon
4 eggs, beaten

For the topping
50g/2oz/scant ½ cup caster
  (superfine) sugar mixed with
  5ml/1 tsp ground cinnamon

1 Preheat the oven to 180°C/ 350°F/Gas 4. Grease and line a 450g/1lb loaf tin (pan) with baking parchment.

2 Tip the chickpeas into a colander, rinse and drain them thoroughly, then rub them between the palms of your hands to loosen and remove any skins.

3 Put the chickpeas into a food processor and process until smooth. Tip the chickpea purée into a mixing bowl, using a spatula to scrape out all the mixture.

4 Stir in the baking powder, orange rind, juice, sugar, cinnamon and eggs.

5 Pour the batter into the tin and smooth the top level. Bake for about 1½ hours, or until a skewer inserted into the centre comes out clean.

6 Leave to cool in the tin for 10 minutes, then turn out on to a wire rack. Sprinkle with cinnamon sugar, then leave to go cold.

Energy 184kcal/780kJ; Protein 5.5g; Carbohydrate 35.2g, of which sugars 28.9g; Fat 3.4g, of which saturates 0.7g; Cholesterol 76mg; Calcium 43mg; Fibre 1.6g; Sodium 118mg.

Pineapple and carrot cake

This is one of the most irresistible cakes ever invented. The poppy seeds and walnut pieces add crunch, and the pineapple and carrot give moisture. A tangy citrus mascarpone icing makes a delicious topping. This will keep for up to four days in an airtight container.

SERVES 10–12

115g/4oz/½ cup butter, melted and
   cooled, plus extra for greasing
250g/9oz/2¼ cups plain
   (all-purpose) flour
10ml/2 tsp baking powder
5ml/1 tsp bicarbonate of soda
   (baking soda)
pinch of salt
5ml/1 tsp ground cinnamon
45ml/3 tbsp poppy seeds
225g/8oz/1 cup soft light
   brown sugar
3 eggs, beaten
finely grated rind of 1 orange
225g/8oz raw carrots,
   finely grated
75g/3oz fresh or canned pineapple,
   drained and finely chopped
75g/3oz/¾ cup walnut pieces

For the icing
150g/5oz/scant ¾ cup
   mascarpone
30ml/2 tbsp icing (confectioners')
   sugar, sifted
finely grated rind of 1 orange

1 Preheat the oven to 180°C/ 350°F/Gas 4. Grease and line a 900g/2lb loaf tin (pan) with baking parchment.

2 Sift the flour, baking powder, bicarbonate of soda, salt and cinnamon into a bowl. Stir in the poppy seeds.

3 In another large bowl, put the sugar, eggs and orange rind. Beat together until smooth and frothy.

4 Squeeze the excess moisture from the carrots and stir them into the egg mixture with the pineapple and walnut pieces.

5 Stir the flour into the egg mixture, then gently fold in the melted butter. Spoon the batter into the prepared tin and smooth the top level.

6 Bake for 1–1¼ hours, or until risen and golden. Leave to cool for 10 minutes, then turn out on a wire rack. Remove the paper when cold.

7 To make the icing, beat the mascarpone with the icing sugar and orange rind. Spread thickly over the top of the cake.

Energy 400kcal/1668kJ; Protein 4.2g; Carbohydrate 39.1g, of which sugars 29.9g; Fat 26.3g, of which saturates 7.2g; Cholesterol 55mg; Calcium 62mg; Fibre 1g; Sodium 67mg.

Courgette and double ginger cake

Both fresh and preserved ginger are used to flavour this unusual teabread, which is made with oil rather than butter. Courgettes, like several other vegetables, bring moisture to a cake mix, making it soft and tasty. Keep this for up to five days in an airtight container or freeze for two months.

4 Sift the flour, baking powder, cinnamon and salt over the batter and stir in.

SERVES 8–10

250ml/8fl oz/1 cup sunflower oil, plus extra for greasing
3 eggs
225g/8oz/generous 1 cup caster (superfine) sugar
5ml/1 tsp vanilla extract
15ml/1 tbsp syrup from a jar of preserved stem ginger
225g/8oz courgettes (zucchini), grated and drained
2.5cm/1in piece fresh root ginger, peeled and grated
350g/12oz/3 cups plain (all-purpose) flour
5ml/1 tsp baking powder
5ml/1 tsp ground cinnamon
pinch of salt
2 pieces preserved stem ginger, chopped
15ml/1 tbsp demerara (raw) sugar

1 Preheat the oven to 190°C/ 325°F/Gas 5. Grease and line a 900g/2lb loaf tin (pan) with baking parchment.

2 In a large bowl, beat together the eggs and sugar until light and fluffy.

3 Slowly beat in the oil until a batter forms. Mix in the vanilla extract and ginger syrup, then stir in the courgettes and fresh ginger.

5 Pour into the prepared tin and smooth level. Sprinkle the chopped ginger and demerara sugar on top.

6 Bake for 1 hour, or until a skewer inserted into the centre comes out clean. Leave to cool for 20 minutes, then turn out on a wire rack.

Energy 252kcal/1060kJ; Protein 5.6g; Carbohydrate 35.6g, of which sugars 8.8g; Fat 10.7g, of which saturates 1.6g; Cholesterol 57mg; Calcium 73mg; Fibre 1.3g; Sodium 82mg.

Sour cherry coffee loaf

Dried sour cherries have a wonderfully concentrated fruit flavour that makes them just right for adding to cakes. Here they are partnered with strong brewed coffee, both in the cake and in the delicious icing. This loaf will keep for up to four days in an airtight container.

SERVES 8–10

175g/6oz/¾ cup butter, softened, plus extra for greasing
175g/6oz/scant 1 cup golden caster (superfine) sugar
5ml/1 tsp vanilla extract
2 eggs, lightly beaten
225g/8oz/2 cups plain (all-purpose) flour
1.5ml/¼ tsp baking powder
75ml/5 tbsp strong brewed instant coffee
175g/6oz/1 cup dried sour cherries

For the icing
50g/2oz/½ cup icing (confectioners') sugar, sifted
20ml/4 tsp strong brewed instant coffee

1 Preheat the oven to 180°C/350°F/Gas 4. Grease and line a 900g/2lb loaf tin (pan).

2 In a large bowl, cream the butter, sugar and vanilla extract until light and fluffy.

3 Gradually add the eggs, beating well after each addition. Add a teaspoon of flour if the mix curdles.

4 Sift the flour and baking powder together over the bowl. Fold into the mixture using a metal spoon, then fold in the coffee and two-thirds of the sour cherries.

5 Spoon the mixture into the prepared tin and smooth the top level. Bake for 1¼ hours, or until firm to the touch.

6 Cool in the tin for 5 minutes, then carefully turn the loaf out on to a wire rack to cool. Remove the lining paper.

7 To make the icing, mix together the icing sugar and coffee, and the remaining cherries. Spoon over the top and sides. Leave to set before slicing.

Energy 307kcal/1283kJ; Protein 2.1g; Carbohydrate 33.1g, of which sugars 33.1g; Fat 19.4g, of which saturates 11.8g; Cholesterol 94mg; Calcium 30mg; Fibre 0.3g; Sodium 152mg.

Lemon and walnut teabread

The unusual combination of earthy walnuts and fresh zesty lemons goes together remarkably well here. Unusually for a teabread, whisked egg whites are added to the batter, making it light and airy. Keep for three days in an airtight container. Freeze for two months wrapped in foil.

SERVES 8–10

115g/4oz/½ cup butter, softened, plus extra for greasing
100g/3¾oz/generous ½ cup caster (superfine) sugar
2 eggs, separated
grated rind of 2 lemons
30ml/2 tbsp lemon juice
200g/7oz/1¾ cups plain (all-purpose) flour
10ml/2 tsp baking powder
120ml/4fl oz/½ cup milk
50g/2oz/½ cup walnuts, chopped
pinch of salt

1 Preheat the oven to 180°C/350°F/Gas 4. Grease and line a 900g/2lb loaf tin (pan) with baking parchment.

2 Beat the butter with the sugar. Beat in the egg yolks, lemon rind and juice. Set aside.

3 Sift the flour and baking powder over the butter mixture in batches, and stir well, alternating with the milk. Fold in the walnuts.

4 Put the egg whites into a clean, grease-free bowl and whisk until they form stiff peaks. Fold a large tablespoon of the egg whites into the walnut mixture to lighten it. Fold in the remaining egg whites until just blended.

5 Pour the batter into the tin and smooth the top level. Bake for 45–50 minutes, or until a skewer inserted into the centre comes out clean.

6 Leave to stand in the tin for 5 minutes then turn out on to a wire rack to go cold. Peel off the lining.

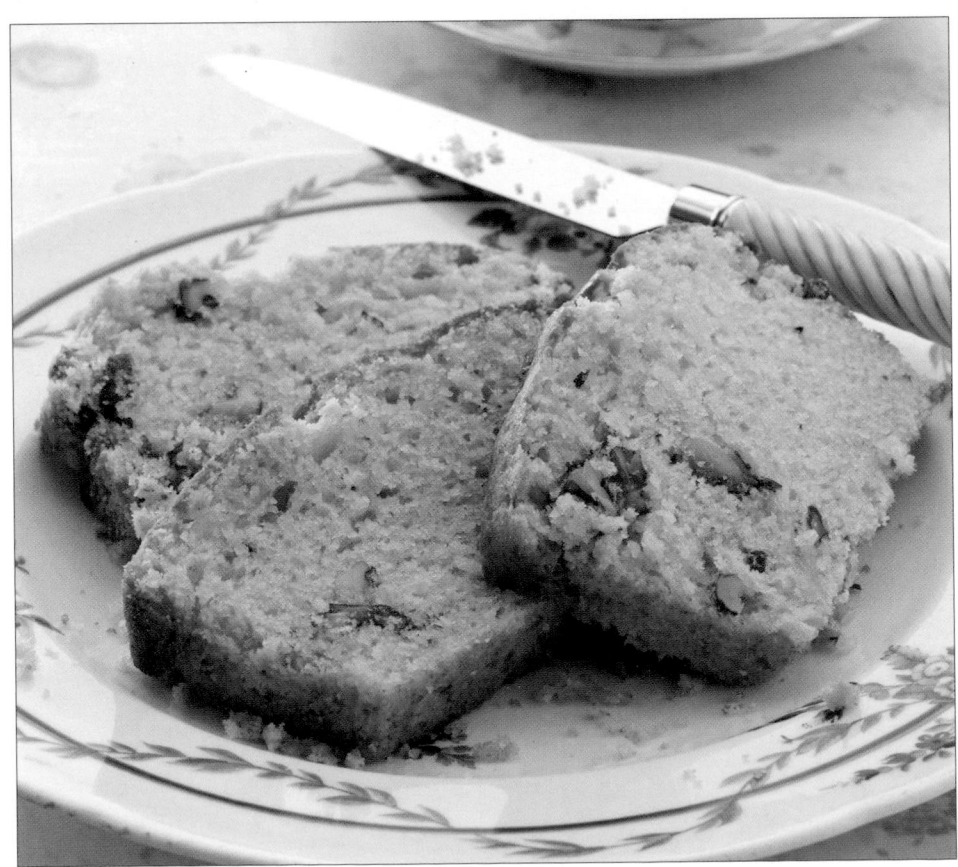

Energy 249kcal/1041kJ; Protein 4.5g; Carbohydrate 26.9g, of which sugars 10.4g; Fat 14.4g, of which saturates 6.7g; Cholesterol 63mg; Calcium 61mg; Fibre 0.8g; Sodium 90mg.

Coconut cake

Sour cream and desiccated coconut make this quick and easy cake wonderfully moist, giving it a full flavour that is lifted by a delicious lemony tang. Buy desiccated coconut as you need it for the best results. It deteriorates with storage. This cake keeps for eight days in an airtight container.

SERVES 8–10

115g/4oz/1 cup butter, softened,
   plus extra for greasing
115g/4oz/generous ½ cup caster
   (superfine) sugar
2 large (US extra large)
   eggs, beaten
115g/4oz/generous 1 cup
   desiccated (dry unsweetened
   shredded) coconut
115g/4oz/1 cup self-raising
   (self-rising) flour
75ml/5 tbsp sour cream or natural
   (plain) yogurt
15ml/1 tbsp finely grated
   lemon rind

1 Preheat the oven to 180°C/350°F/ Gas 4. Grease and line a 900g/2lb loaf tin (pan) with baking parchment.

2 In a large bowl, beat the butter and sugar together until pale and fluffy, then add the eggs in batches, beating well after each addition.

4 Spoon into the tin. Bake for 50 minutes, or until a skewer inserted into the centre comes out clean.

5 Cool in the tin for 5 minutes, then turn out on to a wire rack to go cold. Peel off the lining paper.

COOK'S TIP
To freeze, wrap in foil and freeze for up to 3 months.

3 Add the coconut, flour, sour cream and lemon rind, and beat together until smooth.

VARIATION
Add 75g/3oz/½ cup dried morello cherries at step 3.

Energy 221kcal/924kJ; Protein 3g; Carbohydrate 27.8g, of which sugars 22.1g; Fat 11.6g, of which saturates 8.2g; Cholesterol 61mg; Calcium 31mg; Fibre 1.6g; Sodium 51mg.

Gooseberry cake

Gooseberries can be slightly acidic, so here they are sweetened with sugar and elderflower 30 minutes before they are added to the cake batter. The elderflower infuses the batter with a light, sweet flavour. Serve this fresh as a pudding with a spoonful of crème fraîche.

SERVES 10

75g/3oz/6 tbsp butter, melted,
  plus extra for greasing
150g/5oz gooseberries
22.5ml/4½ tsp golden caster
  (superfine) sugar
15ml/1 tbsp elderflower cordial,
  plus extra for brushing
225g/8oz/2 cups plain
  (all-purpose) flour
10ml/2 tsp baking powder
150g/5oz/¾ cup golden caster
  (superfine) sugar
2.5ml/½ tsp vanilla extract
1 egg, lightly beaten
250ml/8fl oz/1 cup buttermilk
icing (confectioners') sugar,
  for dusting

1 Preheat the oven to 180°C/ 350°F/Gas 4. Grease a 23cm/9in round loose-based cake tin (pan) with butter.

2 Arrange the fruit in a single layer on a plate and sprinkle evenly with the sugar and elderflower cordial. Leave to stand for 30 minutes.

3 Sift the dry ingredients into a large bowl and make a well in the centre.

4 In a separate bowl, lightly whisk together the melted butter, vanilla extract, egg and buttermilk. Pour into the dry ingredients and fold partly together.

5 Lightly combine half the reserved gooseberries and all of the syrupy juices into the batter, then fold together with a metal spoon.

6 Spoon the mixture into the tin and sprinkle the remaining fruit on top.

7 Bake for 30 minutes, but check after 25 minutes. If the centre of the cake is springy to the touch, it is ready. Lightly brush the surface of the warm cake with elderflower cordial, if you like, and serve, dusted with icing sugar.

Energy 273kcal/1144kJ; Protein 3.9g; Carbohydrate 34.6g, of which sugars 18.1g; Fat 14.2g, of which saturates 8.3g; Cholesterol 82mg; Calcium 51mg; Fibre 1g; Sodium 112mg.

Greek yogurt and fig cake

Fresh figs, thickly sliced then baked in honey, make a delectable base that becomes a topping for a featherlight sponge. Figs that are a little on the firm side work best for this particular recipe. Keep refrigerated in an airtight container for two days.

SERVES 8–10

200g/7oz/scant 1 cup butter,
  softened, plus extra for greasing
6 firm fresh figs, thickly sliced
45ml/3 tbsp clear honey, plus extra
  for glazing
175g/6oz/scant 1 cup caster
  (superfine) sugar
grated rind of 1 lemon
grated rind of 1 orange
4 eggs, separated
225g/8oz/2 cups plain
  (all-purpose) flour
5ml/1 tsp baking powder
5ml/1 tsp bicarbonate of soda
  (baking soda)
250ml/8fl oz/1 cup Greek
  (US strained plain) yogurt

1 Preheat the oven to 180C/350°F/ Gas 4. Grease and line the base of a 23cm/9in cake tin (pan) with baking parchment.

2 Arrange the sliced figs over the base of the tin and drizzle over the honey.

3 In a large bowl, beat the butter and sugar together with the citrus rinds until pale and fluffy.

4 Gradually beat in the egg yolks.

5 Sift the dry ingredients into the creamed mixture in batches, alternating with a spoonful of yogurt. Beat well, then repeat this process until all the dry ingredients and yogurt have been incorporated.

6 Put the egg whites into a clean, grease-free bowl and whisk until they form stiff peaks.

7 Stir the egg whites into the cake batter in two batches. Pour the mixture over the figs in the tin and smooth the top level. Bake for 1¼ hours, or until golden and a skewer inserted into the centre of the cake comes out clean.

8 Turn the cake out on to a wire rack, peel off the lining paper and cool. Drizzle the fig topping with extra honey before serving.

Energy 473kcal/1982kJ; Protein 8.2g; Carbohydrate 59.5g, of which sugars 38g; Fat 24.3g, of which saturates 14g; Cholesterol 149mg; Calcium 167mg; Fibre 2g; Sodium 225mg.

Crunchy-topped fresh apricot cake

Almonds are perfect partners for fresh apricots, and this is a great way to use fruits that may be a little too firm for eating. Chopped fresh nectarines make a good alternative when apricots are not available. Serve cold as a cake, or warm with custard for a dessert. It will keep for two days.

SERVES 8

175g/6oz/¾ cup butter, softened, plus extra for greasing
175g/6oz/1½ cups self-raising (self-rising) flour
175g/6oz/¾ cup caster (superfine) sugar
115g/4oz/1 cup ground almonds
3 eggs
5ml/1 tsp almond extract
2.5ml/½ tsp baking powder
8 firm apricots, stoned (pitted) and chopped

For the topping
30ml/2 tbsp demerara (raw) sugar
50g/2oz/½ cup flaked (sliced) almonds

1 Preheat the oven to 160°C/325°F/Gas 3. Grease and line an 18cm/7in round cake tin (pan) with baking parchment.

2 Put all the ingredients, except the apricots, in a large bowl or food processor and whisk or process until light and creamy.

3 Fold the apricots into the cake batter.

4 Spoon the batter into the prepared cake tin and smooth the top level. Make a hollow in the centre with the back of a large spoon.

5 Sprinkle over 15ml/1 tbsp of the demerara sugar, then scatter the flaked almonds over the top.

6 Bake for 1½ hours, or until a skewer inserted into the centre comes out clean.

7 Sprinkle the remaining demerara sugar over the top of the cake and leave to cool for 10 minutes in the tin. Remove from the tin, peel off the paper and finish cooling on a wire rack.

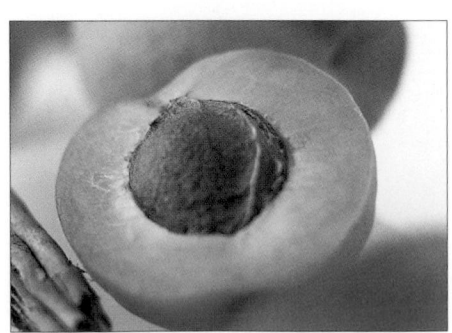

Energy 414kcal/1734kJ; Protein 6.2g; Carbohydrate 46.8g, of which sugars 30.3g; Fat 23.9g, of which saturates 12.3g; Cholesterol 118mg; Calcium 126mg; Fibre 1.8g; Sodium 241mg.

Pumpkin and banana cake

Rather like a cross between a carrot cake and banana bread, this luscious cake is an excellent way of using some of the scooped-out pumpkin flesh from making Hallowe'en lanterns. A cream cheese topping provides a delicious contrast with the dense moist cake. This is best eaten fresh.

SERVES 12

225g/8oz/2 cups self-raising
    (self-rising) flour
7.5ml/1½ tsp baking powder
2.5ml/½ tsp ground cinnamon
2.5ml/½ tsp ground ginger
130g/4½oz/½ cup soft light
    brown sugar
75g/3oz/¾ cup pecan nuts or
    walnuts, chopped
115g/4oz pumpkin flesh,
    coarsely grated
2 small ripe bananas, peeled
    and mashed
2 eggs, lightly beaten
150ml/¼ pint/⅔ cup sunflower oil

For the topping
50g/2oz/¼ cup unsalted butter, at
    room temperature
150g/5oz/⅔ cup soft white
    (farmers') cheese
1.5ml/¼ tsp vanilla extract
115g/4oz/1 cup icing
    (confectioners') sugar
pecan halves, to decorate

1 Preheat the oven to 180°C/350°F/ Gas 4. Line the base and sides of a round deep 20cm/8in cake tin (pan) with baking parchment.

2 Sift the flour, baking powder, cinnamon and ginger into a large bowl to combine.

3 Stir in the sugar, chopped pecan nuts or walnuts and grated pumpkin until thoroughly mixed. Make a slight hollow in the middle of the dry ingredients.

4 In a separate bowl, combine the bananas, eggs and sunflower oil, then stir into the dry ingredients.

5 Spoon into the prepared tin and smooth the top level.

6 Bake for 45–50 minutes, or until a skewer inserted into the centre comes out clean. Cool in the tin for 10 minutes, then turn out to cool completely on a wire rack.

7 To make the topping, put the butter, soft cheese and vanilla extract into a bowl, and beat until blended and smooth. Sift in the icing sugar. Beat again until creamy.

8 Spread the topping over the cake and decorate with pecan halves. Chill for 1 hour before serving, to allow the topping to harden.

Energy 388kcal/1619kJ; Protein 4.5g; Carbohydrate 40.2g, of which sugars 25.4g; Fat 24.4g, of which saturates 7.8g; Cholesterol 53mg; Calcium 64mg; Fibre 1.1g; Sodium 83mg.

Pear and polenta cake

This light polenta sponge has a nutty corn flavour that complements the fruit perfectly. For this upside-down cake, pears and honey are added to the base of the cake tin, then the mixture is added on top. Serve as a dessert with custard or whipped cream, if you like. Eat fresh.

3 Cut the pears into chunky slices and toss them in the lemon juice.

4 Arrange the pears on the base of the cake tin. Drizzle the honey over, and set aside.

SERVES 10

butter, for greasing
175g/6oz/scant 1 cup golden caster (superfine) sugar
4 ripe pears, peeled and cored
juice of ½ lemon
30ml/2 tbsp clear honey
3 eggs
seeds from 1 vanilla pod (bean)
120ml/4fl oz/½ cup sunflower oil
115g/4oz/1 cup self-raising (self-rising) flour
50g/2oz/⅓ cup instant polenta (cornmeal)

1 Preheat the oven to 180°C/350°F/Gas 4. Grease and line a 20cm/8in round cake tin (pan) with baking parchment.

2 Sprinkle 30ml/2 tbsp of the sugar over the base of the prepared tin.

COOK'S TIP
To release the seeds from the vanilla pod, cut down the centre with a sharp knife, then scoop out the seeds with a teaspoon.

5 In a bowl, mix together the eggs, the seeds from the vanilla pod and the remaining sugar. Beat until thick and creamy, then gradually beat in the oil.

6 Sift the flour and polenta into the egg mixture and fold in. Pour the batter over the pears in the tin.

7 Bake for 50 minutes, or until a skewer inserted into the centre comes out clean. Cool in the tin for 10 minutes, then turn the cake out, and peel off the lining paper.

Energy 256kcal/1077kJ; Protein 3.7g; Carbohydrate 38.9g, of which sugars 26.7g; Fat 10.5g, of which saturates 1.5g; Cholesterol 57mg; Calcium 65mg; Fibre 1.8g; Sodium 66mg.

Apricot, prune and cherry cake

This moist cake has a tang of orange. As it stores well for several days, it's useful for tea-time treats during the week. It is one of the easiest cakes to make – just melt the basic ingredients together in a pan. Serve this sliced and buttered, if you like.

SERVES 8–10

175g/6oz/¾ cup butter, plus extra for greasing
175g/6oz/¾ cup soft dark muscovado (molasses) sugar
300ml/½ pint/1¼ cups orange juice
130g/4½oz/generous ½ cup ready-to-eat dried apricots, chopped
130g/4½oz/generous ½ cup ready-to-eat prunes, chopped
125g/4¼oz/ generous ½ cup glacé (candied) cherries, washed, dried and chopped
50g/2oz/⅓ cup chopped mixed (candied) peel
250g/9oz/2¼ cups plain (all-purpose) flour
2.5ml/½ tsp bicarbonate of soda (baking soda)
2 eggs, beaten
45ml/3 tbsp golden (light corn) syrup

1 Preheat the oven to 180°C/350°F/ Gas 4. Grease and line an 18cm/ 7in deep round cake tin (pan) with baking parchment.

2 Put the butter, sugar and orange juice in a pan and heat until the sugar dissolves. Add all the dried fruits, then simmer gently for 15 minutes. Leave to cool.

COOK'S TIP
This cake keeps for 1 week in an airtight tin. Freeze, wrapped in foil, for up to 2 months.

3 Sift the flour and bicarbonate of soda into the cooled fruit mixture with the beaten eggs.

4 Spoon into the tin and bake for 1¼ hours, until a skewer inserted into the cake centre comes out clean.

5 Leave to cool in the tin for 10 minutes, then turn out on to a wire rack, peel away the papers and cool.

6 Warm the golden syrup in a small pan, then brush it over the top of the cake to glaze before serving.

Energy 399kcal/1680kJ; Protein 5.6g; Carbohydrate 62g, of which sugars 43g; Fat 16.1g, of which saturates 9.8g; Cholesterol 78mg; Calcium 94mg; Fibre 3.7g; Sodium 182mg.

Apple cake

This recipe comes from the West of England and uses cooking apples to give the cake a moist texture and a refreshing sweet-and-sour flavour. You can use eating apples, if you prefer, for a sweeter result. This is best eaten fresh with clotted cream or vanilla ice cream.

SERVES 8

115g/4oz/½ cup butter, diced,
  plus extra for greasing
225g/8oz cooking apples, peeled,
  cored and chopped
juice of ½ lemon
225g/8oz/2 cups plain
  (all-purpose) flour
7.5ml/1½ tsp baking powder
165g/5½oz/scant ¾ cup soft
  light brown sugar
1 egg, beaten
30–45ml/2–3 tbsp milk
2.5ml/½ tsp ground cinnamon

1 Preheat the oven to 180°C/
350°F/Gas 4. Grease and line an
18cm/7in round cake tin (pan) with
baking parchment.

2 In a small bowl, toss the apples
with the lemon juice.

3 Sift the flour and baking powder
into a large bowl.

4 With cold hands, rub the butter
into the flour mixture until it
resembles fine crumbs. Stir in
115g/4oz/½ cup of the sugar, and
the apples.

5 Add the egg and enough milk to
give a soft, dropping consistency.

6 Spoon into the prepared tin and
smooth the top level.

7 Mix together the remaining sugar
with the cinnamon, then sprinkle
over the cake batter.

8 Bake for 45–50 minutes, or until
firm to the touch. Leave to cool,
then turn out on to a wire rack to go
cold. Peel off the lining paper.

COOK'S TIP
Steps 3 and 4 can be made
ahead of time and the dry
crumbs stored in the refrigerator.

Energy 476kcal/2003kJ; Protein 4.5g; Carbohydrate 74.6g, of which sugars 56.5g; Fat 19.8g, of which saturates 8.5g; Cholesterol 32.5mg; Calcium 77.1mg; Fibre 2g; Sodium 104.8mg.

Farmhouse apple and sultana cake

This is a traditional, flavourful country cake made very simply and easily using the creaming method. It has a sweet, crispy top, a lovely moist texture and a spicy apple flavour – it makes an ideal tea-time treat. Keep this cake for 2 days in an airtight container in a cool place.

SERVES 12

175g/6oz/¾ cup softened butter, plus extra for greasing
175g/6oz/¾ cup soft light brown sugar
3 eggs
225g/8oz/2 cups self-raising (self-rising) flour, sifted
5ml/1 tsp baking powder, sifted
10ml/2 tsp mixed (apple pie) spice
350g/12oz cooking apples, peeled, cored and diced
175g/6oz/generous 1 cup sultanas (golden raisins)
75ml/5 tbsp milk
30ml/2 tbsp demerara (raw) sugar

1 Preheat the oven to 160°C/325°F/ Gas 3. Grease and line a 20cm/8in round deep cake tin (pan) with baking parchment.

2 Put the butter in a large bowl with the sugar. Beat together until light and fluffy. Beat in the eggs. Sift in the flour, baking powder and spice, then beat until thoroughly mixed.

3 Fold in the apples, sultanas and sufficient milk to make a soft dropping consistency.

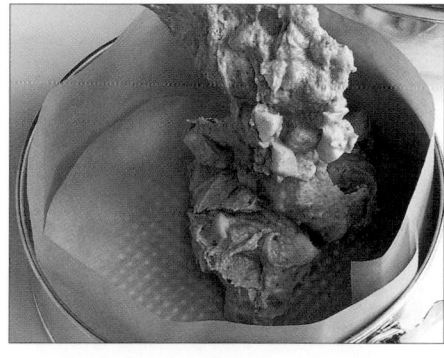

4 Spoon the batter into the prepared tin. Wet a metal spoon by running it under the tap and use the back of the wet spoon to smooth the cake top level.

5 Sprinkle with demerara sugar. Bake for about 1½ hours, or until risen, golden brown and firm to the touch. Cool in the tin for 5 minutes, then turn out on to a wire rack.

Energy 310kcal/1305kJ; Protein 4.2g; Carbohydrate 45.5g, of which sugars 31.2g; Fat 13.7g, of which saturates 8.4g; Cholesterol 81mg; Calcium 63mg; Fibre 1.3g; Sodium 135mg.

Kugelhupf

A special fluted ring mould with a chimney in the middle is a traditional tool of Austrian bakers. These tins can be used to bake rich yeasted mixtures, or this light almond sponge, which is spectacular when decorated with icing, nuts and fruits. Keep for five days in an airtight container.

SERVES 12

225g/8oz/1 cup unsalted butter, softened (plus extra melted butter for greasing)
225g/8oz/generous 1 cup caster (superfine) sugar
3 eggs
225g/8oz/2 cups self-raising (self-rising) flour
finely grated rind of 1 orange
50g/2oz/⅓ cup chopped mixed peel
25g/1oz/¼ cup dried cranberries or dried cherries
50g/2oz/⅓ cup sultanas (golden raisins)
50g/2oz/¼ cup whole almonds, chopped
15ml/1 tbsp milk

For the topping and icing

45ml/3 tbsp clear honey
60ml/4 tbsp orange juice
115g/4oz/1 cup icing (confectioners') sugar
15ml/1 tbsp orange juice
15ml/1 tbsp dried cranberries or cherries
30ml/2 tbsp whole almonds, halved
15ml/1 tbsp whole dried orange and lemon peel, chopped

1 Preheat the oven to 190°C/375°F/ Gas 5. Brush a 1.75 litre/3 pint/ 7½ cup Kugelhupf mould well with melted butter.

2 In a bowl, beat together the butter and sugar. Beat in the eggs, adding 5ml/1 tsp flour with each egg.

3 Sift in the flour, then fold in with the orange rind, mixed peel, cranberries, sultanas, almonds and milk.

4 Spoon into the prepared tin and smooth the top level. Bake for about 1 hour, or until firm and golden. Cool in the tin for 5 minutes, then turn out to cool on a wire rack.

5 For the topping, put the honey and orange juice in a small pan and heat gently until the honey melts. Brush over the cake. Leave to cool.

6 Sift the icing sugar into a bowl, then blend in the orange juice. Spoon the icing over the cake, allowing it to drizzle down the sides. Sprinkle the fruit and nuts around the top and leave to set.

Energy 319kcal/1339kJ; Protein 7g; Carbohydrate 41.8g, of which sugars 14.6g; Fat 14.6g, of which saturates 5.8g; Cholesterol 68mg; Calcium 87mg; Fibre 1.9g; Sodium 83mg.

Flourless fruit cake

Here's a really easy recipe that everyone will enjoy making. Instead of flour, the mixture contains cornflakes, so children can have fun crushing them and stirring the ingredients together. It is packed with fruity flavours too, from mincemeat to soft ready-to-eat figs.

SERVES 12–15

butter, for greasing
450g/1lb/1¼ cups mincemeat
350g/12oz/2 cups dried mixed fruit
115g/4oz/1 cup ready-to-eat dried
    apricots, chopped
115g/4oz/1 cup ready-to-eat dried
    figs, chopped
115g/4oz/½ cup glacé (candied)
    cherries, halved
115g/4oz/1 cup walnut pieces
225g/8oz/8–10 cups
    cornflakes, crushed
4 eggs, lightly beaten
400g/14oz can evaporated milk
5ml/1 tsp mixed (apple pie) spice
5ml/1 tsp baking powder
mixed glacé (candied) fruits,
    chopped, to decorate

1 Preheat the oven to 150°C/300°F/ Gas 2. Grease and line the base and sides of a 25cm/10in round cake tin (pan) with baking parchment.

2 Put all the ingredients into a large bowl and beat together well.

3 Spoon into the prepared tin and smooth the top level.

4 Bake in the centre of the oven for 1¾ hours, or until a skewer inserted into the centre of the cake comes out clean.

5 Cool in the tin for 10 minutes, then turn out to cool on a wire rack. Peel off the lining paper and leave to cool completely.

6 Decorate with the chopped glacé fruits.

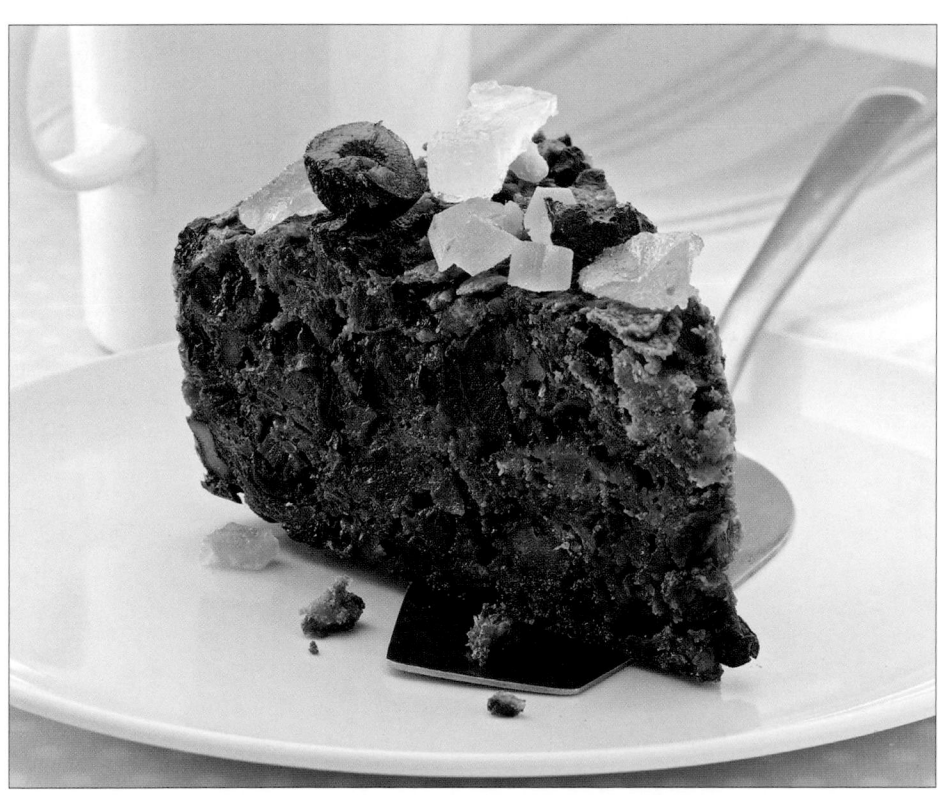

> **COOK'S TIPS**
> • This cake can be kept for up to a week when stored in an airtight container.
> • To crush the cornflakes, put them in a large plastic bag and tap with a rolling pin.

Energy 350kcal/1479kJ; Protein 7.4g; Carbohydrate 62.6g, of which sugars 50.38g; Fat 9.5g, of which saturates 1.5g; Cholesterol 56mg; Calcium 141mg; Fibre 2.4g; Sodium 224mg.

Currant cake

This traditional currant cake, from Norway, known as tiesen lap, uses the rubbed-in method of cake-making for combining the butter with the dry ingredients. Rather like a teabread, this cake is flavoured with nutmeg, and is light and moist with a crisp crust. It will keep for three days.

SERVES 10–12

130g/4½oz/9 tbsp butter, diced, plus extra for greasing
250g/9oz/2¼ cups plain (all-purpose) flour
7.5ml/1½ tsp baking powder
2.5ml/½ tsp freshly grated nutmeg
130g/4½oz/scant ¾ cup caster (superfine) sugar
130g/4½oz/½ cup currants or sultanas (golden raisins)
2 eggs, lightly beaten
150ml/¼ pint/⅔ cup milk or buttermilk

1 Preheat the oven to 190°C/375°F/Gas 5. Grease a shallow 20cm/8in round cake tin (pan).

2 Sift the flour, baking powder and nutmeg into a large bowl and stir in the sugar.

3 Add the butter and, with cold fingertips, rub the butter into the flour until the mixture resembles fine breadcrumbs. Stir in the currants or sultanas.

4 Stir in the eggs with enough milk to make a soft dropping consistency.

5 Spoon the batter into the prepared tin and smooth the top level.

6 Bake for 30–40 minutes, or until risen, golden brown and cooked through, and a skewer inserted in the centre comes out clean. Cool in the tin for 5 minutes, then turn out to go cold on a wire rack.

Energy 283kcal/1190kJ; Protein 4.5g; Carbohydrate 41.9g, of which sugars 22.8g; Fat 12g, of which saturates 7g; Cholesterol 65mg; Calcium 73mg; Fibre 1g; Sodium 105mg.

Irish whiskey cake

For this light cake, Irish whiskey provides moisture and flavour. The lemon icing with its subtle hint of cloves makes a good contrast. Start preparations the night before, as the sultanas are soaked in the whiskey until plump and soft. Keep this for five days in an airtight container.

SERVES 8

225g/8oz/scant 1½ cups sultanas
   (golden raisins)
finely grated rind of 1 lemon
150ml/¼ pint/⅔ cup Irish whiskey
175g/6oz/¾ cup butter, softened,
   plus extra for greasing
175g/6oz/¾ cup soft light
   brown sugar
3 large (US extra large)
   eggs, separated
175g/6oz/1½ cups plain
   (all-purpose) flour
pinch of ground cloves
5ml/1 tsp baking powder

For the icing
juice of 1 lemon
225g/8oz/2 cups icing
   (confectioners') sugar
crystallized lemon slices, to
   decorate (optional)

1 Put the sultanas and lemon rind into a bowl with the whiskey and leave overnight to soak.

2 Preheat the oven to 180°C/ 350°F/Gas 4. Grease and line an 18cm/7in round cake tin (pan) with baking parchment.

3 In a large bowl, beat the butter and sugar until light and fluffy.

4 Beat in the egg yolks one at a time.

5 Sift over the flour, cloves and baking powder. Fold in in batches, alternating with the sultana and whiskey mixture. Do not overbeat.

6 Put the egg whites into a clean, grease-free bowl and whisk until they form stiff peaks. Fold in to the batter with a metal spoon.

7 Spoon the batter into the prepared tin and smooth the top level. Bake for 1½ hours, or until well risen. Turn out to cool on a wire rack.

8 To make the icing, mix the lemon juice with the sifted icing sugar and a few drops of cold water to make a pouring consistency. Put a plate under the cake rack to catch the drips and pour the icing over the cake a spoonful at a time, allowing it to drizzle down the side. Decorate with lemon slices, if you like.

Energy 586kcal/2466kJ; Protein 6g; Carbohydrate 88.9g, of which sugars 72.2g; Fat 20.8g, of which saturates 12.1g; Cholesterol 1mg; Calcium 91.8mg; Fibre 1.2g; Sodium 1.3mg.

Caribbean rum cake

This marvellously moist fruit cake is filled with tropical fruits – pineapple, papaya and mango – that have been soaked in rum. It is sweet and spicy with a fruity, coconut topping. Start preparations the day before for the best results. Keep this for five days in an airtight container.

2 Preheat the oven to 180°C/350°F/Gas 4. Grease and line a 20cm/8in round cake tin (pan) with baking parchment.

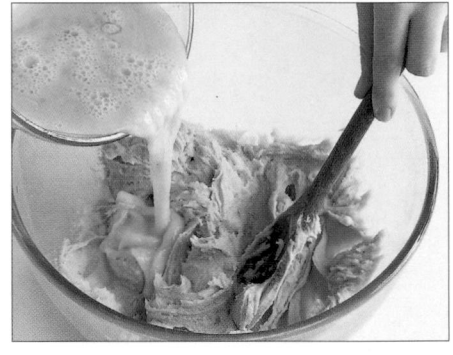

3 Cream the butter with the sugar. Beat in the eggs, a little at a time.

4 Sift over the flour and mixed spice, then fold in. Stir in the soaked fruits and mix thoroughly. Spoon into the cake tin and smooth the top level.

SERVES 10–12

50g/2oz/scant ⅓ cup sultanas (golden raisins)
175g/6oz/1 cup ready-to-eat dried pineapple, chopped
175g/6oz/1 cup ready-to-eat dried papaya, chopped
175g/6oz/1 cup ready-to-eat dried mango, chopped
60ml/4 tbsp rum
225g/8oz/1 cup butter, softened, plus extra for greasing
225g/8oz/1 cup soft light brown sugar
4 eggs, beaten
225g/8oz/2 cups plain (all-purpose) flour
10ml/2 tsp mixed (apple pie) spice

For the topping
75g/3oz/1 cup desiccated (dry unsweetened shredded) coconut
50g/2oz/⅓ cup ready-to-eat dried papaya, chopped
50g/2oz/⅓ cup ready-to-eat dried pineapple, chopped

1 Combine the sultanas with the dried pineapple, papaya and mango in a bowl. Spoon the rum over, then cover and leave for a few hours, or preferably overnight.

5 To make the topping, mix the coconut, papaya and pineapple in a small bowl. Sprinkle over the batter.

6 Bake for 1½–1¾ hours, or until a skewer inserted into the centre comes out clean. Cool in the tin for 15 minutes, then turn out on to a wire rack. Remove the lining paper.

Energy 434kcal/1826kJ; Protein 5.6g; Carbohydrate 63.2g, of which sugars 49.1g; Fat 18g, of which saturates 10.3g; Cholesterol 118mg; Calcium 86mg; Fibre 2.1g; Sodium 172mg.

Porter cake

Stout and porter are dark, full-flavoured beers and they can add real depth of flavour in cooking. This recipe originated in Ireland during the 19th century, where those drinks were popular, and it makes a fruit cake rich and tasty. Store this cake for one week before eating.

SERVES 10–12

225g/8oz/1 cup butter, at room
    temperature, plus extra
    for greasing
225g/8oz/1 cup soft dark
    brown sugar
350g/12oz/3 cups plain
    (all-purpose) flour
5ml/1 tsp baking powder
5ml/1 tsp mixed (apple pie) spice
3 eggs
450g/1lb/2⅓ cups mixed
    dried fruit
115g/4oz/½ cup glacé
    (candied) cherries
115g/4oz/⅔ cup mixed
    (candied) peel
50g/2oz/½ cup chopped almonds
    or walnuts
about 150ml/¼ pint/⅔ cup stout

1 Preheat the oven to 160°C/ 325°F/Gas 3. Grease and line a 20cm/8in round cake tin (pan) with baking parchment.

2 In a large bowl, cream the butter and sugar until light and fluffy.

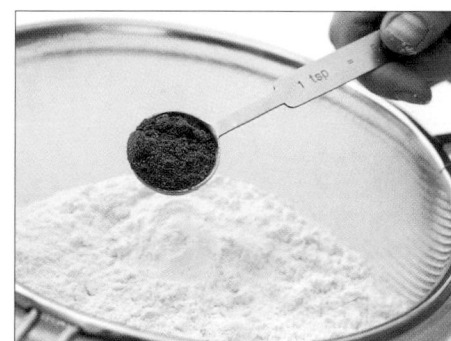

3 Sift the flour, baking powder and spice into another bowl.

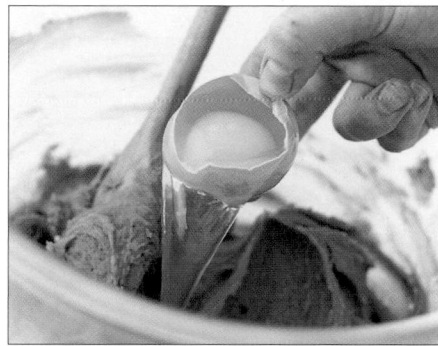

4 Add the eggs to the butter and sugar mixture, beating well and adding 5ml/1 tsp of the flour mixture with each addition to prevent the batter from curdling. Mix well and fold in the remaining flour.

5 Add the dried fruit and nuts and enough stout to make a soft dropping consistency. Mix well. Spoon into the prepared tin and smooth the top level.

6 Bake for 1 hour. Reduce the heat to 150°C/300°F/Gas 2 and bake for another 1½–2 hours, or until a skewer inserted into the centre comes out clean. Allow to go cold in the tin.

7 Remove the lining paper, wrap in fresh baking parchment and store in an airtight container.

Energy 510kcal/2150kJ; Protein 6.7g; Carbohydrate 80.4g, of which sugars 58g; Fat 20g, of which saturates 10.4g; Cholesterol 0.9mg; Calcium 0.1mg; Fibre 2.5g; Sodium 0.1mg.

Rich fruit cake

Use a food processor to chop and combine whole citrus fruits and dates to make this incredibly moist cake that is bursting with fruity and spicy flavours. This traditional cake is ideal for decorating for Christmas or special occasions. It will keep for one month in an airtight container.

SERVES 10–12

75g/3oz/scant ½ cup butter, plus extra for greasing
1 large orange, unpeeled, washed, cut into pieces and seeded
1 large lemon, unpeeled, washed, cut into pieces and seeded
1 large cooking apple, unpeeled, washed, cored and cut into pieces
90g/3½oz/generous ½ cup stoned (pitted) dates
75g/3oz/6 tbsp hazelnut butter
90g/3½oz/generous ½ cup raisins
90g/3½oz/generous ½ cup currants
90g/3½oz/generous ½ cup sultanas (golden raisins)
90g/3½oz/generous ½ cup ready-to-eat stoned (pitted) prunes, chopped
50g/2oz/½ cup cashew nut pieces
5ml/1 tsp ground cinnamon
5ml/1 tsp freshly grated nutmeg
2.5ml/½ tsp mace
2.5ml/½ tsp ground cloves
115g/4oz/1 cup wholemeal (whole-wheat) flour
7.5ml/1½tsp baking powder
115g/4oz/generous 1 cup rolled oats, processed until smooth
3 large (US extra large) eggs, beaten
45–60ml/3–4 tbsp unsweetened coconut milk, if needed

COOK'S TIP
Hazelnut butter is available in health-food stores and some larger supermarkets.

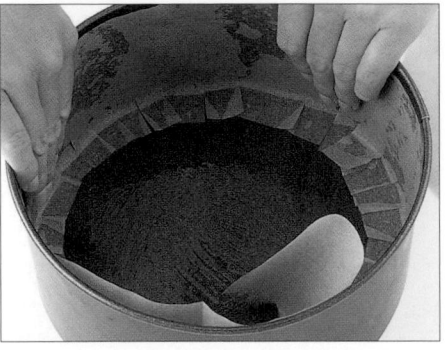

1 Preheat the oven to 150°F/300°C/ Gas 2. Grease and line a 20cm/8in round deep cake tin (pan) with baking parchment.

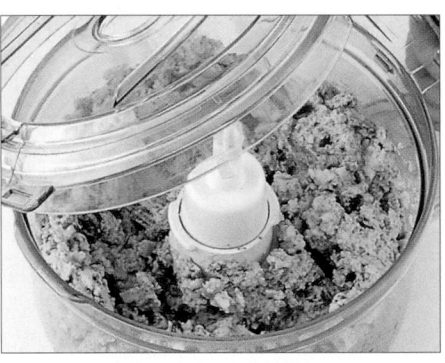

2 Put the first six ingredients in a food processor and process to make a rough purée.

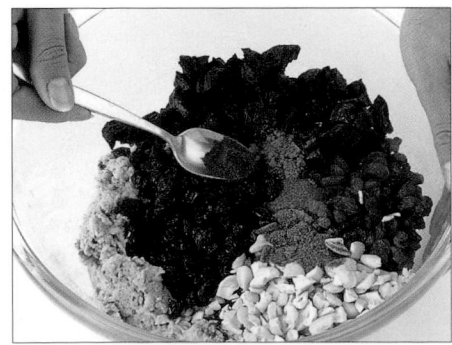

3 Scrape the mixture into a bowl and stir in the raisins, currants, sultanas, prunes, nuts and spices.

4 Stir in the flour, baking powder and oats, alternating with the eggs.

5 If the mixture seems very dry, stir in the coconut milk.

6 Spoon the batter into the prepared tin and smooth the top level. Bake for 1 hour, or until a skewer inserted into the centre comes out clean. Cool for 15 minutes, then turn out to cool on a wire rack.

Energy 376kcal/1576kJ; Protein 2.4g; Carbohydrate 52.4g, of which sugars 52.4g; Fat 18.4g, of which saturates 7.9g; Cholesterol 30mg; Calcium 54mg; Fibre 1.2g; Sodium 123mg.

Sugar-free fruit cake

Ask your guests to guess what's in this cake. Although it tastes sweet, it contains no added sugar – all the sweetness comes from date purée and dried fruit. The cake is packed with healthy minerals and it's lower in calories than the average fruit cake, too. Keep this for two weeks.

3 Sift the flour and spice into a large bowl, then add the cooled purée and butter, eggs, dried fruit and ground almonds.

4 Beat with a wooden spoon for about 3 minutes, or until light and fluffy. Spoon into the tin and smooth the top level.

5 Sprinkle with the sliced almonds.

6 Bake for about 1¼ hours, or until a skewer inserted into the centre comes out clean.

SERVES 8–10

130g/4½oz/generous ½ cup
   softened butter, plus extra
   for greasing
175g/6oz/1 generous cup dried
   stoned (pitted) dates, chopped
finely grated rind of 1 small orange
225g/8oz/2 cups self-raising
   wholemeal (self-rising
   whole-wheat) flour
5ml/1 tsp mixed (apple pie) spice
3 eggs, beaten
450g/1lb/2⅔ cups mixed
   dried fruit
25g/1oz/¼ cup ground almonds
50g/2oz/½ cup flaked
   (sliced) almonds
15ml/1 tbsp clear honey,
   warmed, to glaze

1 Preheat the oven to 180°C/350°F/Gas 4. Grease and line a 20cm/8in round deep cake tin (pan) with baking parchment.

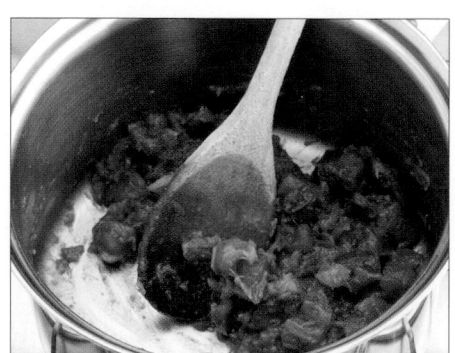

2 Put the dates in a heavy pan with the orange rind and 150ml/¼ pint/⅔ cup water. Simmer gently for 3–4 minutes, or until the dates form a purée, then leave to cool for 10 minutes.

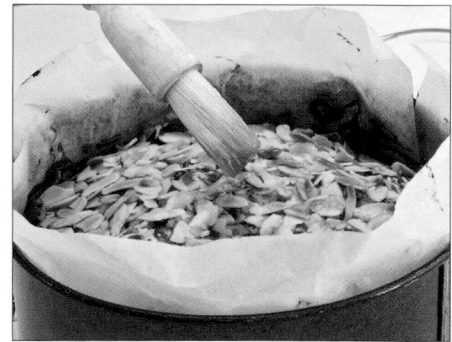

7 Brush the warmed melted honey lightly over the flaked almonds on top of the cake, for a shiny glaze. Leave to cool in the tin for 15 minutes, then turn out to go cold and peel away the paper.

Energy 406kcal/1709kJ; Protein 7.1g; Carbohydrate 60.1g, of which sugars 43.2g; Fat 17g, of which saturates 7.9g; Cholesterol 87mg; Calcium 148mg; Fibre 2.9g; Sodium 224mg.

All-in-one mixed fruit cake

This cake couldn't be easier to make, as all the ingredients are added in one go. Serve it plain or use it as a base for a decorated celebration cake. If you bake it a week before you need it, the flavour will develop and the texture will improve, making it easier to cut as well.

SERVES 8–10

175g/6oz/³⁄₄ cup butter, softened, plus extra for greasing
225g/8oz/2 cups self-raising (self-rising) flour
2.5ml/¹⁄₂ tsp mixed (apple pie) spice
175g/6oz/³⁄₄ cup muscovado (molasses) sugar
3 eggs, beaten
350g/12oz/2 cups luxury mixed dried fruit
50g/2oz/¹⁄₂ cup glacé (candied) cherries, washed, dried and chopped
15ml/1 tbsp treacle (molasses)

2 Sift the flour and spice into a large bowl, then add all the remaining ingredients.

3 Beat with a wooden spoon for about 3 minutes, or until the mixture is well combined, thick and creamy.

4 Spoon into the prepared tin and smooth the top level.

5 Bake for 2–2¹⁄₄ hours, or until a skewer inserted into the centre comes out clean. Leave to cool in the tin for 15 minutes, then turn out to go cold on a wire rack.

1 Preheat the oven to 160°C/325°F/ Gas 3. Grease and line the base and sides of a deep 20cm/8in round cake tin (pan) with a double layer of baking parchment snipped at the bottom edge to make a neat seal.

COOK'S TIP
This cake keeps for 1 month in an airtight tin. Freeze whole or in slices wrapped tightly in foil, for up to 4 months.

Energy 346kcal/1454kJ; Protein 4.3g; Carbohydrate 52.4g, of which sugars 39.1g; Fat 10.7g, of which saturates 6.2g; Cholesterol 62mg; Calcium 66mg; Fibre 2.1g; Sodium 90mg.

Mincemeat cake

If you have part of a jar of fruit mincemeat and a few small oranges left over after the Christmas holiday, they make a great basis for a tangy, quick and easy cake. Enrich the batter with some plain chocolate to make the cake even more special. Keep for one week in an airtight container.

SERVES 8–10

115g/4oz/½ cup soft tub margarine, plus extra for greasing
3 small mandarins or tangerines
75g/3oz/⅓ cup soft dark brown sugar
2 eggs, beaten
175g/6oz/1½ cups self-raising (self-rising) flour
2.5ml/½ tsp baking powder
15ml/1 tbsp milk
225g/8oz/⅔ cup luxury fruit mincemeat
50g/2oz plain (semisweet) chocolate, grated

For the decoration
175g/6oz/1½ cups icing (confectioners') sugar

1 Preheat the oven to 160°C/325°F/Gas 3. Grease and line a 20cm/8in round deep cake tin (pan) with baking parchment.

2 Finely grate the rind from two oranges and put it in a large bowl.

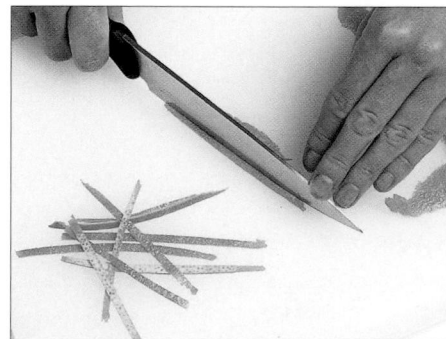

3 Pare long shreds of peel from the third orange, then set aside.

4 Squeeze the juice from two oranges and keep 30ml/2 tbsp aside for the icing.

5 Put the remaining juice and all the other cake ingredients into a large bowl. Beat with a wooden spoon for about 2 minutes, or until the mixture is soft and smooth. Spoon into the tin and smooth the top level.

6 Bake for 40–45 minutes, or until firm and a warmed skewer inserted into the centre comes out clean. Cool in the tin for 10 minutes, then turn out to cool on a wire rack and peel away the papers.

7 To make the decoration, mix the icing sugar with the reserved orange juice until smooth. Spread over the top of the cold cake and allow the icing to run in drizzles down the sides. Sprinkle the orange shreds on top of the cake and leave to set for 30 minutes.

Energy 292kcal/1227kJ; Protein 2g; Carbohydrate 44.6g, of which sugars 44.4g; Fat 13g, of which saturates 7.9g; Cholesterol 66mg; Calcium 37mg; Fibre 0.5g; Sodium 135mg.

Vinegar cake

This fruit cake is sweet and moist, and not in the least sour from the white wine vinegar. It is made using an old-fashioned recipe, which contains no eggs, and the vinegar helps the mixture to rise. Keep in an airtight tin for one week and freeze whole or in slices for up to two months.

SERVES 12

150g/5oz/10 tbsp butter or block
  margarine, diced, plus extra
  for greasing
300g/11oz/2⅔ cups plain
  (all-purpose) flour
150g/5oz/generous ½ cup soft dark
  brown sugar
75g/3oz/generous ¾ cup raisins
75g/3oz/¾ cup sultanas
  (golden raisins)
50g/2oz/⅓ cup chopped mixed
  (candied) peel
2.5ml/½ tsp bicarbonate of soda
  (baking soda)
250ml/8fl oz/1 cup milk
25ml/1½ tbsp white wine vinegar

1 Preheat the oven to 180°C/350°F/ Gas 4. Grease and line a 20cm/8in round deep cake tin (pan).

2 Sift the flour into a large bowl. Add the butter and rub in until the mixture resembles fine breadcrumbs. Add the sugar and dried fruits, and stir together.

3 Dissolve the bicarbonate of soda in 75ml/5 tbsp of the milk and add to the dry ingredients.

4 Stir the vinegar into the remaining milk and pour into the bowl. Beat with a wooden spoon until smooth, then spoon into the prepared tin and smooth the top level. Indent the centre slightly.

5 Bake for 1 hour, then reduce the heat to 160°C/325°F/Gas 3 and bake for a further 20 minutes, or until a warmed skewer inserted into the centre comes out clean.

6 Cool in the tin for 5 minutes, then turn out to go cold on a wire rack.

Energy 276kcal/1159kJ; Protein 3.6g; Carbohydrate 43.4g, of which sugars 24.3g; Fat 11g, of which saturates 7g; Cholesterol 30mg; Calcium 78mg; Fibre 1.1g; Sodium 110mg.

Dundee cake

This classic Scottish fruit cake is made with mixed peel, dried fruit, almonds and spices. It is decorated in the traditional way, topped with whole blanched almonds. Make in advance so that the flavour can mature. Keep for one month in an airtight container.

SERVES 10–12

175g/6oz/¾ cup butter, plus
   extra for greasing
175g/6oz/¾ cup soft light
   brown sugar
3 eggs
225g/8oz/2 cups plain
   (all-purpose) flour
10ml/2 tsp baking powder
5ml/1 tsp ground cinnamon
2.5ml/½ tsp ground cloves
pinch of freshly grated nutmeg
225g/8oz/1½ cups sultanas
   (golden raisins)
175g/6oz/¾ cup glacé
   (candied) cherries
115g/4oz/⅔ cup chopped mixed
   (candied) peel
50g/2oz/½ cup blanched almonds,
   roughly chopped
grated rind of 1 lemon
30ml/2 tbsp brandy
75g/3oz/¾ cup whole blanched
   almonds, to decorate

1 Preheat the oven to 160°C/325°F/ Gas 3. Grease and line a 20cm/8in round deep cake tin (pan).

2 Beat the butter and sugar together in a bowl. Add each egg, beating thoroughly after each addition.

COOK'S TIP
The flavour of this cake improves if left in a cool place for up to 3 weeks. Wrap it in baking parchment and a double layer of foil.

3 Sift the flour, baking powder and spices together. Fold into the creamed mixture, alternating with the remaining ingredients. Mix until evenly blended.

4 Spoon into the prepared tin and smooth the top level, then make a dip in the centre.

5 Decorate the top by arranging the whole almonds in decreasing circles over the entire surface. Bake in the preheated oven for 2–2¼ hours, or until a skewer inserted into the centre comes out clean.

6 Cool in the tin for 30 minutes, then turn out to cool on a wire rack.

Energy 292kcal/1229kJ; Protein 4.37g; Carbohydrate 41.5g, of which sugars 32.8g; Fat 12.9g, of which saturates 5.2g; Cholesterol 47mg; Calcium 69mg; Fibre 1.7g; Sodium 91mg.

Boiled fruit cake

The texture of this cake is quite distinctive – moist and plump as a result of boiling the dried fruit with the butter, sugar and milk prior to baking. For special occasions, arrange cherries and nuts on the surface of the batter before baking. It will keep for two weeks in an airtight container.

SERVES 10–15

225g/8oz/1 cup butter, plus
   extra for greasing
350g/12oz/2 cups mixed dried fruit
225g/8oz/1 cup soft dark
   brown sugar
400ml/14fl oz/1⅔ cups milk
450g/1lb/4 cups self-raising
   (self-rising) flour
5ml/1 tsp bicarbonate of soda
   (baking soda)
5ml/1 tsp mixed (apple pie) spice
2 eggs, beaten

1 Preheat the oven to 160°C/325°F/
Gas 3. Grease and line a 20cm/8in
round cake tin (pan).

2 Put the dried fruit in a large pan
and add the butter, sugar and milk.
Bring to the boil. Stir occasionally.

3 When the butter has melted and
the sugar has dissolved, allow the
mixture to bubble gently for about
2 minutes. Remove from the heat
and leave to cool slightly.

4 Sift the flour with the bicarbonate
of soda and mixed spice. Stir into
the fruit mixture with the eggs, and
mix together well.

5 Spoon into the prepared tin and
smooth the top level.

6 Bake for 1½ hours, or until firm
to the touch and a skewer inserted
into the centre comes out clean.

7 Cool in the tin for 20–30 minutes,
then turn out to go cold on a wire
rack. Remove the lining paper.

Energy 343kcal/1445kJ; Protein 4.8g; Carbohydrate 53g, of which sugars 33.2g; Fat 13.9g, of which saturates 8.3g; Cholesterol 58mg; Calcium 156mg; Fibre 1.3g; Sodium 219mg.

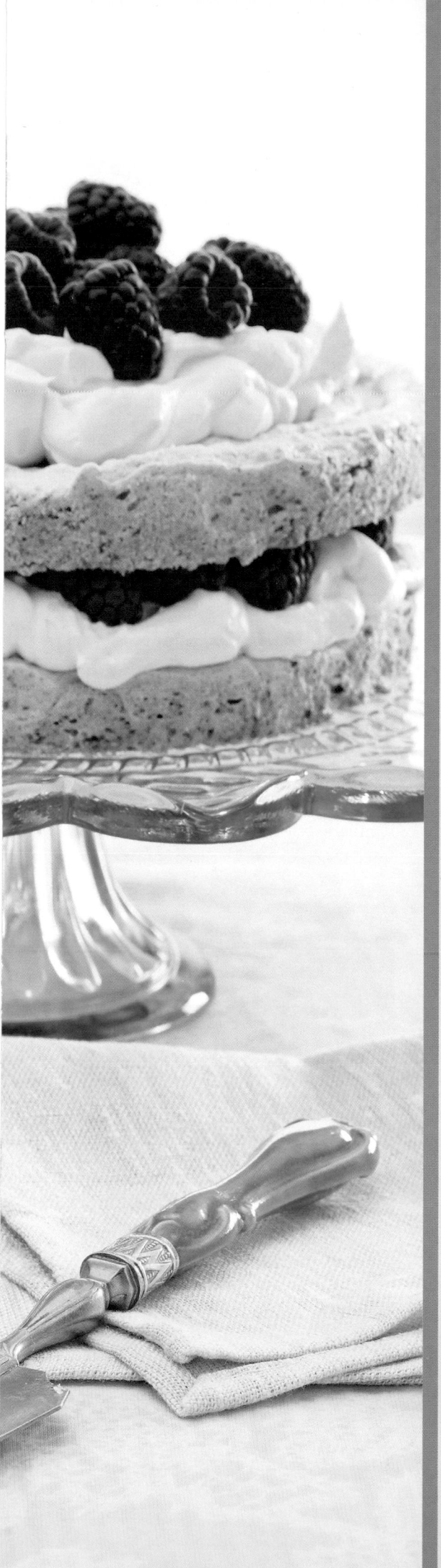

Dessert cakes

Many of us have been tempted to buy beautiful gateaux from a pâtisserie and serve these as a dessert for a special occasion, but you can also create these elegant specialities in your own kitchen. Gateaux do take a little more time and effort to make than many other cakes, but most can be prepared ahead or in stages. Allow plenty of time to enjoy the finishing and decorations. Although the cakes are a little more complicated, you will be surprised how simple skills can achieve a spectacular, mouthwatering centrepiece. Cheesecakes make an ideal dinner party dessert that can be made in advance. You have plenty of choice here: delicious Polish Cheesecake, Rum and Raisin Cheesecake, Baked Coffee Cheesecake, and more. There are also exquisite chocolate dessert cakes – White Chocolate Cappuccino Gateau or Chocolate Brandy-snap Gateau. You will impress friends and family with your own home-made pâtisserie.

Left: Coconut Lime Gateau and Raspberry and Hazelnut Meringue Cake.

Raspberry and hazelnut meringue cake

Toasted and ground hazelnuts add a nutty flavour to this simple cake of meringue rounds sandwiched together with fresh cream and raspberries. This combination will appeal to all dessert lovers. Store the baked meringue bases, unfilled, for one week. Once filled, eat fresh.

SERVES 8

butter, for greasing
140g/5oz/1¼ cups hazelnuts
4 egg whites
200g/7oz/1 cup caster
   (superfine) sugar
2.5ml/½ tsp vanilla extract

For the filling
300ml/½ pint/1¼ cups
   whipping cream
700g/1lb 8oz/4 cups raspberries

1 Preheat the oven to 180°C/350°F/ Gas 4. Grease and line the bases of two 20cm/8in round cake tins (pans) with baking parchment.

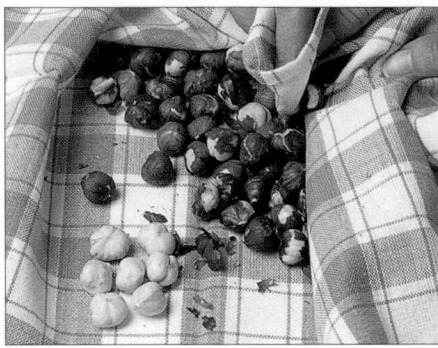

2 Spread the hazelnuts on a baking sheet and bake for 8 minutes, or until lightly toasted. Leave to cool slightly. Rub the hazelnuts vigorously in a clean dish towel to remove the skins. Reduce the oven temperature to 150°C/ 300°F/Gas 2.

3 Grind the nuts in a food processor, until they are the consistency of coarse sand.

4 Put the egg whites into a clean, grease-free bowl and whisk until they form stiff peaks. Beat in 30ml/ 2 tbsp of the sugar, then, using a plastic spatula, fold in the remaining sugar, a few spoonfuls at a time.

5 Fold in the vanilla and hazelnuts.

6 Divide the mixture between the cake tins and smooth the top level. Bake for 1¼ hours until firm.

7 Leave to cool in the tin for 5 minutes, then run a knife around the inside edge of the tins to loosen the meringues. Turn out to go cold on a wire rack.

8 For the filling, whip the cream. Spread half on one cake round and top with half the raspberries.

9 Top with the other cake round. Spread the remaining cream on top and arrange the rest of the raspberries over the surface. Chill for 1 hour before serving.

Energy 298kcal/1252kJ; Protein 3.2g; Carbohydrate 39.5g, of which sugars 39.5g; Fat 15.3g, of which saturates 9.5g; Cholesterol 39mg; Calcium 55mg; Fibre 1.4g; Sodium 44mg.

Raspberry mousse cake

A lavish amount of raspberries gives this freezer gateau its vibrant colour and flavour. Make it at the height of summer when these deliciously scented fruits are plentiful and their flavour is at its best. Keep this cake frozen for three months. Thaw it in the refrigerator.

SERVES 8–10

2 eggs
50g/2oz/¼ cup sugar
50g/2oz/½ cup plain
  (all-purpose) flour
30ml/2 tbsp unsweetened
  cocoa powder
600g/1lb 5oz/3½ cups raspberries
115g/4oz 1 cup icing
  (confectioners') sugar
300ml/½ pint/1¼ cups
  whipping cream
2 egg whites

1 Preheat the oven to 180°C/350°F/ Gas 4. Grease and line a 23cm/9in round cake tin (pan).

2 Whisk the eggs and sugar in a bowl set over a pan of simmering water until the beaters leave a trail when lifted. Remove from the heat.

3 Sift over the flour and cocoa and fold it in with a metal spoon. Spoon into the tin. Bake for 12–15 minutes, or until just firm. Turn out to cool on a wire rack.

4 Reline the tin with baking paper and replace the cake. Freeze.

5 Set aside 175g/6oz/1 cup of raspberries.

6 Put the rest of the raspberries in a a food processor bowl, stir in the icing sugar and process to a purée.

7 Whip the cream to form soft peaks.

8 Put the egg whites into a clean, grease-free bowl and whisk until they form stiff peaks.

9 Using a large metal spoon, fold the cream, then the egg whites into the raspberry purée.

10 Spread half the raspberry mixture on to the cake. Sprinkle with the reserved raspberries. Spread the remaining raspberry mixture on top. Freeze overnight, then thaw for at least 2 hours before serving.

Energy 238kcal/996kJ; Protein 4.4g; Carbohydrate 25g, of which sugars 20.9g; Fat 14.1g, of which saturates 8.3g; Cholesterol 70mg; Calcium 58mg; Fibre 2g; Sodium 65mg.

Iced raspberry pavlova roulade

This melt-in-the-mouth meringue, rolled around vanilla cream and luscious raspberries, is a star dinner-party attraction, and is surprisingly quick and simple to make. Eat it fresh, or store it in the freezer in a rigid plastic container. Keep frozen for up to three months, and defrost for four hours.

5 Spoon the mixture into the prepared tin and smooth it level.

6 Put the meringue into a cold oven and turn the temperature to 150°C/300°F/Gas 2. Bake for 1 hour, or until the top is crisp and the meringue feels springy.

7 Turn out on to baking parchment sprinkled with sifted icing sugar, and leave to go cold.

8 Meanwhile, whip the cream and vanilla. Stir in the raspberries.

SERVES 6–8

10ml/2 tsp cornflour (cornstarch)
225g/8oz/generous 1 cup caster (superfine) sugar
4 egg whites, at room temperature
icing (confectioners') sugar, sifted, for dusting
300ml/½ pint/1¼ cups double (heavy) cream or whipping cream
a few drops of vanilla extract
175g/6oz/1 cup raspberries, partly frozen, plus extra to serve

1 Line a 33 x 23cm/13 x 9in Swiss roll tin (jelly roll pan) with baking parchment.

2 Sift the cornflour into a bowl and blend evenly with the sugar.

3 Put the egg whites into a clean, grease-free bowl and whisk until stiff peaks form.

4 Whisk in the caster sugar, a few spoonfuls at a time, until the mixture becomes stiff and glossy.

VARIATIONS
• Flavour the cream with liqueur or lemon curd.
• Fill with soft ice cream.

9 Spread the raspberry cream over the meringue, then roll up, using the paper as a support. Freeze for 1 hour before serving. Dust with icing sugar and top with more raspberries, to serve.

Energy 243kcal/1015kJ; Protein 2g; Carbohydrate 26g, of which sugars 26g; Fat 15.3g, of which saturates 9.5g; Cholesterol 39mg; Calcium 34mg; Fibre 0.5g; Sodium 33mg.

White chocolate cappuccino gateau

A fabulous dessert for a special occasion, this gateau is made with light sponge layers filled with coffee liqueur cream. On top is a fluffy coating of white chocolate and coffee liqueur frosting, with a layer of chocolate curls dusted with cocoa. This will keep chilled, for two days.

SERVES 8

butter, for greasing
4 eggs
115g/4oz/generous ½ cup caster
    (superfine) sugar
15ml/1 tbsp strong black coffee
2.5ml/½ tsp vanilla extract
115g/4oz/1 cup plain
    (all-purpose) flour
75g/3oz white chocolate, grated
white chocolate curls, to decorate,
    see page 84
unsweetened cocoa powder or
    powdered cinnamon, for dusting

For the filling
120ml/4fl oz/½ cup double
    (heavy) cream
15ml/1 tbsp coffee liqueur

For the white chocolate frosting
175g/6oz white chocolate
75g/3oz/6 tbsp unsalted butter
115g/4oz/1 cup icing
    (confectioners') sugar
90ml/6 tbsp double (heavy) cream
15ml/1 tbsp coffee liqueur

1 Preheat the oven to 180°C/350°F/
Gas 4. Grease and line two 18cm/
7in round shallow cake tins (pans).

2 Combine the eggs, sugar, coffee
and vanilla extract in a large bowl
set over a pan of hot water. Whisk
until the mixture is pale and holds
its shape when the beaters are lifted.

3 Sift half the flour over the mixture,
and fold in. Fold in the rest of the
flour with the grated chocolate.

4 Divide between the cake tins. Bake
for 20–25 minutes, until golden.
Turn out to cool on wire racks.

5 Whip the filling ingredients in a
bowl until stiff. Spread over one cake
and put the second cake on top.

6 To make the frosting, melt the
chocolate with the butter in a
heatproof bowl set over a pan of
simmering water. Remove from the
heat and beat in the icing sugar.

7 Whip the cream in another bowl
until it just holds its shape, then
beat into the chocolate mixture.
Allow to cool, stirring occasionally.
Stir in the coffee liqueur.

8 Spread over the top and sides of
the cake. Top with chocolate curls
and dust with cocoa or cinnamon.
Serve with fresh berries. Freeze any
leftover slices wrapped in foil.

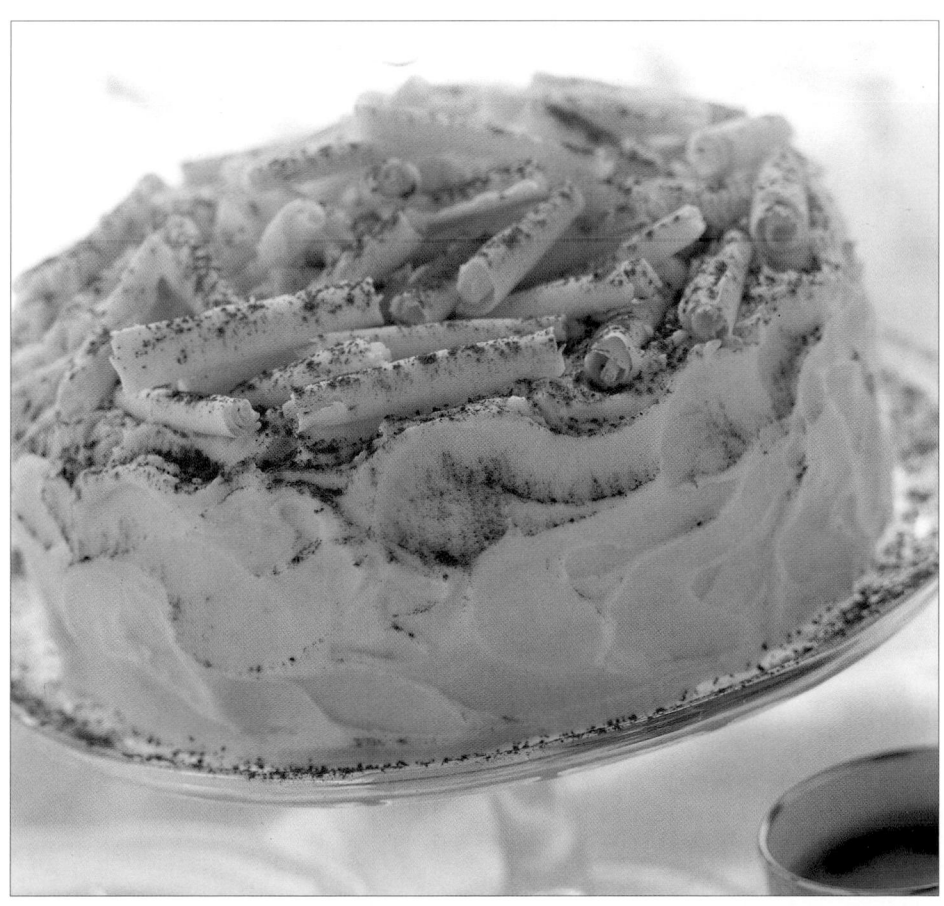

Energy 337kcal/1418kJ; Protein 5.3g; Carbohydrate 50.5g, of which sugars 39.5g; Fat 13.6g, of which saturates 7.4g; Cholesterol 116mg; Calcium 61mg; Fibre 0.7g; Sodium 41mg.

Chocolate brandy-snap gateau

Savour every mouthful of this sensational dark chocolate gateau. The cake is rich with chocolate and hazelnuts, then filled and topped with ganache – a cream and chocolate icing. Crisp brandy-snap frills look wonderful and contrast beautifully with the soft cake. Eat fresh.

SERVES 8

225g/8oz/1 cup unsalted butter,
  softened, plus extra for greasing
225g/8oz plain (semisweet)
  chocolate, broken into pieces
200g/7oz/scant 1 cup muscovado
  (molasses) sugar
6 eggs, separated
5ml/1 tsp vanilla extract
150g/5oz/1¼ cups ground
  hazelnuts
60ml/4 tbsp fresh white
  breadcrumbs
finely grated rind of 1 large orange
icing (confectioners') sugar,
  for dusting

For the brandy snaps
50g/2oz/¼ cup unsalted butter
50g/2oz/¼ cup caster
  (superfine) sugar
75g/3oz/¼ cup golden (light
  corn) syrup
50g/2oz/½ cup plain
  (all-purpose) flour
5ml/1 tsp brandy

For the chocolate ganache
250ml/8fl oz/1 cup double
  (heavy) cream
225g/8oz plain (semisweet)
  chocolate, broken into pieces

1 Preheat the oven to 180°C/
250°F/Gas 4.

2 Grease and line two 20cm/8in round shallow cake tins (pans) and two baking sheets with baking parchment.

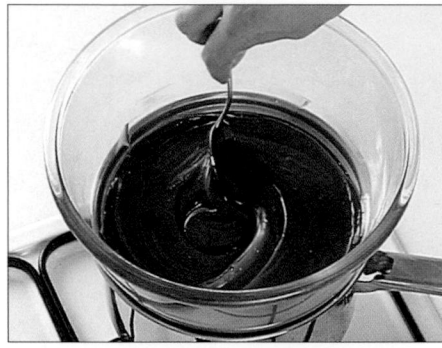

3 To make the cake, melt the chocolate in a heatproof bowl set over a pan of gently simmering water. Stir occasionally. Remove from the heat to cool slightly.

4 Beat the butter and sugar in a large bowl until pale and fluffy. Beat in the egg yolks and vanilla extract. Add the melted chocolate and mix thoroughly.

5 Put the egg whites into a clean, grease-free bowl and whisk until they form soft peaks.

6 Fold a tablespoon of the whites into the chocolate mixture to slacken it, then fold in the rest in batches with the ground hazelnuts, breadcrumbs and orange rind.

7 Divide the cake batter between the prepared tins and smooth the tops level.

8 Bake for 25–30 minutes, or until well risen and firm, then turn out to cool on wire racks. Remove the lining paper.

9 To make the brandy snaps, melt the butter, sugar and syrup in a pan over a low heat, stirring occasionally.

10 Remove from the heat and stir in the flour and brandy until smooth.

11 Place small spoonfuls well apart on the baking sheet leaving enough space to allow each biscuit to spread out, and bake for 10–15 minutes, or until golden.

Energy 870kcal/3622kJ; Protein 10.7g; Carbohydrate 70g, of which sugars 59g; Fat 62.7g, of which saturates 31.2g; Cholesterol 244mg; Calcium 102mg; Fibre 2.3g; Sodium 424mg.

12 Cool for a few seconds until firm enough to lift.

13 Immediately pinch the edges of each brandy snap to make a frilled effect. If the biscuits become too firm, pop them back into the oven for a few minutes. Leave to set on a wire rack.

14 Meanwhile, to make the chocolate ganache, heat the cream and chocolate together in a pan over a low heat, stirring frequently until the chocolate has melted.

15 Pour into a bowl. Leave to cool, then stir until the mixture begins to hold its shape.

16 Sandwich the cake layers together with half the chocolate ganache, transfer to a plate and spread the remaining ganache on top.

17 Arrange the brandy snap frills over the gateau and dust with icing sugar. Serve immediately.

Layer cake

Three light cakes enclose one layer of crushed raspberries and another of custard, then the whole cake is covered with vanilla-flavoured cream. Make when raspberries are at their sweetest and best. Bake the cake layers the day before for the best flavour, then assemble the cake and eat it fresh.

SERVES 10–12

115g/4oz/½ cup unsalted butter,
  plus extra for greasing
200g/7oz/1 cup caster
  (superfine) sugar
4 eggs, separated
45ml/3 tbsp milk
175g/6oz/1½ cups plain
  (all-purpose) flour
25ml/1½ tbsp cornflour
  (cornstarch)
7.5ml/1½ tsp baking powder
5ml/1 tsp vanilla sugar
fresh raspberries, to decorate

For the custard filling
2 eggs
90g/3½oz/½ cup caster
  (superfine) sugar
15ml/1 tbsp cornflour (cornstarch)
350ml/12fl oz/1½ cups milk

For the cream topping
475ml/16fl oz/2 cups double
  (heavy) cream or whipping cream
25g/1oz/½ cup icing
  (confectioners') sugar
5ml/1 tsp vanilla sugar

For the raspberry filling
375g/13oz/generous 2 cups
  raspberries
sugar, to taste

COOK'S TIP
To make vanilla sugar, put a vanilla pod in a jar with a well-fitting lid, and fill with caster (superfine) sugar.

1 Preheat the oven to 230°C/450°F/ Gas 8. Lightly grease and flour three 23cm/9in shallow cake tins (pans).

2 Cream the butter with the sugar in a large bowl until light and fluffy. Beat in the egg yolks, one at a time. Stir in the milk until blended.

3 In a separate bowl, sift together the flour, cornflour, baking powder and vanilla sugar. Beat the flour mixture into the egg mixture.

4 Put the egg whites into a clean, grease-free bowl and whisk until they form stiff peaks. Gently fold the egg whites into the cake mixture.

5 Divide the batter evenly among the tins and smooth to the edges. Bake for 12 minutes. Leave the cakes to cool for 10 minutes, then turn out to go cold on a wire rack.

6 To make the custard filling, whisk together the eggs and sugar in a pan. Whisk in the cornflour and the milk. Cook over a low heat, stirring, for about 6 minutes or until thickened. Remove from the heat and leave to cool.

7 Beat the cream in a bowl until soft peaks form. Stir in the icing sugar and vanilla sugar and continue beating until stiff.

8 To make the raspberry filling, crush the raspberries in a bowl and add a little sugar to taste.

9 To assemble the cake, place one layer on a serving plate and spread with the raspberry filling.

10 Place a second cake layer over the first and spread with the cooled custard. Top with the final layer.

11 Spread whipped cream over the sides and top of the cake.

12 Chill the cake until ready to serve, and decorate with raspberries.

Energy 433kcal/1811kJ; Protein 6.1g; Carbohydrate 44.6g, of which sugars 30.4g; Fat 27g, of which saturates 15.9g; Cholesterol 157mg; Calcium 86mg; Fibre 1.2g; Sodium 109mg.

Polish cheesecake

There are many different versions of cheesecake. Unlike others, this rich, creamy baked version is not made on a biscuit base, but includes raisins and semolina, giving it sweetness and a firm texture. Keep this cheesecake refrigerated for two days, and freeze for up to two months.

SERVES 6–8

100g/3¾oz/scant ½ cup butter,
    softened, plus extra for greasing
500g/1¼lb/2¼ cups curd cheese
2.5ml/½ tsp vanilla extract
6 eggs, separated
150g/5½oz/scant ¾ cup caster
    (superfine) sugar
10ml/2 tsp grated lemon rind
15ml/1 tbsp cornflour (cornstarch)
15ml/1 tbsp semolina
50g/2oz/⅓ cup raisins
icing (confectioners') sugar,
    for dusting

1 Preheat the oven to 200°C/400°F/ Gas 6. Grease and line the base and sides of a 20cm/8in loose-based cake tin (pan) with baking parchment.

2 In a large bowl, cream together the curd cheese, butter and vanilla extract.

3 Put the egg whites into a clean, grease-free bowl and add 15ml/ 1 tbsp sugar. Whisk until the whites form stiff peaks.

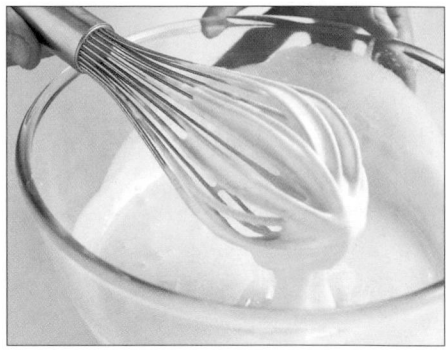

4 Whisk the egg yolks with the remaining sugar until thick and creamy. Add to the cheese mixture with the lemon rind, and stir to combine.

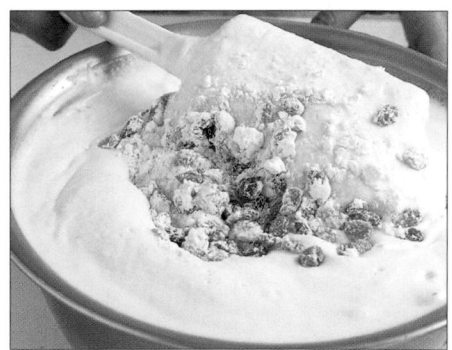

5 Gently fold in the egg whites, then fold in the cornflour, semolina and raisins.

6 Transfer to the lined tin and bake for 1 hour, or until the cake is set and golden brown.

7 Leave to cool in the tin. Remove the sides of the tin and papers, then dust with icing sugar and serve.

Energy 347kcal/1488kJ; Protein 10.8g; Carbohydrate 24.8g, of which sugars 21.6g; Fat23.6g, of which saturates 13.4g; Cholesterol 196mg; Calcium 34mg; Fibre 0g; Sodium131mg.

Baked coffee cheesecake

This rich, baked and chilled cheesecake, flavoured with coffee and orange liqueur, has a wonderfully dense, velvety texture and makes a lovely dessert served with single cream. Keep for two days refrigerated. Freeze for up to two months.

SERVES 8

75g/3oz/6 tbsp butter, plus extra
   for greasing
115g/4oz/1 cup plain
   (all-purpose) flour
5ml/1 tsp baking powder
50g/2oz/¼ cup caster
   (superfine) sugar
1 egg, lightly beaten
30ml/2 tbsp cold water
single (light) cream, to serve

For the filling
45ml/3 tbsp near-boiling water
30ml/2 tbsp ground coffee
4 eggs
225g/8oz/generous 1 cup caster
   (superfine) sugar
450g/1lb/2 cups cream cheese, at
   room temperature
30ml/2 tbsp orange liqueur
40g/1½ oz/⅓ cup plain
   (all-purpose) flour, sifted
300ml/½ pint/1¼ cups
   whipping cream
30ml/2 tbsp icing (confectioners')
   sugar, for dusting

1 Preheat the oven to 160°C/325°F/Gas 3. Grease and line a 20cm/8in round loose-based cake tin (pan) with baking parchment.

2 Sift the flour and baking powder into a bowl. Rub in the butter until the mixture resembles fine crumbs.

3 Stir in the sugar, then add the egg and the cold water, and mix to a dough. Press the mixture into the base of the tin.

4 For the filling, pour the water over the coffee and leave for 4 minutes. Strain through a fine sieve (strainer).

5 Whisk the eggs and sugar until thick.

6 Using a wooden spoon, beat the cream cheese until softened, then beat in the liqueur, a spoonful at a time.

7 Gradually mix in the whisked eggs. Fold in the flour. Finally, stir in the whipping cream and coffee.

8 Pour over the base and bake for 1½ hours. Turn off the heat. Leave in the oven to go cold with the door ajar.

9 Chill for 1 hour. Remove from the tin and dust with icing sugar.

Energy 713kcal/2969kJ; Protein 8.4g; Carbohydrate 53.4g, of which sugars 38.6g; Fat 52.8g, of which saturates 32g; Cholesterol 233mg; Calcium 143mg; Fibre 0.6g; Sodium 301mg.

Sponge cake with strawberries and cream

This classic treat is delicious in the summer, filled with ripe, fragrant strawberries. The sponge is exceptionally light because it is made without fat. To ensure you have a perfect sponge, have all the ingredients at room temperature. Eat this cake on the day it is made.

SERVES 8–10

oil, for greasing
115g/4oz/generous ½ cup caster
    (superfine) sugar, plus extra
    for dusting
90g/3½oz/¾ cup plain
    (all-purpose) flour, sifted, plus
    extra for dusting
4 eggs
icing (confectioners') sugar,
    for dusting

For the filling
300ml/½ pint/1¼ cups double
    (heavy) cream
about 5ml/1 tsp icing
    (confectioners') sugar, sifted
450g/1lb/4 cups strawberries,
    washed and hulled
a little orange liqueur (optional)

1 Preheat the oven to 190°C/375°F/ Gas 5. Grease a round 20cm/8in cake tin (pan). Dust the tin with 10ml/2 tsp caster sugar and flour combined. Tap out the excess.

COOK'S TIP
Freeze, unfilled, for 2 months.

2 Put the eggs and sugar into a bowl and use an electric whisk at high speed until the mixture is light and thick, and the mixture leaves a trail as it drops from the whisk. (To whisk by hand: set the bowl over a pan one quarter filled with hot water and whisk until thick and creamy, then remove from the heat.)

3 Sift the flour over the whisked eggs and carefully fold it in with a metal spoon, mixing thoroughly but losing as little volume as possible.

4 Pour the batter into the cake tin and smooth the top level. Bake for 25–30 minutes, or until the sponge feels springy to the touch.

5 Leave in the tin for 5 minutes to set slightly, then loosen the sides with a knife and invert on to a wire rack to go cold.

6 To make the filling, whip the cream with a little icing sugar until it is stiff enough to hold its shape.

7 Slice the sponge across the middle with a long sharp knife to make two even layers.

8 Divide half the cream between the two inner cut sides of the sandwich.

9 Reserve some strawberries for the cake top, and then slice the rest.

10 Put the first sponge half on a serving plate and arrange the sliced strawberries on the cream. Sprinkle with liqueur, if using.

11 Cover with the second cake half and press down gently.

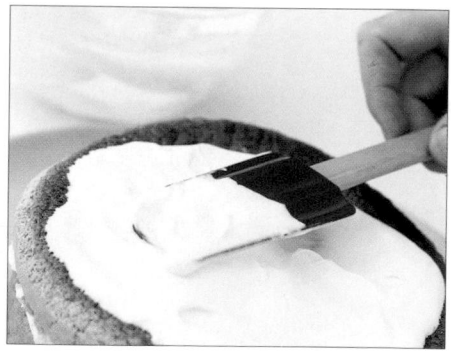

12 Spread the remaining cream on top of the cake, and arrange the reserved strawberries, whole or halved according to size, on top.

13 Set aside for an hour or so for the flavours to develop, then dust lightly with icing sugar and serve.

Energy 333kcal/1387kJ; Protein 5.3g; Carbohydrate 27.8g, of which sugars 19.2g; Fat 23.1g, of which saturates 13.3g; Cholesterol 147mg; Calcium 65mg; Fibre 1g; Sodium 48mg.

Cinnamon apple gateau

Make this unusual cake for an autumn celebration. A light sponge is split and filled with a honey and cream cheese layer as well as softly cooked cinnamon apples and sultanas, then topped with glazed apples. Keep the sponge, unfilled, for two days in an airtight container; fill and eat it fresh.

SERVES 8–10

butter, for greasing
3 eggs
115g/4oz/generous ½ cup caster
 (superfine) sugar
75g/3oz/⅔ cup plain
 (all-purpose) flour
5ml/1 tsp ground cinnamon

For the filling and topping
4 large eating apples
60ml/4 tbsp clear honey
75g/3oz/generous ½ cup sultanas
 (golden raisins)
2.5ml/½ tsp ground cinnamon
350g/12oz/1½ cups soft cheese
60ml/4 tbsp fromage frais or
 crème fraîche
10ml/2 tsp lemon juice
45ml/3 tbsp apricot jam, strained
mint sprigs, to decorate

1 Preheat the oven to 190°C/ 375°F/Gas 5. Grease and line a 23cm/9in round cake tin (pan) with baking parchment.

2 Put the eggs and sugar in a bowl and beat with an electric whisk until thick and mousse-like and the beaters leave a trail on the surface.

3 Sift the flour and cinnamon over the egg mixture and carefully fold in with a large spoon.

4 Pour into the prepared tin and bake for 25–30 minutes, or until the cake springs back when lightly pressed in the centre.

5 Slide a knife between the cake and the tin to loosen the edge, then turn the cake on to a wire rack to cool.

6 To make the filling, peel, core and slice three apples and put them in a pan. Add 30ml/ 2 tbsp of the honey and 15ml/1 tbsp water. Cover and cook over a low heat for 10 minutes, or until the apples have softened.

7 Add the sultanas and cinnamon, stir, replace the lid and leave to cool.

8 Put the soft cheese in a bowl with the remaining honey, the fromage frais or crème fraîche and half the lemon juice. Beat until smooth.

9 Cut the cake into two equal rounds. Put half on a plate and drizzle over any liquid from the apple mixture.

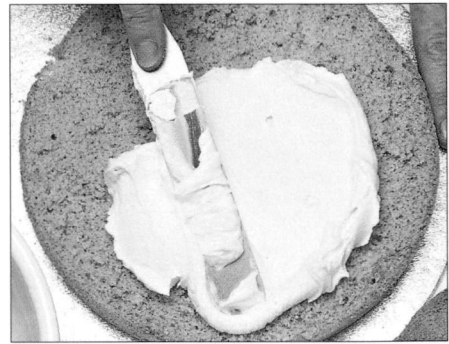

10 Spread with two-thirds of the cheese mixture, then top with the apple filling. Fit the top of the cake in place.

11 Swirl the remaining cheese mixture over the top of the sponge. Core and slice the remaining apple, sprinkle with lemon juice and use to decorate the edge of the cake. Brush the apple with apricot glaze and place mint sprigs on top to decorate.

Energy 239kcal/1010kJ; Protein 10.8g; Carbohydrate 39.9g, of which sugars 32.8g; Fat 5.8g, of which saturates 2.9g; Cholesterol 82mg; Calcium 97mg; Fibre 1.1g; Sodium 225mg.

Sponge cake with strawberries and cream

This classic treat is delicious in the summer, filled with ripe, fragrant strawberries. The sponge is exceptionally light because it is made without fat. To ensure you have a perfect sponge, have all the ingredients at room temperature. Eat this cake on the day it is made.

SERVES 8–10

oil, for greasing
115g/4oz/generous ½ cup caster
  (superfine) sugar, plus extra
  for dusting
90g/3½oz/¾ cup plain
  (all-purpose) flour, sifted, plus
  extra for dusting
4 eggs
icing (confectioners') sugar,
  for dusting

For the filling
300ml/½ pint/1¼ cups double
  (heavy) cream
about 5ml/1 tsp icing
  (confectioners') sugar, sifted
450g/1lb/4 cups strawberries,
  washed and hulled
a little orange liqueur (optional)

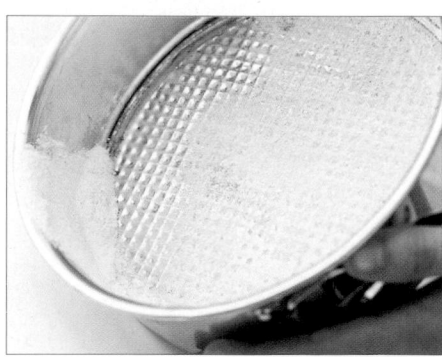

1 Preheat the oven to 190°C/375°F/ Gas 5. Grease a round 20cm/8in cake tin (pan). Dust the tin with 10ml/2 tsp caster sugar and flour combined. Tap out the excess.

COOK'S TIP
Freeze, unfilled, for 2 months.

2 Put the eggs and sugar into a bowl and use an electric whisk at high speed until the mixture is light and thick, and the mixture leaves a trail as it drops from the whisk. (To whisk by hand: set the bowl over a pan one quarter filled with hot water and whisk until thick and creamy, then remove from the heat.)

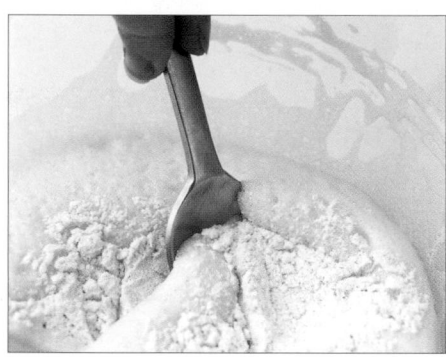

3 Sift the flour over the whisked eggs and carefully fold it in with a metal spoon, mixing thoroughly but losing as little volume as possible.

4 Pour the batter into the cake tin and smooth the top level. Bake for 25–30 minutes, or until the sponge feels springy to the touch.

5 Leave in the tin for 5 minutes to set slightly, then loosen the sides with a knife and invert on to a wire rack to go cold.

6 To make the filling, whip the cream with a little icing sugar until it is stiff enough to hold its shape.

7 Slice the sponge across the middle with a long sharp knife to make two even layers.

8 Divide half the cream between the two inner cut sides of the sandwich.

9 Reserve some strawberries for the cake top, and then slice the rest.

10 Put the first sponge half on a serving plate and arrange the sliced strawberries on the cream. Sprinkle with liqueur, if using.

11 Cover with the second cake half and press down gently.

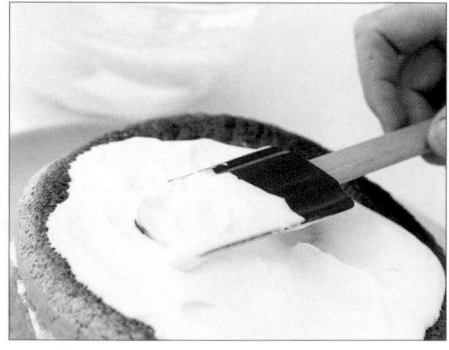

12 Spread the remaining cream on top of the cake, and arrange the reserved strawberries, whole or halved according to size, on top.

13 Set aside for an hour or so for the flavours to develop, then dust lightly with icing sugar and serve.

Energy 333kcal/1387kJ; Protein 5.3g; Carbohydrate 27.8g, of which sugars 19.2g; Fat 23.1g, of which saturates 13.3g; Cholesterol 147mg; Calcium 65mg; Fibre 1g; Sodium 48mg.

Princess cake

A light sponge cake is layered and topped with vanilla custard cream, then covered with home-made marzipan to make an unusual and special dessert gateau. You can make the marzipan in advance, if you like. Serve a slice of the cake with strawberries. Keep for two days in a cool place.

SERVES 8–10

200g/7oz/scant 1 cup unsalted
   butter, plus extra for greasing
400g/14oz/2 cups caster
   (superfine) sugar
3 eggs
350g/12oz/3 cups plain
   (all-purpose) flour
5ml/1 tsp baking powder
10ml/2 tsp vanilla sugar
fresh strawberries, to serve

For the filling and topping
3 gelatine leaves
1 litre/1¾ pints/4 cups double
   (heavy) cream
10ml/2 tsp sugar
10ml/2 tsp cornflour (cornstarch)
2 egg yolks
10ml/2 tsp vanilla sugar

For the marzipan
200g/7oz/1¾ cups ground almonds
200g/7oz/1¾ cups icing
   (confectioners') sugar
1 egg white
a few drops of green food colour

1 To make the marzipan, put the ground almonds in a bowl and add the icing sugar and egg white. Mix to form a paste.

2 Add a few drops of green food colour and knead until evenly coloured. Refrigerate in a plastic bag for up to 3 days until required.

3 Preheat the oven to 180°C/350°F/ Gas 4. Grease and line a 20cm/8in round cake tin (pan).

4 Put the butter and sugar in a large bowl and beat until fluffy. Add the eggs and whisk together. Sift in the flour, baking powder and vanilla sugar and stir together.

5 Spoon the batter into the cake tin and bake for 1 hour, or until firm to the touch. Leave to cool in the tin. When cold, slice in half horizontally.

6 To make the filling, soak the gelatine in cold water according to the directions on the packet. Put half of the cream, the sugar, cornflour and egg yolks in a pan and heat gently, stirring constantly, until the mixture thickens. Do not allow it to boil or the eggs will curdle.

7 Pour into a bowl, and stir in the soaked gelatine leaves. Leave to cool.

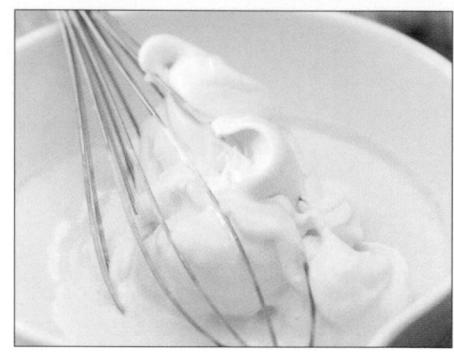

8 Put the remaining cream with the vanilla sugar in a bowl and whisk until stiff.

9 Fold into the cooled custard and quickly spread half the mixture over the bottom layer of cake. Put the other cake layer on top and spread the remaining custard over the top and sides.

10 Put the marzipan between two sheets of foil. Roll out a thin round. Remove the top sheet of foil and, using a 30cm/12in diameter plate as a guide, cut a marzipan circle.

11 Use the foil to lift the marzipan circle over the top of the cake and smooth it down the sides. Trim the edge around the cake base. Decorate with fresh strawberries.

Energy 1326kcal/5512kJ; Protein 11.3g; Carbohydrate 112g, of which sugars 77.6g; Fat 95.7g, of which saturates 56.1g; Cholesterol 346mg; Calcium 191mg; Fibre 1.9g; Sodium 218mg.

Coconut lime gateau

American frosting is what makes this zesty lime and coconut gateau so attractive. Made by whisking egg white and a sugar mixture over heat, the frosting is like a soft meringue icing. It tastes divine scattered with toasted coconut. Eat the gateau fresh or refrigerate it for two days.

SERVES 10–12

225g/8oz/1 cup butter, at
   room temperature, plus extra
   for greasing
225g/8oz/2 cups plain
   (all-purpose) flour
12.5ml/2½ tsp baking powder
225g/8oz/generous 1 cup caster
   (superfine) sugar
grated rind of 2 limes
4 eggs
60ml/4 tbsp fresh lime juice (from
   about 2 limes)
85g/3oz/1 cup desiccated (dry
   unsweetened shredded) coconut

For the frosting
275g/10oz/scant 1½ cups caster
   (superfine) sugar
2.5ml/½ tsp cream of tartar
2 egg whites
60ml/4 tbsp cold water
15ml/1 tbsp liquid glucose
10ml/2 tsp vanilla extract

1 Preheat the oven to 180°C/350°F/ Gas 4. Grease and line two 23cm/9in round shallow cake tins (pans) with baking parchment.

2 Sift together the flour and baking powder into a bowl.

3 In another large bowl, beat the butter until soft. Add the sugar and lime rind, then beat until pale and fluffy. Beat in the eggs, one at a time, adding 5ml/1 tsp of the flour mixture with each addition to stop the batter from curdling. Beat the mixture well between each addition.

4 Using a wooden spoon, fold in the flour mixture in small batches, alternating with the lime juice. When the batter is smooth, stir in two-thirds of the coconut.

5 Divide the batter between the tins and spread it evenly to the sides.

6 Bake for 30–35 minutes, or until a skewer inserted into the centre comes out clean. Leave to cool in the tins for 10 minutes, then turn out to cool on a wire rack. Remove the lining paper. Leave to go cold.

7 Spread the remaining coconut in another cake tin. Bake until golden brown, stirring occasionally. Watch carefully so that the coconut does not get too dark. Allow to cool in the tin.

8 To make the frosting, put the sugar in a large heatproof bowl and add the cream of tartar, egg whites, water and glucose. Stir to mix.

9 Set the bowl over a pan of boiling water. Beat with an electric whisk at high speed for 7 minutes or until thick and stiff peaks form. Remove from the heat.

10 Add the vanilla extract and continue beating for 3 minutes or until the frosting has cooled slightly.

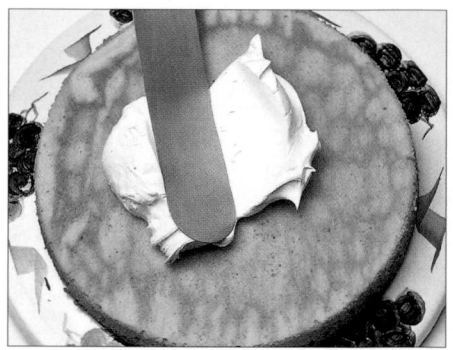

11 Invert one cake on a serving plate. Spread a layer of frosting on top.

12 Set the second cake on top. Swirl the rest of the frosting all over the cake. Sprinkle with the toasted coconut and leave to set.

Energy 732kcal/3079kJ; Protein 7.3g; Carbohydrate 111g, of which sugars 59g; Fat 32g, of which saturates 20.5g; Cholesterol 155mg; Calcium 105.7mg; Fibre 2.1g; Sodium 221mg.

Lemon chiffon cake

Split a light lemon sponge cake in half horizontally, then fill with a lovely thick layer of lemon mousse to give it a tangy centre. Top with a lemon icing and lemon zest and you have the most lemony cake. Keep this for one day in the refrigerator, or freeze for two months, undecorated.

SERVES 8

butter, for greasing
2 eggs
75g/3oz/6 tbsp caster (superfine) sugar
grated rind of 1 lemon
50g/2oz/½ cup plain (all-purpose) flour, sifted
lemon shreds, to decorate

For the filling
2 eggs, separated
75g/3oz/6 tbsp caster (superfine) sugar
grated rind and juice of 1 lemon
15ml/1 tbsp gelatine
120ml/4fl oz/½ cup fromage frais or crème fraîche

For the icing
15ml/1 tbsp lemon juice
115g/4oz/1 cup icing (confectioners') sugar, sifted

1 Preheat the oven to 180°C/350°F/Gas 4. Grease and line a 20cm/8in round loose-based cake tin (pan).

2 Whisk the eggs, sugar and lemon rind until mousse-like. Fold in the flour, then pour into the cake tin.

3 Bake for 20–25 minutes, or until the cake springs back when lightly pressed in the centre. Turn on to a rack to go cold. Clean the cake tin.

4 Remove the lining paper. Split the cake in half horizontally and return the lower half to the clean cake tin.

5 To make the filling, put the egg yolks, sugar, lemon rind and juice in a bowl. Beat with an electric whisk until thick, pale and creamy.

6 Pour 30ml/2 tbsp water into a small heatproof bowl and sprinkle the gelatine on top. Leave until spongy, then set the bowl over simmering water and stir until dissolved. Cool slightly, then whisk into the yolk mixture. Fold in the fromage frais or crème fraîche.

7 When the filling mixture begins to set, whisk the egg whites in a clean, grease-free bowl until they form soft peaks. Stir a spoonful into the mousse mixture to lighten it, then fold in the rest.

8 Pour the filling over the sponge in the cake tin, spreading it to the edges. Put the second layer of sponge on top and chill until set.

9 Slide a knife dipped in hot water between the tin and the cake to loosen it, then transfer the cake to a serving plate.

10 To make the icing, add enough lemon juice to the icing sugar to make a thick, spreadable icing. Pour over the cake and spread to the edges. Decorate with lemon shreds.

Energy 356kcal/1491kJ; Protein 6.7g; Carbohydrate 43.6g, of which sugars 29.8g; Fat 18.4g, of which saturates 4g; Cholesterol 118mg; Calcium 68mg; Fibre 0.6g; Sodium 227mg.

Special occasion cakes

In this chapter you will find some fabulous cakes to help celebrate many occasions, such as family gatherings, weddings, christenings and parties, all of which call for a centrepiece. Give yourself plenty of time to make these cakes. The detailed step-by-step photographs will help to take you through the complicated techniques. A freshly baked Strawberry Shortcake couldn't be better to take to a summer barbecue party, or you could make a present of a Simnel Cake for Easter. For a christening or naming party, Lemon Daisy Christening Cake could be served with a Meringue Mountain as part of a special tea. Take the worry out of the festive season celebrations by making the Traditional Christmas Cake, Yule Log or White Christmas Cake, all of which can be prepared well ahead of time.

Left: Mother's Day Cake and Celebratory Anniversary Cake.

Lemon daisy christening cake

This delicate sponge cake is drizzled with a lemon syrup, making it moist with good keeping qualities. Use sugarpaste to give it the perfect finish, decorated with hand-moulded daisies. Make it up to four days ahead, so you have plenty of time to concentrate on decorating it.

SERVES 16–18

350g/12oz/1½ cups butter or block
  margarine, plus extra for greasing
350g/12oz/1¾ cups caster
  (superfine) sugar
6 eggs, beaten
115g/4oz/1 cup plain
  (all-purpose) flour
275g/10oz/2½ cups self-raising
  (self-rising) flour
finely grated rind and juice
  of 2 lemons

For the syrup and decorations
100g/3¼ oz/generous ½ cup caster
  (superfine) sugar
finely grated rind and juice
  of 2 lemons
1 quantity buttercream icing, *see
  page 23*
icing (confectioners') sugar,
  for dusting
1kg/2¼ lb sugarpaste icing,
  see page 26
yellow and pink edible paste
  food colourings
small tube writing icing
Materials: lemon satin ribbon

1 Preheat the oven to 160°C/325°F/Gas 3. Grease and line a 23cm/9in deep, round cake tin (pan) with baking parchment.

2 In a bowl, beat the butter and sugar together until light and fluffy.

3 Gradually beat in the eggs a little at a time, adding 5ml/1 tsp flour with each addition to prevent the mixture from curdling.

4 Sift the flours into the bowl and fold into the egg mixture with the lemon rind and juice until smooth.

5 Spoon into the tin and smooth the top level. Bake for 1¼ hours, or until a warmed skewer inserted into the middle comes out clean.

6 Leave in the tin until just warm, then prick over the top of the cake with a skewer.

7 To make the syrup, put the sugar, lemon juice and rind in a pan and heat gently until the sugar dissolves completely. Allow to cool slightly.

8 Brush the syrup over the cake and leave to cool completely in the tin. Remove the lining paper. Wrap the cake in baking parchment, then in foil until needed.

9 Cut the cake in half horizontally, sandwich together with buttercream icing, then spread the remainder thinly around the outside.

10 Put the sugarpaste icing on a surface lightly dusted with icing sugar, and roll out to a circle large enough to cover the top and sides of the cake.

11 Lift the sugarpaste over the cake, smooth down with your hands to remove any bubbles or pleats, then trim the excess away carefully with a sharp knife.

COOK'S TIP
Keeps for 5 days, undecorated.

Energy 591kcal/2503kJ; Protein 5.5g; Carbohydrate 117.6g, of which sugars 108.3g; Fat 11.6g, of which saturates 2.4g; Cholesterol 38mg; Calcium 112mg; Fibre 2g; Sodium 140mg.

14 Position the flowers on the cake in a daisy circle and stick each in place using a little blob of writing icing.

15 Write the name or message in the centre of the cake, if you like, and finish by tying a deep ribbon in a bow around the sides of the cake.

12 Roll the trimmings into small pea-sized balls, then shape each one into a cone. Flatten out one edge thinly. Using clean scissors, snip the edge to represent petals. Mark the centre with the scissor points.

13 Put a dot each of yellow and pink paste colours on to a plate and, using a paintbrush, dilute slightly with water. Paint the centres of the flowers lemon and the outer petal tips pale pink. Leave to dry out.

COOK'S TIP
To bake ahead, cool the cake, cover it with syrup and freeze, undecorated, for up to 3 months.

Celebration bow cake

Adding a little glycerine to this delicate almond cake helps it retain its moisture for longer, so you can make it ahead of time. The cake is ideal for any type of celebration, and you can vary the icing colours to suit. Small icing cutters are useful for quick-and-easy cake decorating.

SERVES 12

275g/10oz/2½ cups self-raising
   (self-rising) flour
2.5ml/½ tsp baking powder
50g/2oz/¼ cup ground almonds
275g/10oz/1¼ cups soft tub
   margarine, plus extra for greasing
275g/10oz/scant 1½ cups natural
   caster (superfine) sugar
5 eggs, beaten
a few drops of almond extract
15ml/1 tbsp milk
15ml/1 tbsp glycerine

For the decoration
90ml/6 tbsp sieved (strained)
   apricot glaze
700g/1lb 9oz almond paste
1kg/2¼lb sugarpaste icing
paste food colourings, such as
   yellow, pink and blue

1 Preheat the oven to 160°C/325°F/ Gas 3. Grease and line the base and sides of a 20cm/8in square cake tin (pan).

2 Sift the flour, baking powder and almonds into a large bowl. Add the margarine, caster sugar, eggs, almond extract, milk and glycerine and beat for about 2 minutes with an electric mixer until smooth.

3 Spoon into the tin and smooth level. Bake for 50 minutes to 1 hour, or until well risen, golden and firm in the middle.

4 Cool in the tin for 5 minutes, then turn out to cool on a wire rack.

5 When cold, remove the lining paper. Brush the cake with apricot glaze. Roll out the almond paste large enough to cover the cake. Lift on to the cake, smooth down the sides and trim. Leave for 24 hours.

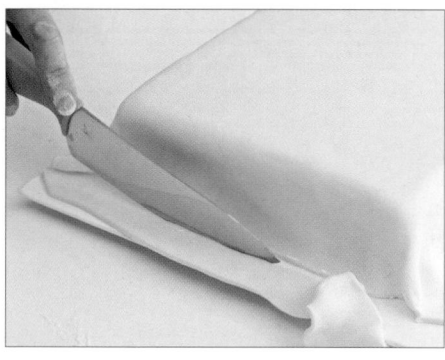

6 Colour half of the sugarpaste pale yellow and roll out to a square large enough to cover the cake. Brush the cake with a little cold boiled water, then lift the icing on to the cake and smooth down. Trim the edges neatly.

7 Colour half of the remaining sugarpaste blue and the rest pink.

COOK'S TIP
The cake keeps for 5 days in an airtight container. Do not freeze.

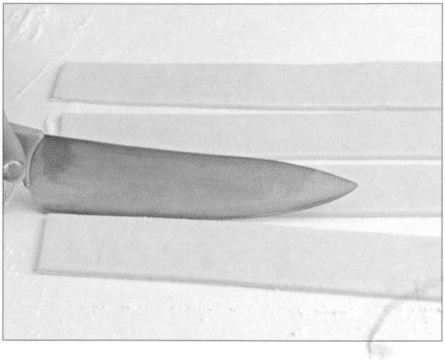

8 Roll out the pink icing and cut four strips 4 x 20cm/1½ x 8in and eight strips 4 x 10cm/1½ x 4in.

9 Roll out the blue icing and cut four strips 2.5 x 20cm/1 x 8in and eight strips 2.5 x 10cm/1 x 4in.

10 Centre matching length blue strips on top of the pink strips. Using a little water, stick the longer lengths to the cake top in a cross.

11 Form loops with four shorter strips. Leave to dry out overnight over the handle of a wooden spoon.

12 Trim the ends of the remaining strips and stick to the cake top like ribbons. Stick the loops in place. Stamp the leftover icing into small shapes and use to decorate the cake.

Energy 483kcal/2024kJ; Protein 4.2g; Carbohydrate 63.6g, of which sugars 49.6g; Fat 25.4g, of which saturates 15.3g; Cholesterol 124mg; Calcium 105mg; Fibre 0.6g; Sodium 265mg.

Fun kitty cake

Buttercream icing is a great way to cover a cake simply and easily. This jolly children's birthday cake is textured to look like a cat's fur and can be coloured to match the child's favourite cat. It is a simple party centrepiece – but it looks good and has a lovely citrus tang, too.

SERVES 14

350g/12oz/1½ cups soft tub
   margarine, plus extra for greasing
350g/12oz/1¾ cups natural caster
   (superfine) sugar
350g/12oz/3 cups self-raising
   (self-rising) flour
10ml/2 tsp baking powder
finely grated zest of 1 orange
60ml/4 tbsp orange juice
30ml/2 tbsp milk
6 eggs, beaten
60ml/4 tbsp orange marmalade

For the decoration

225g/8oz/1 cup unsalted butter
450g/1lb/4 cups natural icing
   (confectioners') sugar
30ml/2 tbsp warm milk
food colouring, brown or orange
bootlace liquorice, liquorice allsorts
   and sweets (candies)

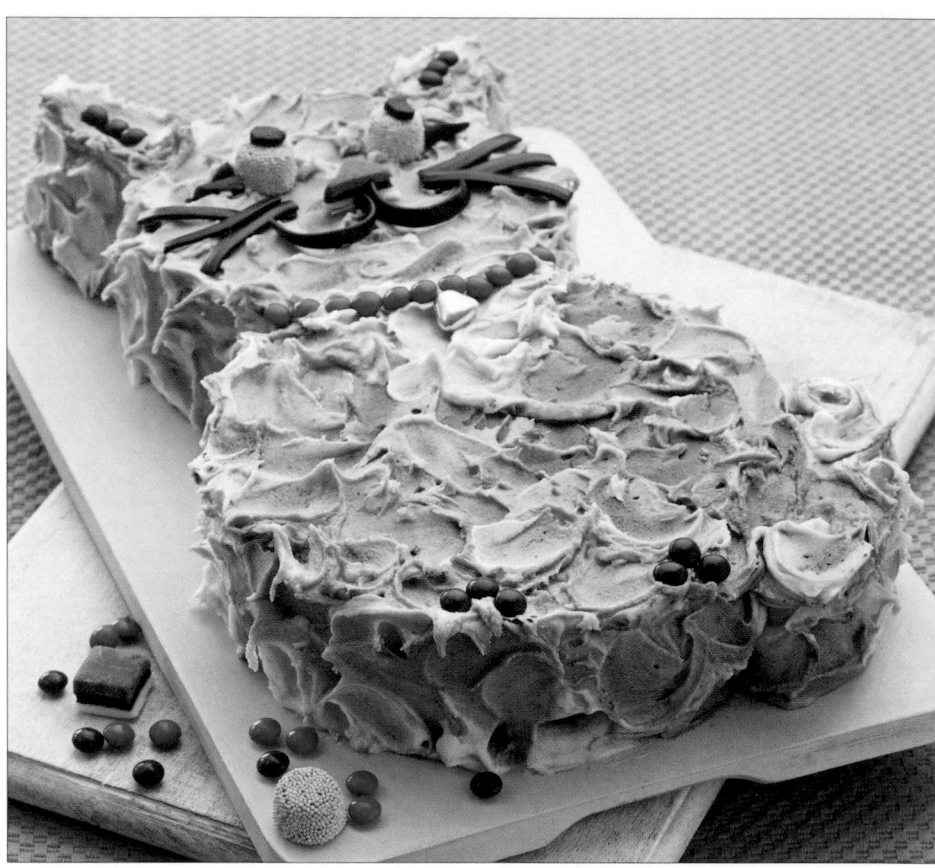

1 Preheat the oven to 190°C/375°F/ Gas 5. Grease and line the bases of two 20cm/8in deep round cake tins (pans) with baking parchment.

2 Put the margarine and sugar in a bowl and sift in the flour and baking powder. Beat thoroughly to combine.

3 Add the orange zest, 30ml/2 tbsp of the juice, the milk and eggs. Beat for about 2 minutes, or until the mixture is smooth.

4 Spoon into the tins and bake for 30–35 minutes, or until golden. Cool in the tins for 5 minutes, then turn out to cool on a wire rack.

5 Make the buttercream with the butter, icing sugar, remaining orange juice and milk, and whisk until light. Colour the icing if required.

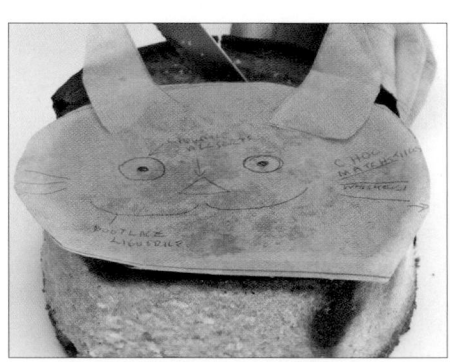

6 Put one cake on a board for the body. Cut the other cake into the head, ears and tail.

7 Cut the cakes in half horizontally. Sandwich together with marmalade.

8 Assemble the cake and secure with buttercream. Cover with buttercream, flicking up into a furry effect using a spatula. Make eyes, nose, mouth, whiskers and paws from liquorice.

Energy 435kcal/1828kJ; Protein 5.3g; Carbohydrate 62.6g, of which sugars 54.7g; Fat 19.9g, of which saturates 4.5g; Cholesterol 48mg; Calcium 65mg; Fibre 1.4g; Sodium 150mg.

Easy birthday cake

Make celebrating a birthday simple with this scrumptious caramel cake, which can be decorated to make it suitable for either children or adults. The fudgy icing is made in a pan then swirled over the top and sides of the cake in moments – it really couldn't be easier.

SERVES 10–12

175g/6oz/¾ cup soft tub
   margarine, plus extra for greasing
225g/8oz/2 cups self-raising
   (self-rising) flour
2.5ml/½ tsp baking powder
225g/8oz/1 cup soft light
   brown sugar
3 eggs, beaten
30ml/2 tbsp golden (light corn)
   syrup
60ml/4 tbsp milk
5ml/1 tbsp vanilla extract

For the caramel icing
115g/4oz/½ cup unsalted butter
225g/8oz/1 cup soft light
   brown sugar
60ml/4 tbsp milk
115g/4oz/1 cup icing
   (confectioners') sugar
sweets (candies) and candles,
   to decorate

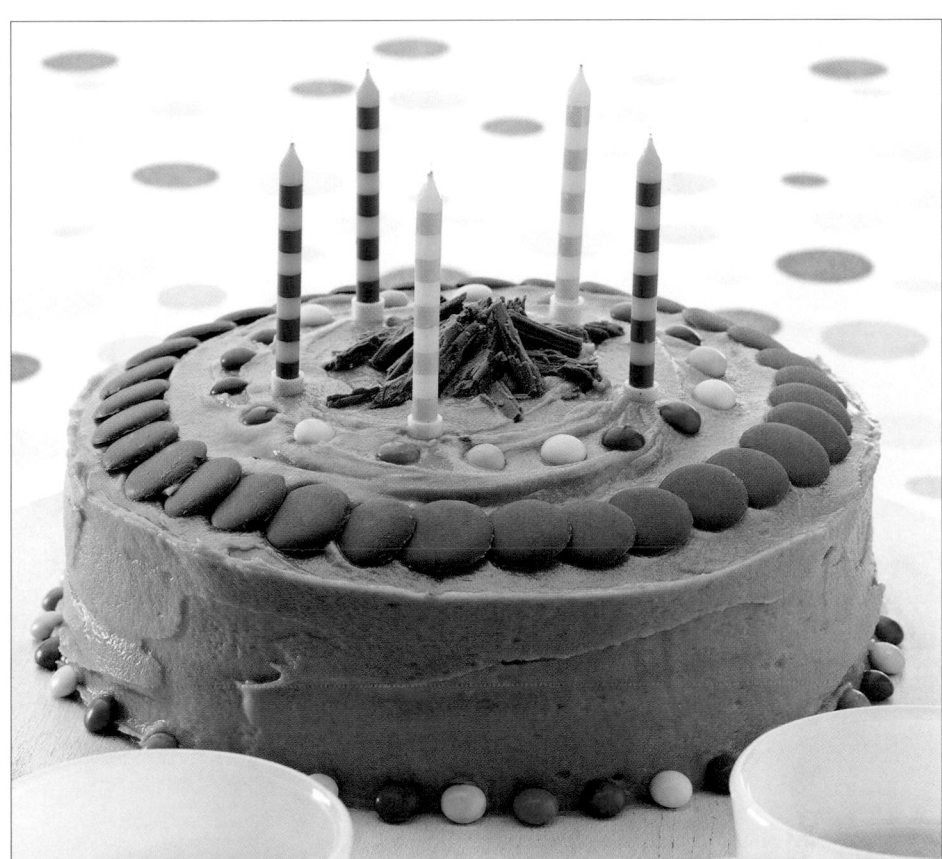

1 Preheat the oven to 180°C/350°F/ Gas 4. Grease and line the bases of two 20cm/8in shallow round cake tins (pans) with baking parchment.

2 Sift the flour and baking powder into a large bowl, then add the margarine, soft light brown sugar, eggs, syrup, milk and vanilla extract. Beat with an electric mixer for about 2 minutes, or until smooth, then divide between the tins.

3 Bake for 30 minutes, or until firm to the touch. Allow to cool for 5 minutes, then turn out on a wire rack. Remove the lining paper.

4 To make the icing, melt the butter in a pan, add the brown sugar and the milk, and bring to the boil. Reduce the heat and simmer for 2 minutes, then pour into a bowl and leave to cool.

5 When cold, beat in the icing sugar.

6 Swirl the icing over the top and sides of the cake. Decorate with sweets and candles or use chocolate buttons and broken flaked chocolate, as desired.

7 The undecorated cake keeps for 4 days in an airtight tin.

Energy 570kcal/2408kJ; Protein 3.8g; Carbohydrate 108.8g, of which sugars 95.1g; Fat 16.3g, of which saturates 9.6g; Cholesterol 18mg; Calcium 64mg; Fibre 0.6g; Sodium 293mg.

Mother's Day cake

Almonds, orange and vanilla give this special cake its delicate flavour, which can be further enhanced by drizzling over orange liqueur. To get the full citrus tang of the fresh orange you will need a food processor to grind the orange rind finely.

SERVES 12

200g/7oz/scant 1 cup butter, softened, plus extra for greasing
2 small oranges
100g/3¾oz/scant 1 cup toasted flaked (sliced) almonds
200g/7oz/1 cup soft light brown sugar
4 eggs, beaten
5ml/1 tsp vanilla extract
175g/6oz/1½ cups self-raising (self-rising) flour
40g/1¾oz/generous ¼ cup natural icing (confectioners') sugar, plus extra dusting
5ml/1 tbsp orange liqueur (optional)

For the decoration
½ quantity buttercream icing, *see page 22*
675g/1½lb sugarpaste
Materials: 1.5m/1yd fancy ribbon; bought sugarpaste or silk flowers

1 Preheat the oven to 180°C/350°F/ Gas 4. Grease and line a 20cm/8in round springform cake tin (pan) with baking parchment.

2 Peel the oranges in strips, then put in a food processor. Process for a few seconds until the peel forms a fine powder, then put into a bowl.

COOK'S TIP
Store the cake undecorated in an airtight container for up to 5 days, or decorated in a cool place for up to 2 days.

3 Process the almonds until fine, then mix with the powdered rind.

4 Beat the butter and sugar together until light and fluffy. Whisk in the eggs gradually, adding 5ml/1 tsp flour with each addition to prevent the mixture from curdling.

5 Fold in the remaining flour with the almond and rind mixture until smooth, then spoon into the tin.

6 Bake for about 40 minutes, or until golden and firm to the touch.

7 Meanwhile, squeeze the juice from 1 orange and put in a small pan with the icing sugar and 3 tbsp/ 45ml cold water, and simmer for 10 minutes, or until syrupy. Add the orange liqueur, if using.

8 Remove the lining paper. Prick over the top of the cake with a skewer and spoon the syrup over, then leave to cool in the tin. Cut the cake in half horizontally.

9 Spread one cut cake side with buttercream icing. Sandwich the other layer on top and spread thinly all over with buttercream.

10 Roll out the sugarpaste icing on a surface dusted with icing sugar and use to cover the cake, smoothing down over the top and sides. Trim the base neatly.

11 Tie a ribbon around the sides and into a bow. Decorate the top with sugarpaste or silk flowers. You can freeze the undecorated base for up to 2 months.

Energy 573kcal/2419kJ; Protein 10.2g; Carbohydrate 98.7g, of which sugars 95.6g; Fat 18g, of which saturates 1.9g; Cholesterol 73mg; Calcium 138mg; Fibre 2.4g; Sodium 52mg.

Easter simnel cake

This cake is traditionally served at Easter. The marzipan balls on top represent the 11 faithful apostles. It is also sometimes made for Mothering Sunday, when the almond paste top is decorated with fresh or crystallized spring flowers.

SERVES 8–10

175g/6oz/¾ cup butter, plus extra
   for greasing
175g/6oz/¾ cup soft brown sugar
3 large (US extra large) eggs, beaten
225g/8oz/2 cups plain
   (all-purpose) flour
2.5ml/½ tsp ground cinnamon
2.5ml/½ tsp freshly grated nutmeg
450g/15oz/3 cups total weight
   currants, sultanas (golden
   raisins) and raisins
85g/3oz/scant ½ cup glacé
   (candied) cherries, quartered
85g/3oz/scant ½ cup chopped
   mixed (candied) peel,
grated rind of 1 large lemon
450g/1lb almond paste
icing (confectioners') sugar,
   for dusting
1 egg white, lightly beaten

1 Preheat the oven to 160°C/325°F/ Gas 3. Grease and line an 18cm/7in round cake tin (pan).

2 In a large bowl, beat the butter and sugar, then beat in the eggs. Lightly fold in the flour, spices, dried fruits, cherries, mixed peel and the lemon rind.

3 Roll half the almond paste to a 16cm/6¼in circle on a surface dusted with icing sugar.

4 Spoon half the cake batter into the prepared tin. Put the circle of almond paste on top of the mixture.

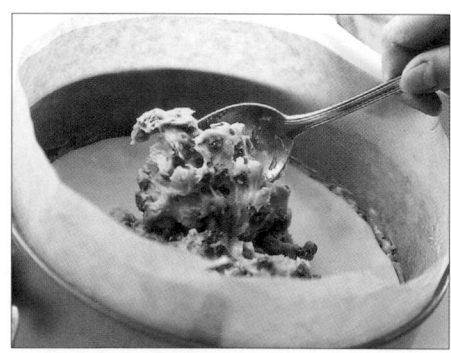

5 Spoon the remaining cake mixture on top of the almond paste and level the surface. Bake for 1 hour.

6 Reduce the temperature to 150°C/ 300°F/Gas 2 and bake for 2 more hours. Leave to cool in the tin.

7 Brush the cake with egg white. and use the remaining almond paste to cover the cake. Roll the remaining paste into 11 balls and attach with egg white. Brush the cake top with more egg white and grill (broil) until lightly browned.

Energy 810kcal/3416kJ; Protein 10.4g; Carbohydrate 132g, of which sugars 111g; Fat 30.4g, of which saturates 13.2g; Cholesterol 144mg; Calcium 156mg; Fibre 33g; Sodium 208mg.

Summer celebration shortcake

A departure from the usual summer shortcake, this crisp dessert contains crunchy almonds, which go particularly well with the juicy strawberries and cream filling. The top layer is already divided into portions, giving it an attractive appearance as well as making it easier to serve.

SERVES 8

175g/6oz/¾ cup butter, plus extra
   for greasing
150g/5oz/1¼ cups plain
   (all-purpose) flour
115g/4oz/1 cup ground almonds
50g/2oz/¼ cup caster
   (superfine) sugar
25g/1oz/¼ cup flaked
   (sliced) almonds

For the filling and decoration
450g/1lb/4 cups fresh strawberries
300ml/½ pint/1¼ cups double
   (heavy) cream
15ml/1 tbsp amaretto (optional)
icing (confectioners') sugar,
   for dusting

1 Preheat the oven to 180°C/350°F/
Gas 4. Grease two baking sheets.

2 Rub the butter into the flour until it forms fine crumbs, then stir in the ground almonds and sugar. Mix to a soft dough and knead until smooth.

3 Roll half of the dough into a 20cm/8in round and cut out neatly. Put on a baking sheet and sprinkle over half the almonds.

4 Knead the trimmings and the rest of the dough to make a second shortcake round. Sprinkle over the almonds. Prick each with a fork.

5 Bake for 20 minutes, or until pale golden. While still warm, mark the flattest one into eight even triangles and leave to cool. Cut the triangles when cold.

6 For the filling, reserve nine strawberries. Hull and chop the rest.

7 Whip the cream until it forms soft peaks. Place one quarter in a piping (pastry) bag fitted with a star nozzle.

8 Fold the berries into the remaining cream with the liqueur, if using.

9 Put the whole shortbread on a serving plate. Pile the fruit filling on top and arrange the eight triangles on top with points facing inwards.

10 Pipe a cream rosette on each one and top with a strawberry, then put the last strawberry in the centre. Dust lightly with icing sugar. Serve immediately.

Energy 364kcal/1515kJ; Protein 4.3g; Carbohydrate 29.9g, of which sugars 8.5g; Fat 25.6g, of which saturates 15.6g; Cholesterol 87mg; Calcium 70mg; Fibre 1.2g; Sodium 76mg.

Meringue mountain

A meringue can make a stunning centrepiece and is actually quite easy to make. Bake it ahead of time, if you like – it then takes just a few minutes to put together before serving. For best results bake the meringues slowly and leave them in the oven overnight to make them extra crisp.

SERVES 8–10

8 egg whites
450g/1lb/2 cups caster
  (superfine) sugar
pink food colouring
450ml/¾ pint/scant 2 cups double
  (heavy) cream
Materials: tiny rosebuds and
  candles, to decorate

1 Preheat the oven to 110°C/
225°F/Gas ½. Line three baking
sheets with baking parchment. Rinse
out a large, grease-free bowl with
boiling water, then dry completely.

2 Put the egg whites into the bowl
of an electric mixer. Whisk the
egg whites until they form soft
peaks. Whisk in the sugar, 15ml/
1 tbsp at a time, until the mixture
forms stiff peaks.

COOK'S TIPS
• Bake the meringues ahead and
store in an airtight tin in a dry
place for up to a week.
• This cake is not suitable
for freezing.

3 Remove a quarter of the mixture
and put it into a clean bowl. Colour
it a pale pink with food colouring.

4 Spoon the pink meringue
mixture into a piping (pastry) bag
fitted with a star nozzle and pipe
15 pink rosettes.

5 Spoon the remaining white
mixture into a piping bag fitted
with a star nozzle and pipe a thin
20cm/8in circle on to one of the
baking sheets. Pipe about 15
small white rosettes with the
remaining meringue.

6 Bake for 4 hours, swapping the
trays over in the oven halfway
through. Turn off the heat and
allow the meringues to dry out in
the oven overnight if possible.

7 To assemble, whip the cream until
it forms soft peaks, then spoon into
a piping bag.

8 Pipe a cone shape of cream on to
the circular base. Pipe a little cream
on the base of each meringue
rosette, then assemble them in a
conical shape.

9 Decorate with rosebuds and
candles, and serve immediately.

Energy 389kcal/1628kJ; Protein 3.3g; Carbohydrate 48.2g, of which sugars 48.2g; Fat 24.2g, of which saturates 13.5g; Cholesterol 59mg; Calcium 48mg; Fibre 0g; Sodium 68mg.

Croquembouche

This stunning tower is made from tiny, light-as-air choux buns filled with cream and delicately drizzled with caramel. Croquembouche is served in France for special occasions such as weddings and tastes wonderful. Be careful when you make the caramel, as it can easily burn.

SERVES 10

75g/3oz/6 tbsp unsalted butter, plus extra for greasing
115g/4oz/1 cup plain (all-purpose) flour, sifted
3 eggs

For the filling
600ml/1 pint/2¼ cups double (heavy) cream
60ml/4 tbsp caster (superfine) sugar

For the caramel
115g/4oz/generous ½ cup caster (superfine) sugar

1 Preheat the oven to 200°C/400°F/Gas 6. Grease four baking sheets.

2 Melt the butter in a pan with 250ml/8fl oz/1 cup water and bring to the boil. Remove from the heat.

3 Sift the flour on to a paper sheet and immediately pour into the pan.

COOK'S TIP
Bake the buns a day ahead and store unfilled in an airtight box.

4 Quickly beat together until the mixture forms a ball.

5 Transfer to a bowl and whisk in the eggs, using an electric whisk, until a smooth, thick paste forms.

6 Fill a piping (pastry) bag fitted with a 1cm/½in plain nozzle and pipe small balls about 2.5cm/1in wide on to the baking sheets, spaced well apart.

COOK'S TIP
Freeze unfilled buns in a plastic box. Keep for 2 months. Thaw, then re-heat in the oven at 180°C/350°F/Gas 4 for 10 minutes. Cool, then fill as step 9.

7 Bake for 20 minutes, or until golden. Pierce a large hole in the base of each to release the steam, then return to the oven for a further 5 minutes. Cool on a wire rack.

8 To make the filling, whip the cream together with the 60ml/4 tbsp sugar, until it forms soft peaks.

9 Spoon into a piping bag fitted with a 5mm/¼in nozzle and pipe cream into each bun through the hole in the base.

10 Arrange the buns in a pyramid.

11 To make the caramel, slowly heat the sugar until liquid in a pan.

12 Drizzle the hot caramel over the pyramid, allowing it to drizzle down over the buns. Serve immediately.

Energy 579kcal/2400kJ; Protein 6g; Carbohydrate 32.6g, of which sugars 24.4g; Fat 46.8g, of which saturates 28.3g; Cholesterol 159mg; Calcium 123mg; Fibre 0.3g; Sodium 138mg.

Celebratory anniversary cake

Sugarpaste makes a perfectly smooth finish for a celebration cake and can also be used to mould decorations, as for these delicate arum lilies. When you colour the centre of the lilies, use silver to indicate 25 years of marriage or gold for 50 years.

SERVES 30

175g/6oz/¾ cup butter, plus extra
   for greasing
450g/1lb/2⅔ cups mixed
   dried fruit
50g/2oz/¼ cup glacé (candied)
   cherries, chopped
150g/5oz/generous ½ cup ready-to-
   eat dried apricots, chopped
115g/4oz/scant 1 cup dried, stoned
   (pitted) dates, chopped
165g/5½oz/scant 1½ cups dried,
   stoned (pitted) prunes, chopped
50g/2oz/¼ cup dried
   peaches, chopped
175g/6oz/¾ cup muscovado
   (molasses) sugar
2 oranges and 1 lemon
15ml/1 tbsp mixed (apple
   pie) spice
15ml/1 tbsp treacle (molasses)
4 eggs, beaten
250g/9oz/2¼ cups plain
   (all-purpose) flour
5ml/1 tsp baking powder

For the decoration
60ml/4 tbsp apricot glaze
900g/2lb almond paste
1.2kg/2½lb ivory-coloured
   sugarpaste
Materials: 8 strands of green
   floristry wire; gold or silver
   food colouring or dusting
   powder; 10 strands of bear
   grass; 1.5m/1¾yd silver or gold
   fine net ribbon

1 Put the butter in a large, heavy pan and add the dried fruits and the muscovado sugar.

2 Grate in the rind from one orange and the lemon. Squeeze in the juice from both oranges and the lemon with 75ml/2½fl oz/⅓ cup water. Heat gently, stirring, for 10 minutes, or until the butter melts and the sugar dissolves.

3 Pour into a large bowl, stir in the mixed spice and treacle, and leave to stand overnight.

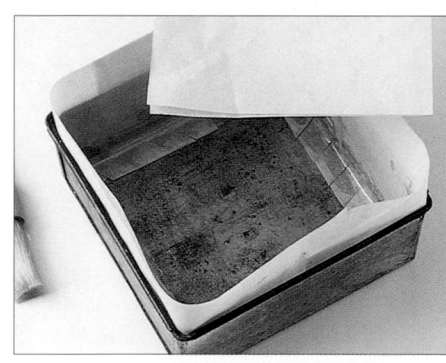

4 Preheat the oven to 160°C/325°F/ Gas 3. Grease and triple-line a 20cm/8in square tin (pan) or a 23cm/9in round cake tin, and wrap four layers of newspaper around the outside.

5 Add the eggs to the fruit mixture, then sift in the flour and baking powder. Mix until smooth.

6 Pour into the prepared tin and level the top. Cover with two layers of baking parchment to prevent over-browning.

7 Bake for 2 hours, then lower the temperature to 150°C/300°F/Gas 2 and bake for a further 1¾ –2 hours. Test with a skewer inserted into the centre; it will come out clean when the cake is cooked. Cool in the tin, then turn out and wrap in foil to mature for 2–3 months.

8 Remove the lining paper. To decorate the cake, brush with the apricot glaze and cover with almond paste. Leave for 24 hours.

9 Roll out the sugarpaste icing to a square large enough to cover the cake. Brush the cake with cooled boiled water, position the sugarpaste on the cake, smooth over the top and sides, and trim neatly.

COOK'S TIP
Keep for 4–6 months, wrapped in foil in an airtight tin. Freeze undecorated for up to 4 months.

Energy 224kcal/936kJ; Protein 2.4g; Carbohydrate 26.7g, of which sugars 20.5g; Fat 12.6g, of which saturates 7.6g; Cholesterol 17mg; Calcium 26mg; Fibre 0.7g; Sodium 168mg.

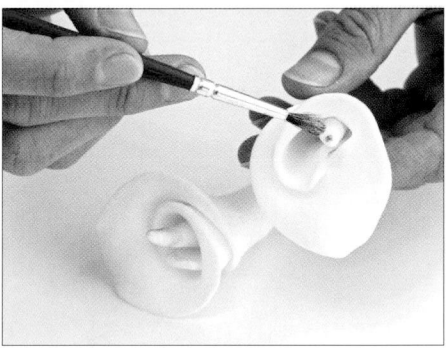

10 Make a small flat loop at the top of each piece of floristry wire. The loop helps the sugarpaste adhere to the wire. Re-roll the sugarpaste scraps to make 8 thin sausages and wrap these around the floristry wires. Leave to dry for 24 hours on waxed or non-stick paper.

11 Roll out the remaining sugarpaste thinly and cut into small rectangles 10 × 9cm/4 × 3in. Wrap each rectangle into a cone around the centre as shown, leaving a long, pointed tip. Flute out the edges to soften. Leave to dry out upside down in egg boxes for 24 hours.

12 Paint the tips of the lily stamens silver or gold, or dust the powder over with a dry paintbrush. Arrange a bunch of lilies with a few strands of bear grass and tie this together with a ribbon to secure. Arrange the flowers on the cake. Trim the sides with matching ribbon.

Rose-petal wedding cake

This special two-tiered cake looks very dainty with its pink and white glossy buttercream icing decorated with rose petals. You can bake the cake bases a day or two before you need them, then decorate them with the simple icing on the day.

SERVES 18

For the small cake
115g/4oz/½ cup butter, softened, plus extra for greasing
115/4oz/1 cup self-raising (self-rising) flour
2.5ml/½ tsp baking powder
115g/4oz/generous ½ cup natural caster (superfine) sugar
2 eggs, beaten
15ml/1 tbsp milk
a few drops of rose water

For the large cake
350g/12oz/1½ cups butter, softened, plus extra for greasing
350g/12oz/3 cups self-raising (self-rising) flour
5ml/1 tsp baking powder
350g/12oz/1½ cups natural caster (superfine) sugar
6 eggs, beaten
30ml/2 tbsp milk
a few drops of rose water

For the decoration
4 egg whites
275g/10oz/ 2½ cups icing (confectioners') sugar
275g/10 oz/1¼ cups unsalted butter, beaten
a few drops of rose water
pink food colouring
120ml/4fl oz/½ cup apricot jam
crystallized rose petals

1 Make and bake the two cakes separately. Preheat the oven to 160°C/325°F/Gas 3. Grease and line a 15cm/6in round deep cake tin (pan) with baking parchment.

2 To make the small cake, sift the flour and baking powder into a bowl. Add the sugar, butter, eggs, milk and rose water. Beat for 2 minutes, until smooth. Spoon into the cake tin and smooth the top.

3 Bake for 30–40 minutes, until firm and golden. Turn out to cool on a wire rack.

4 Repeat steps 1–3 to make the large cake, using a 25cm/10in round cake tin. Bake for 1 hour 5–10 minutes.

5 Whisk the egg whites and icing sugar in a bowl set over a pan of hot water until the beaters leave a trail when lifted. Remove from the heat. Continue whisking until soft peaks form. Cool slightly, then beat into the softened butter and rose water.

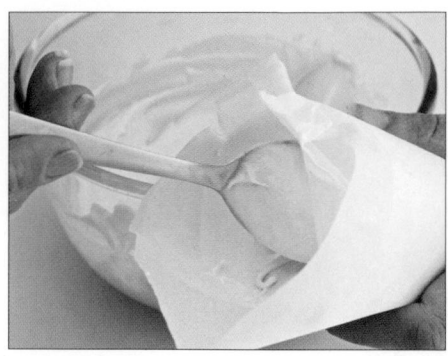

6 Put 45ml/3 tbsp of the mixture into a piping (pastry) bag and snip a tiny hole off the end.

7 Colour one-third of the remaining icing pale pink and put 60ml/4 tbsp in another paper icing bag, then snip off the end.

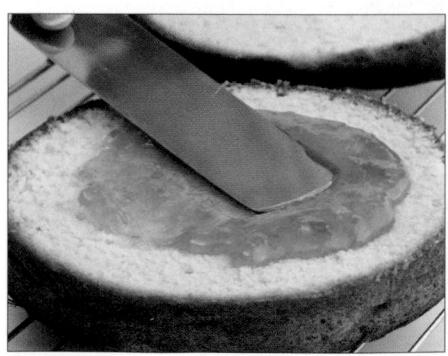

8 Remove the paper linings. Slice each cake in half horizontally and sandwich together with apricot jam.

COOK'S TIPS
• Cover in foil for up to 3 days until ready to decorate.
• Freeze the undecorated sponge cake bases, wrapped in foil or strong plastic bags, for up to 2 months.

Energy 253kcal/1071kJ; Protein 2.5g; Carbohydrate 48.8g, of which sugars 44.6g; Fat 5.5g, of which saturates 1.1g; Cholesterol 17mg; Calcium 49mg; Fibre 0.9g; Sodium 63mg.

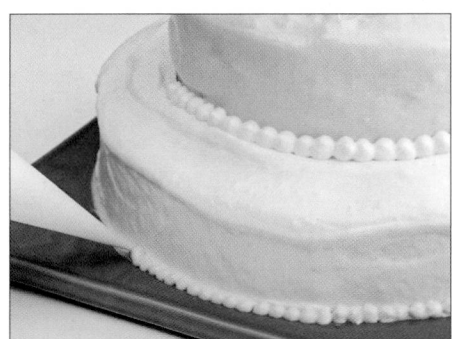

9 Cover the small cake with pink icing and smooth flat with a metal spatula. Cover the large cake with white icing and smooth it flat.

10 Using a metal spatula, put the small cake on top of the large one. Remove the spatula carefully to avoid spreading cake crumbs.

11 Pipe tiny beads around the base of each cake. Sprinkle crystallized rose petals over the cakes and around the base, and serve.

Traditional Christmas cake

Make this cake four to six weeks before Christmas to give it time to mature. Once or twice during this time, pierce the cake with a skewer and spoon over 30–45ml/2–3 tbsp brandy to make it beautifully moist and rich. Top it with almond paste and sugarpaste just before eating.

SERVES 20

225g/8oz/1⅓ cups sultanas
   (golden raisins)
225g/8oz/1 cup currants
225g/8oz/1⅓ cups raisins
115g/4oz/½ cup prunes, stoned
   (pitted) and chopped
50g/2oz/¼ cup glacé (candied)
   cherries, halved
50g/2oz/⅓ cup chopped mixed
   (candied) peel,
45ml/3 tbsp brandy or sherry
225g/8oz/1 cup butter, plus extra
   for greasing
225g/8oz/2 cups plain
   (all-purpose) flour
pinch of salt
2.5ml/½ tsp ground cinnamon
2.5ml/½ tsp freshly grated nutmeg
15ml/1 tbsp unsweetened
   cocoa powder
225g/8oz/1 cup soft dark
   brown sugar
4 large (US extra large) eggs
finely grated rind of 1 orange
   or 1 lemon
50g/2oz/½ cup ground almonds
50g/2oz/½ cup chopped almonds

For the decoration
60ml/4 tbsp apricot jam
icing (confectioners') sugar
   for dusting
450g/1lb almond paste, *see page 24*
30ml/2 tbsp Kirsch or brandy
450g/1lb white sugarpaste icing,
   see page 26
225g/8oz royal icing, *see page 25*
Materials: red or green ribbon

1 The day before you want to bake the cake, put all the dried fruit in a large bowl. Pour in the brandy or sherry, cover with clear film (plastic wrap) and leave overnight.

2 Preheat the oven to 170°C/325°F/ Gas 3. Grease and line the base and sides of a 20cm/8in round cake tin (pan) with a double thickness of baking parchment.

3 Sift together the flour, salt, spices and cocoa powder into a large bowl.

4 In a large bowl, beat the butter and sugar together until light and fluffy, then beat in each egg.

5 Mix in the citrus rind, both almonds, dried fruits (with any liquid) and the flour mixture.

6 Spoon into the prepared tin and smooth the surface level. Give the cake tin a gentle tap on the work surface to settle the batter and disperse any air bubbles.

7 Bake for 3 hours, or until a skewer inserted into the centre comes out clean.

8 Leave the cake to cool in the tin for an hour. Turn the cake out on to a wire rack, but leave the paper on, as it will help to keep the cake moist during storage. When the cake is cold, wrap it tightly in foil and store in a cool place until ready to decorate.

9 Put the apricot jam in a pan and heat to warm, then sieve (strain) it to make a glaze.

Energy 6637kcal/28042kJ; Protein 60.6g; Carbohydrate 1245.8g, of which sugars 1129.2g; Fat 166.7g, of which saturates 85.9g; Cholesterol 940mg; Calcium 1515mg; Fibre 31.1g; Sodium 1896mg.

10 Remove the lining paper and centre the cake on a cake board.

11 Brush the cake with hot jam.

12 Dust the work surface with sifted icing sugar. Roll out the almond paste until large enough to cover the top and sides of the cake. Pick the almond paste up on the rolling pin and fit over the surface. Smooth out any air bubbles with your hands. Trim away any excess.

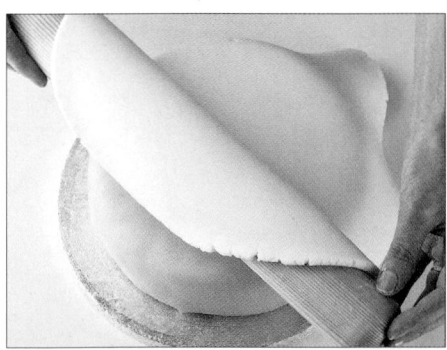

13 Brush 2 tbsp Kirsch over the almond paste. Roll out the sugarpaste as before and use to cover the cake. Trim the excess.

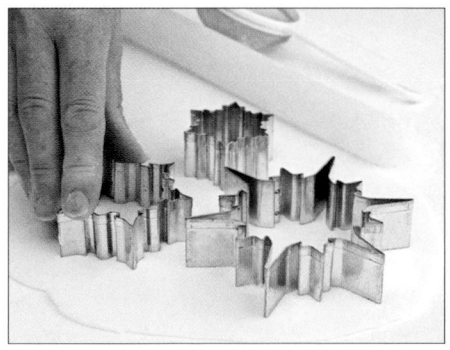

14 Roll out any sugarpaste trimmings and stamp out festive decorations using cutters. Lift in place with a small palette knife, then stick them in place with a little royal icing.

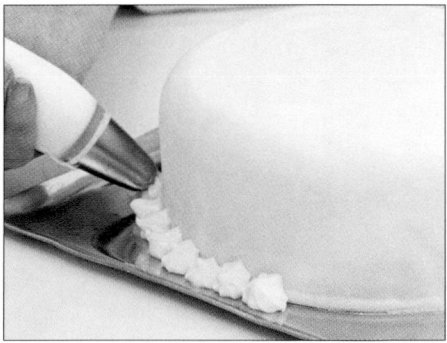

15 Use a star nozzle in a piping (pastry) bag and one-third fill it with royal icing. Pipe a border of rosettes around the base of the cake. Leave to dry thoroughly. Tie a ribbon around the sides of the cake.

Festive Yule log

The chocolate-covered Yule log has its origins in France. It makes a good alternative for those who don't like the traditional rich fruit cake, or it can be served during the Christmas holidays as a dessert with a fresh fruit compote. Eat this fresh or freeze it, unfilled, for two months.

SERVES 8

butter, for greasing
90g/3½oz/¾ cup self-raising (self-rising) flour
30ml/2 tbsp unsweetened cocoa powder
pinch of salt
4 eggs
115g/4oz/generous ½ cup golden caster (superfine) sugar, plus extra for dusting

For the filling and icing
150ml/¼ pint/⅔ cup double (heavy) cream
50g/2oz plain (semisweet) chocolate
30ml/2 tbsp unsweetened cocoa powder
15ml/2 tbsp boiling water
115g/4oz/½ cup unsalted butter, softened
225g/8oz/2 cups natural icing (confectioners') sugar, sifted, plus extra for dusting
almond paste or chocolate holly leaves, to decorate

1 Preheat the oven to 220°C/425°F/Gas 7. Grease and line a 33 x 23cm/13 x 9in Swiss roll tin (jelly roll pan).

2 Sift the flour, cocoa and salt into a bowl.

COOK'S TIP
The sponge mixture for a Swiss roll is rolled up while it is still hot, to avoid it cracking.

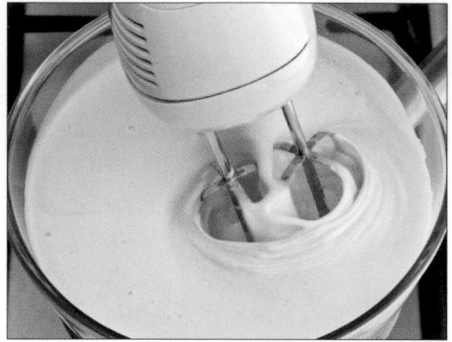

3 Put the eggs and sugar into a large heatproof bowl and place this over a pan of hot water. Whisk for 10 minutes, or until the mixture is thick. Remove the bowl from the water and whisk until the mixture is thick and pale, and leaves a trail when the beaters are lifted away.

4 Using a large metal spoon, gently fold in half the flour and cocoa using a figure-of-eight movement. Fold in the remaining flour with 15ml/1 tbsp cold water. Pour the mixture into the prepared tin and smooth level.

5 Bake for 10 minutes, or until springy to the touch. Sprinkle a sheet of baking parchment with caster sugar and place this on a clean dish towel.

6 Turn the hot sponge out on to the paper.

7 Peel away the lining paper. Trim away the crusty sponge edges. Using the dish towel, roll up the sponge loosely, with the paper inside, then leave to cool on a wire rack.

8 Carefully unwrap the cold sponge cake and remove the paper. Whip the cream until stiff, spread over the sponge, then roll up and chill until needed.

9 Melt the chocolate in a heatproof bowl over a pan of gently simmering water, then leave to cool.

10 Dissolve the cocoa in the boiling water, stir until blended, then leave to cool.

Energy 478kcal/2003kJ; Protein 7.1g; Carbohydrate 55.4g, of which sugars 44.1g; Fat 26.1g, of which saturates 15g; Cholesterol 130mg; Calcium 75mg; Fibre 1.4g; Sodium 47mg.

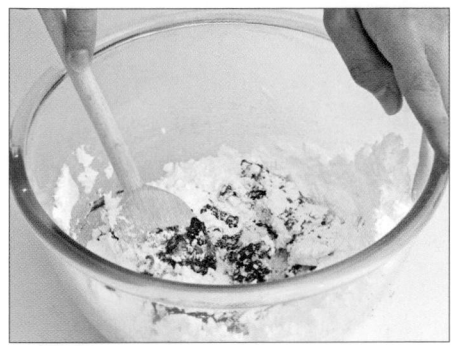

11 Beat the butter until fluffy, then beat in the icing sugar and cooled cocoa with the melted chocolate.

12 Put the cake on a long serving dish. Spread the chocolate icing over the top and sides of the cake with a metal spatula, in deep swirls and ridges.

13 Decorate the top with almond paste or chocolate holly leaves and dust very lightly with a sprinkle of icing sugar before serving.

White Christmas cake

This light and zesty cake makes a refreshing change to a traditional heavy fruit cake. Make the moist sponge bases a day ahead, or bake and freeze them to make life simple over the holiday, so that all you have to do is add the very easy filling and decoration. Eat on the day it is made.

SERVES 12

225g/8oz/1 cup unsalted butter,
  softened, plus extra for greasing
finely grated rind and juice
  of 2 limes
75g/3oz block creamed coconut,
  grated or 150ml coconut cream
225g/8oz/generous 1 cup caster
  (superfine) sugar
4 large (US extra large) eggs
225g/8oz/2 cups self-raising
  (self-rising) flour

For the filling and decoration
200g/7oz/scant ¾ cup lemon curd
 225g/8oz/1 cup cream cheese
75g/3oz/6 tbsp unsalted butter
275g/10oz/2½ cups icing
  (confectioners') sugar
finely grated rind of 1 lime
175g/6oz/2 cups shredded coconut
crystallized sprigs of bay leaf,
  rosemary and cranberries,
  or silver Christmas baubles
  or snowflake ornaments,
  to decorate

1 Preheat the oven to 180°C/350°F/ Gas 4. Grease and line two 20cm/ 8in round cake tins (pans).

COOK'S TIP
To make frosted leaves and berries, whisk 1 egg white until frothy, then brush it over a bay leaf, sprigs of rosemary and a few cranberries. Put on a wire rack. Dust with plenty of caster (superfine) sugar. Leave to dry.

2 Put the lime juice and 30ml/2 tbsp water in a small pan with the creamed coconut and heat gently to dissolve, then cool.

3 Put the lime rind, butter, sugar, eggs, flour and cooled coconut mixture into a bowl and whisk for 2–3 minutes, or until smooth and soft.

4 Divide the batter equally between the cake tins and smooth the tops level.

5 Bake for 20–25 minutes, or until golden and risen, and firm to the touch in the centre.

6 Cool in the tin for 5 minutes, then turn out to cool on a wire rack and peel away the lining papers.

7 Cut each cake in half horizontally with a sharp knife, then sandwich each together with lemon curd. Put one cake on a plate, spread the top with the remaining lemon curd and sandwich both cakes together.

8 To make the coating, put the cream cheese, butter, icing sugar and lime rind in a bowl and beat until smooth. Spread the coating over the top and sides of the cake.

9 Sprinkle the coconut over the top and pat on to the sides, then tidy the base.

10 Decorate the centre of the cake with sprigs of rosemary and cranberries, or bought silver Christmas baubles or snowflake ornaments, if you like.

Energy 698kcal/2912kJ; Protein 8.9g; Carbohydrate 63g, of which sugars 51.8g; Fat 47.5g, of which saturates 34.7g; Cholesterol 193mg; Calcium 78mg; Fibre 6.4g; Sodium 188mg.

Index

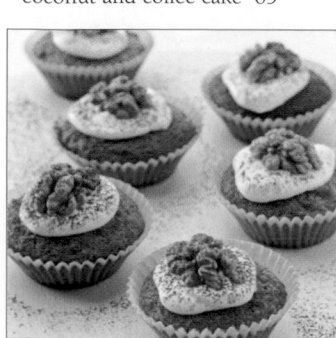

Lemon chiffon cake

Split a light lemon sponge cake in half horizontally, then fill with a lovely thick layer of lemon mousse to give it a tangy centre. Top with a lemon icing and lemon zest and you have the most lemony cake. Keep this for one day in the refrigerator, or freeze for two months, undecorated.

SERVES 8

butter, for greasing
2 eggs
75g/3oz/6 tbsp caster
   (superfine) sugar
grated rind of 1 lemon
50g/2oz/½ cup plain (all-purpose)
   flour, sifted
lemon shreds, to decorate

For the filling
2 eggs, separated
75g/3oz/6 tbsp caster
   (superfine) sugar
grated rind and juice of 1 lemon
15ml/1 tbsp gelatine
120ml/4fl oz/½ cup fromage frais
   or crème fraîche

For the icing
15ml/1 tbsp lemon juice
115g/4oz/1 cup icing
   (confectioners') sugar, sifted

1 Preheat the oven to 180°C/350°F/
Gas 4. Grease and line a 20cm/8in
round loose-based cake tin (pan).

2 Whisk the eggs, sugar and lemon rind until mousse-like. Fold in the flour, then pour into the cake tin.

3 Bake for 20–25 minutes, or until the cake springs back when lightly pressed in the centre. Turn on to a rack to go cold. Clean the cake tin.

4 Remove the lining paper. Split the cake in half horizontally and return the lower half to the clean cake tin.

5 To make the filling, put the egg yolks, sugar, lemon rind and juice in a bowl. Beat with an electric whisk until thick, pale and creamy.

6 Pour 30ml/2 tbsp water into a small heatproof bowl and sprinkle the gelatine on top. Leave until spongy, then set the bowl over simmering water and stir until dissolved. Cool slightly, then whisk into the yolk mixture. Fold in the fromage frais or crème fraîche.

7 When the filling mixture begins to set, whisk the egg whites in a clean, grease-free bowl until they form soft peaks. Stir a spoonful into the mousse mixture to lighten it, then fold in the rest.

8 Pour the filling over the sponge in the cake tin, spreading it to the edges. Put the second layer of sponge on top and chill until set.

9 Slide a knife dipped in hot water between the tin and the cake to loosen it, then transfer the cake to a serving plate.

10 To make the icing, add enough lemon juice to the icing sugar to make a thick, spreadable icing. Pour over the cake and spread to the edges. Decorate with lemon shreds.

Energy 356kcal/1491kJ; Protein 6.7g; Carbohydrate 43.6g, of which sugars 29.8g; Fat 18.4g, of which saturates 4g, Cholesterol 118mg; Calcium 68mg; Fibre 0.6g; Sodium 227mg.

Easter simnel cake

This cake is traditionally served at Easter. The marzipan balls on top represent the 11 faithful apostles. It is also sometimes made for Mothering Sunday, when the almond paste top is decorated with fresh or crystallized spring flowers.

SERVES 8–10

175g/6oz/¾ cup butter, plus extra
    for greasing
175g/6oz/¾ cup soft brown sugar
3 large (US extra large) eggs, beaten
225g/8oz/2 cups plain
    (all-purpose) flour
2.5ml/½ tsp ground cinnamon
2.5ml/½ tsp freshly grated nutmeg
450g/15oz/3 cups total weight
    currants, sultanas (golden
    raisins) and raisins
85g/3oz/scant ½ cup glacé
    (candied) cherries, quartered
85g/3oz/scant ½ cup chopped
    mixed (candied) peel,
grated rind of 1 large lemon
450g/1lb almond paste
icing (confectioners') sugar,
    for dusting
1 egg white, lightly beaten

1 Preheat the oven to 160°C/325°F/ Gas 3. Grease and line an 18cm/7in round cake tin (pan).

2 In a large bowl, beat the butter and sugar, then beat in the eggs. Lightly fold in the flour, spices, dried fruits, cherries, mixed peel and the lemon rind.

3 Roll half the almond paste to a 16cm/6¼in circle on a surface dusted with icing sugar.

4 Spoon half the cake batter into the prepared tin. Put the circle of almond paste on top of the mixture.

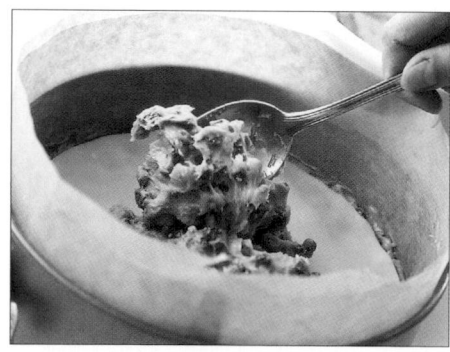

5 Spoon the remaining cake mixture on top of the almond paste and level the surface. Bake for 1 hour.

6 Reduce the temperature to 150°C/ 300°F/Gas 2 and bake for 2 more hours. Leave to cool in the tin.

7 Brush the cake with egg white. and use the remaining almond paste to cover the cake. Roll the remaining paste into 11 balls and attach with egg white. Brush the cake top with more egg white and grill (broil) until lightly browned.

Energy 810kcal/3416kJ; Protein 10.4g; Carbohydrate 132g, of which sugars 111g; Fat 30.4g, of which saturates 13.2g; Cholesterol 144mg; Calcium 156mg; Fibre 33g; Sodium 208mg.

This edition is published by Lorenz Books, an imprint of Anness Publishing Ltd, Blaby Road, Wigston, Leicestershire LE18 4SE

info@anness.com

www.lorenzbooks.com;
www.annesspublishing.com

If you like the images in this book and would like to investigate using them for publishing, promotions or advertising, please visit our website www.practicalpictures.com for more information.

© Anness Publishing Ltd 2012

A CIP catalogue record for this book is available from the British Library.

Publisher: Joanna Lorenz
Editorial Director: Helen Sudell
Editor: Simona Hill
Photographer: William Lingwood
Stylist: Liz Hippisley
Home Economist: Lucy McKelvie
Designer: Nigel Partridge
Production Controller: Pirong Wang

Main front cover image shows Meringue Mountain – for recipe, see page 240

NOTES
Bracketed terms are intended for American readers.
• For all recipes, quantities are given in both metric and imperial measures and, where appropriate, in standard cups and spoons. Follow one set of measures, but not a mixture, because they are not interchangeable.
• Standard spoon and cup measures are level. 1 tsp = 5ml, 1 tbsp = 15ml, 1 cup = 250ml/8fl oz.
• Australian standard tablespoons are 20ml. Australian readers should use 3 tsp in place of 1 tbsp for measuring small quantities.
• American pints are 16fl oz/ 2 cups. American readers should use 20fl oz/2.5 cups in place of 1 pint when measuring liquids.
• Electric oven temperatures in this book are for conventional ovens. When using a fan oven, the temperature will probably need to be reduced by about 10–20°C/ 20–40°F. Since ovens vary, check with your manufacturer's instruction book for guidance.
• The nutritional analysis given for each recipe is calculated per portion (i.e. serving or item), unless otherwise stated. If the recipe gives a range, such as Serves 4–6, then the nutritional analysis will be for the smaller portion size, i.e. 6 servings. The analysis does not include optional ingredients, such as salt added to taste.
• Medium (US large) eggs are used unless stated.
• Recipes containing raw eggs should not be eaten by pregnant women, babies, the very young and elderly people. You can use dried egg whites instead which give excellent results and can be substituted in recipes.

The following companies provide an excellent postal service for all cake decorating and baking supplies.
For all cake decorating supplies:
Squires Kitchen
www.squires-group.co.uk
www.squires-shop.com
For all baking supplies:
Lakeland
www.lakeland.co.uk